EXPANDING DIMENSIONS OF CONSCIOUSNESS

A. ARTHUR SUGERMAN, M.D., Med. D. Sc., is director
of research and education, the Carrier Foundation,
Belle Mead, New Jersey. He is clinical professor of
Psychiatry at Rutgers Medical School and a contributing
faculty member of the Rutgers University Graduate
School of Applied and Professional Psychology.

RALPH E. TARTER, Ph.D., is research psychologist at
the Carrier Foundation, and is clinical assistant
professor of Psychiatry at Rutgers Medical School and
a contributing faculty member of the Rutgers University
Graduate School of Applied and Professional Psychology.

EXPANDING DIMENSIONS OF CONSCIOUSNESS

A. Arthur Sugerman and
Ralph E. Tarter, editors
with contributors

 SPRINGER PUBLISHING COMPANY ■ New York

Springer Publishing Company, Inc.
200 Park Avenue South
New York, N.Y. 10003

78 79 80 81 82 / 10 9 8 7 6 5 4 3 2 1

Library of Congress Cataloging in Publication Data
Main entry under title:

Expanding dimensions of consciousness.

Includes bibliographies and index.
1. Consciousness—Addresses, essays, lectures.
I. Sugerman, A. Arthur. II. Tarter, Ralph E.
III. Title. [DNLM: 1. Consciousness—Congresses.
2. Biofeedback (Psychology)—Congresses. BF311 E96
1976]
BF311.E88   154   78–59650
ISBN 0–8261–2340–6
ISBN 0–8261–2341–4 pbk.

Printed in the United States of America

Contents

■ TWO
Induction of Altered States of Consciousness

Contributors

Roderick A. Borrie, Ph.D., research associate, Department of Psychology, University of British Columbia.

Patricia Carrington, Ph.D., lecturer, Department of Psychology, Princeton University; psychologist in private practice.

Andrew M. Elmore, M.A., research physiologist, Veterans Administration Hospital, Northport, New York.

Lester G. Fehmi, Ph.D., director of the Behavioral Medicine Learning Clinic; affiliate staff member, The Medical Center at Princeton.

Roland Fischer, Ph.D., lecturer and clinical professor, Departments of Psychiatry, The Johns Hopkins University and Georgetown University Medical Schools; professorial lecturer in Pharmacology, George Washington University Medical School.

Steven M. Fishkin, Ph.D., associate professor of Psychiatry and Behavioral Sciences, University of Oklahoma Health Sciences Center; research psychologist, Veterans Administration Hospital, Oklahoma City.

Bernard C. Glueck, M.D., director of research, Institute of Living, Hartford, Connecticut; lecturer, Department of Psychiatry, Yale University School of Medicine; professor, Department of Psychiatry, University of Connecticut Health Center and Medical School.

Ben Morgan Jones, Ph.D., research psychologist, the Carrier Foundation, Belle Mead, New Jersey.

Charles F. Stroebel, Ph.D., M.D., director, Psychophysiology Clinic and Laboratories, Institute of Living, Hartford, Connecticut; lecturer, Department of Psychiatry, Yale University School of Medicine; professor, Department of Psychiatry, University of Connecticut Health Center and Medical School.

Peter E. Suedfeld, Ph.D., professor and head, Department of Psychology, University of British Columbia.

Charles T. Tart, Ph.D., professor of Psychology, University of California at Davis.

Bernard Tursky, codirector, Laboratory for Behavioral Research, and professor, Department of Political Science; professor of Psychiatry and adjunct professor of Psychology, State University of New York at Stony Brook.

Andre M. Weitzenhoffer, Ph.D., professor of Psychiatry and Behavioral Sciences; University of Oklahoma Health Sciences Center, clinical research psychologist, Veterans Administration Hospital, Oklahoma City.

David L. Wilson, Ph.D., associate professor, Department of Physiology and Biophysics, University of Miami School of Medicine.

Michael R. Zales, M.D., assistant clinical professor of Psychiatry, Albert Einstein College of Medicine; lecturer in Human Relations, Hebrew Union College—Jewish Institute of Religion; lecturer in Psychiatry, Yale University.

Preface

This volume originated from a symposium held at the Carrier Clinic Foundation in October of 1976. Under the leadership of Dr. Robert S. Garber, the annual symposia have been conducted for the past two decades on contemporary issues and problems in psychiatry and behavioral science.

Because of the unusually large response to this symposium and requests for written transcriptions, we decided to organize and expand the presentations of five of the speakers (Tart, Fehmi, Glueck, Carrington, and Tursky) and to invite other contributors to present overviews of their areas of specialization. Our objective was to gain some perspective on the vast and complex field of consciousness and to allow discussion of those aspects of consciousness which are currently engaging the interest of scientists, philosophers, and laymen.

We thank the authors for their effort and forbearance during many stages of revision. Appreciation is also extended to Cynthia Sansom for her editorial assistance and to Thomas Buonpane for his contribution to the artwork. We thank Charlotte Hardy, Daryl Hoffman, and Carol Ryan, whose secretarial help, often under conditions of frantic pressure and deadlines, kept the book moving along at a steady pace. And, finally, we are grateful to Dr. Cyril Franks, who gave of his time unfailingly in helping organize the original symposium, bringing the publisher in contact with our efforts, and suggesting several of the contributors.

A. Arthur Sugerman
Ralph E. Tarter

Belle Mead, N.J.
February 3, 1978

Introduction

The topics discussed in this volume have fascinated thinkers for thousands of years. Some of them have been studied scientifically since the origins of experimental psychology over one hundred years ago, when attention began to be focused on the content of consciousness. Psychologists of the structuralist and functionalist schools then tried to measure sensation and to elucidate the flow of experience in the stream of consciousness. With the behavioral revolution, overt performance became the target of study as sophisticated apparatus was developed for its measurement and control. Lacking comparable direct means of empirical analysis and ultimately dependent on either overt verbal or nonverbal responses anyway, the study of consciousness as an integral aspect of human psychology receded in importance as a topic for scientific inquiry.

In the middle 1960s, the social disruptions caused by civil rights movements, political assassinations, the Vietnam war, and the plethora of mind-altering drugs brought about a dramatic shift away from the idea of the good life provided by advanced technology and material wealth and towards the search for inner-directed growth of human potential. This led to attempts to expand awareness by inducing altered states of consciousness and to a great interest in Eastern approaches to meditation and contemplation. But, even in America, such developments were not new. William James, physician, philosopher, and one of America's greatest psychologists, wrote at the beginning of this century: "The mind-cure principles are beginning so to pervade the air that one catches their spirit second hand. One hears of 'The Gospel of Relaxation,' of the 'Don't Worry Movement,' of people who repeat to themselves 'Youth, health, vigor!' when dressing in the morning . . ." (p. 93). Although James was one of the fathers of American positivism, he gave introspection a status equal to that of experiment. He wrote of the effects of alcohol and anesthetics on the mind, finding links between mystical experience and intoxication that can provide a useful perspective from which to view some of the chapters of this book:

> The sway of alcohol over mankind is unquestionably due to the power to stimulate the mystical faculties of human nature, usually crushed to earth by the cold facts and dry criticisms of the sober hour. Sobriety diminishes, discriminates, and says no; drunkenness expands, unites, and says yes. . . . To the poor and unlettered it stands in the place of symphony concerts and of literature; and it is part of the deeper mystery and tragedy of life that whiffs and gleams of something that we immediately recognize as excellent should be vouchsafed to so many of us only in the fleeting earlier phases of what in its totality is so degrading a poisoning. The drunken consciousness is one bit of the mystic consciousness, and our total opinion of it must find its place in our opinion of that larger whole. [p. 377]

James goes on to speak of the stimulating effects of nitrous oxide and ether on the mystical consciousness; he says that depth beyond depth of truth seems revealed to the inhaler, and even after he comes to, the sense of profound meaning persists; "I know more than one person who is persuaded that in nitrous oxide trance we have a genuine metaphysical revelation" (p. 378).

He describes very vividly his own experiences with one of these agents.

> Some years ago I myself made some observations on this aspect of nitrous oxide intoxication. . . . One conclusion was forced upon my mind at that time, and my impression of its truth has ever since remained

unshaken. It is that our normal waking consciousness, rational consciousness as we call it, is but one special type of consciousness, whilst all about it, parted from it by the filmiest of screens, there lie potential forms of consciousness entirely different. We may go through life without suspecting their existence; but apply the requisite stimulus, and at a touch they are there in all completeness, definite types of mentality which probably somewhere have their field of application and adaptation. No account of the universe in its totality can be final which leaves these other forms of consciousness quite disregarded. How to regard them is the question—for they are so discontinuous with ordinary consciousness. Yet they may determine attitudes though they cannot furnish formulas, and open a region though they fail to give a map. [pp. 378–379]

We are today no further advanced than James was at the turn of the century in explaining the operations and potential of consciousness. We have many theories and models, some of which may be found in various chapters of this volume, and we also have many techniques for altering consciousness, some of which were not available in James' day. We are close to finding a happy balance in which research technology can be integrated with human values. Biofeedback strategies can be used to train people to regulate their own physiological processes and to achieve altered conscious states. This application of modern technology to age-old medical problems and to the extension of consciousness beyond the limits of the normal, waking, rational consciousness promises humane and useful methods of studying the capacity of the human mind.

We offer the reader an overview of the state of the art in some of the varied approaches to the alteration of consciousness. It will be readily apparent that some areas have had a great deal of empirical study and that others are quite virgin, their depths mysterious and unplumbed.

Our first three contributors offer conceptual orientation rather than specific techniques. Wilson discusses the inadequacies of psychoanalysis and behaviorism as foundations for neuroscience, and looks forward to an understanding of mind and consciousness based on introspection and physiological research. He considers altered states of consciousness within an identity theory of mind.

Fischer provides an ambitious theory in which consciousness is viewed within a circular schema. Conscious states range from increasing ergotrophic dominance on the one hand to increasing trophotrophic dominance on the other; at the one extreme there are the hyperaroused states of psychosis and at the other, the hypoaroused states of meditation and contemplation. His perspective incorporates the psychopharmacology of hallucinogenic drugs, the electroencephalogram of ecstasy, and both oriental and occidental paths to enlightment.

Tart offers us a "systems approach" to altered states of consciousness. He points out the value system implicit and often unnoticed in their investigation and the cultural biases that impel us to perceive the world selectively and thus organize our psychological potentials into certain patterns. Discrete states of consciousness are defined by the selection of potentials and their pattern of organization. A discrete altered state of consciousness is induced by destabilizing and disrupting the ongoing pattern. This framework provides a psychological approach to ordinary consciousness, sleep, dreaming, and alcohol and drug intoxication.

In the first of the chapters devoted to specific techniques used in altering consciousness, Carrington discusses the value of meditation as an adjunct to psychotherapy. She is also careful to point out the limitations of meditation without accompanying psychotherapy in the care of neurotic patients. Glueck and Stroebel give an overview of their research into relaxation techniques. They clarify the relative advantages and disadvantages of meditation and biofeedback for different conditions and individuals, discuss reasons for individuals dropping out of treatment, and ask pertinent questions about the role of the mantra in influencing brain functions and state of consciousness. Elmore and Tursky provide a scholarly history of the evolution of the concept of biofeedback and its therapeutic applications. They review representative studies, and show that with currently used techniques, few clinically significant lasting changes are observed. They suggest that more powerful techniques may be developed by selecting response consequences appropriately, and that these may produce long-lasting and meaningful effects.

Fehmi also recommends that the feedback signal should be relevant to the task to be learned, and points out the technical problems that can occur in EEG biofeedback training. He provides a lucid outline of his pioneering technique of multichannel EEG synchrony.

Another approach to the alteration of consciousness is shown by Weitzenhoffer, who has devoted many years to the study of hypnosis and hypnosuggestive phenomena. Although both consciousness and hypnosis are elusive entities, he shows quite clearly that altered states of consciousness can be produced hypnotically; the evidence suggests that the alteration is in the content and not the structure of consciousness.

Suedfeld and Borrie show that sensory deprivation can produce altered states of consciousness, but these are not commonly the qualitative changes or changes in pattern of Tart's model. They are usually characterized by quantitative changes in perception reminiscent of the alterations described by Weitzenhoffer of hypnotic states.

Zales writes on the changes of consciousness noted throughout history in the mystic, who seeks detachment from the world by contemplation. He distinguishes the experiences of the mystic from those produced by schizophrenia, by hallucinogenic drugs, and by temporal lobe epilepsy.

In the final chapter, Fishkin and Jones describe a model of consciousness based on attention that has applications to both normal consciousness and the altered states produced by alcohol and drugs.

Our contributors have not tried to cover all of the aspects of their subject matter that might be of interest to researchers. Such a task would be beyond the scope of a single volume. Rather, the objective has been to place the problems and methods associated with the study of consciousness into a contemporary perspective. Because of the varied nature of the means of altering consciousness, some contributors can show the results of experimental research and others must be content with reports of experience. Although little is sacred to the experimental psychologist, we are unlikely to see statistical treatments of the mystical experiences of saints, and must be satisfied with the apprehension that there are many gates to knowledge, just as there are many dimensions along which consciousness may be changed.

REFERENCE

James, W. *The Varieties of Religious Experience.* First published 1902; page numbers from Modern Library Edition, New York, 1936.

one
THEORETICAL
PERSPECTIVES

1
Brain Mechanisms, Consciousness, and Introspection

DAVID L. WILSON

> The brain is waking and with it the mind
> is returning. It is as if the Milky Way
> entered upon some cosmic dance. Swiftly
> the head-mass becomes an enchanted
> loom where millions of flashing shuttles
> weave a dissolving pattern, always a
> meaningful pattern though never an
> abiding one. [Sherrington, 1951, p. 178]

Introduction

The number of neurons in a human brain is about equal to the number of stars in the Milky Way—over 10,000,000,000. Although the principles of organization of our galaxy were put forward by Newton 300 years ago and have undergone revision by modern cosmologists such as Einstein, our knowledge of the principles of organ-

This research was supported in part by a Biomedical Research Support Grant.
I thank Michael Edwards, Margaret Wilson, George Stone, and Michael Hall for their helpful comments on drafts of the manuscript.

3

ization of the human brain has come more recently. In the last hundred years considerable information has been obtained from anatomy concerning the gross-level or macro-organization of the brain. We also know a substantial amount about the molecular and cellular processes occurring in the brain. Finally, we have a knowledge of higher brain (mental) functions from psychology, psychiatry, linguistics, and from centuries of philosophical analysis. Unfortunately, as scientific disciplines have become more subdivided, attempts at a synthesis of these separate bodies of knowledge have become rare.

I would like to indicate how the chief reigning paradigms in psychiatry and psychology are both inadequate as foundations for neuroscience. I propose that the foundation for understanding mental functions should ultimately rest upon such "harder" sciences as physiology, anatomy, and biochemistry. There is some justification for considering these biological sciences to be capable of dealing with the phenomena of mind and consciousness (Wilson, 1976). Making this assumption, I will proceed to discuss some relationships between brain events and conscious experience.

Freud versus Skinner

At present there is no unified position that can guide psychologists and psychiatrists as they attempt to treat mentally ill patients. There exist a number of competing theories, no one of which explains all cases of mental order or disorder. Especially noticeable is the separation between psychology and psychiatry. A number of schools are included in each of these disciplines. Perhaps the most important school in psychology today is B. F. Skinner's (1971, 1974) version of behaviorism, which stands in sharp contrast with the major school of Freudian psychiatry. There appear to be irreconcilable differences between the two schools, and these differences are reflected in the clinical treatments that have evolved from each. In Skinner's latest book, *About Behaviorism,* he is on the attack against Freudian views. He strongly criticizes the theory that instincts are driving forces in human behavior, calling such an idea a "serious mistake," whereas this concept is a cornerstone of Freudian psychiatry: "The forces which we assume to exist behind the tensions caused by the needs of the Id are called *instincts.* They represent the somatic demands upon mental life" (Freud, 1949, p. 19). And again: "Instincts fill the Id; to put it shortly, all energy in the Id comes from them. The forces in the Ego, too, have no other origin, they are all derived from those in the Id" (Freud, 1969, p. 42). But Skinner (1974, p. 154) goes even further: "What behaviorism rejects is the unconscious as an agent, and of course it rejects the conscious mind as an agent, too. . . . Freudian dynamisms or defense mechanisms . . . are not psychic processes taking place in the depths of the mind, conscious or unconscious; they are the effects of contingencies of reinforcement, almost always involving punishment." Thus, it is unlikely that behaviorists will be able to view psychoanalysis as capable of being encompassed by their theories of human behavior since "the contribution of psychoanalysis to science consists precisely in having extended research to the region of the mind" (Freud, 1933, pp. 217–218).

But we cannot conclude that in the future either Freudian psychiatry or behaviorism will prove to be correct while the other is rejected. Both are inadequate as a scientific basis for mental function or human behavior. One difficulty with Freudian psychiatry appears to be its failure to allow for falsification. Indeed, it has been criticized by Karl Popper (1965) as unscientific because all observations can be accommodated within its framework. Popper argues that its endless explanatory strength is in fact a great weakness, and that one should be able to imagine some possible observations that would disprove the theory, even if such observations never actually occur. Another problem with Freudian psychiatry is the difficulty in linking its framework with other aspects of neuroscience, such as neuroanatomy or neurochemistry. The Freudian paradigm does not appear to be designed to allow correction or modification on the basis of new knowledge in other disciplines. Freud has contributed to the acceptability of the idea of a self and to the concepts of a conscious and unconscious mind, but these concepts are in need of clarification or revision on the basis of physiology and psychology.

There also are problems with any attempt to use behaviorism as a basis for a science of higher brain functions. In its early forms, behaviorism appeared to reject consciousness and mind altogether: "Behaviorism claims that consciousness is neither a definable nor a usable concept" (Watson, 1924, p. 3). Some more recent forms of behaviorism resemble epiphenomenalism: "We do not need to try to discover what personalities, states of mind, feelings, traits of character, plans, purposes, or other perquisites of autonomous man really are in order to get on with a scientific analysis of behavior. . . . We do feel certain states of our bodies associated with behavior . . . ; they are by-products and not to be mistaken for causes" (Skinner, 1971, pp. 13–14).

The behaviorists have narrowed the scope of the psychologist's program. Wundt, one of the first psychologists, declared (1904) that "physiological psychology . . . is competent to investigate the relations that hold between the process of the physical and those of the mental life" (p. 3), and "the relations existing between determinate conditions of the physical organization, on the one hand, and the process of consciousness, on the other, are primarily of interest to the psychologist" (p. 4). In contrast, the behaviorist has attempted to reduce mind to stimulus-response relationships. "Mind" becomes "behavior," and "attributes of mind" become "relations between stimulus characteristics and responses" (Thompson, 1967, pp. 4–5).

Scientific frameworks, or paradigms (Kuhn, 1962), can be inadequate not only because of a failure to correspond with data but also because such frameworks can unnecessarily restrict the set of problems considered relevant to a particular scientific community. It is likely that all frameworks have some limitations (Kuhn, 1962), but part of scientific development consists of evolving theories of higher levels of generality (Popper, 1959) capable of dealing with a broader range of observations and experiences. Perhaps psychologists have now developed the groundwork of behavioral studies enough to allow us to go beyond stimulus-response to the "black-box" in between.

In a sense, behaviorism is not a predictive science. One needs a response before one can define the stimulus and its relevant aspects. If a particular stimulus first displays its influence on behavior in a response that occurs ten years after the stimulus, it is only after the response that behaviorism explains the response. There is no emphasis in behaviorism on determining brain states and processes. With such determinations one can deal with the impact of the experience (rather than the stimulus) on the individual's thoughts, and so forth. An approach using knowledge of inner states and processes would allow for prediction rather than after-the-fact explanation.

Introspective reports of mental states and processes by subjects during psychological testing can be used as experimental data useful for understanding how inner (brain) processes are involved in producing behavior. Of course, verbal responses are routinely used in numerous behavioral experiments, but it is not universally accepted that these responses can be used to give us information concerning mental states. Such information can be useful in understanding and explaining behavior. These inner processes or mental events, which the individual can be aware of through introspection, are causally related to subsequent behavior. By asking individuals to make verbal reports concerning their inner states and processes, we can add to our knowledge of the underlying causes of human behavior.

The behavioristic view, by concentrating on externally observed behavior, has produced theories that are deficient because they eliminate consideration of brain processes. For example, the operant conditioning model of human learning (Skinner, 1971) is oversimplified—a surface view of complex internal phenomena. Even with lower animals, numerous experiments (Bolles, 1972) indicate that the rate of learning as well as the ability to learn certain tasks at all is species-specific, and thus dependent upon internal organization. Human responses to stimuli are often under voluntary (conscious) control, and this participation by higher brain centers requires a very different analysis of the learning process. Of course, learning can occur in an individual without his being aware of it. This does not contradict the fact that with much human learning, thought processes do participate in, and generally speed, the learning process.

To give a particular example, consider an individual asked to predict each utterance of a speaker, and suppose that each utterance is a single letter, either A or B. If the speaker alternates A, B, A, B, A, B, A, B. . . . , we can ask how long it will take before the individual correctly predicts, say, ten utterances. Consider that such an individual could be in one of a number of states—what one might loosely call mental sets. In one of these he suspects a sequence will be involved in the utterances and tries, from the beginning, to detect what the sequence is. Most individuals with such a set will quickly determine the correct sequence, but the process cannot accurately be described as operant conditioning. That is, it is not at all the kind of slow, gradual improvement of score, leading to 80%–90% correct responses, that we would expect of a rat or pigeon. Instead, the individual will examine the first few utterances, test out various hypotheses for sequences, and generally recognize the correct one in a "eureka" manner. The answers, at first guesses, become 100% correct in a "jump."

In order to emphasize further the role of internal states in the learning process, consider the same situation but with another mental set: the individual believes, at the outset, that the experiment is a test of extrasensory perception, and that he should try to obtain the correct utterance through mental telepathy. Clearly, with this set the recognition that a pattern exists, and hence the learning, will be much slower and actually will not come until the mental set has changed or the individual becomes unconsciously conditioned (a different, slower process).

Either of the sets described above, or others, could be functioning in an individual. The determination of which particular mental set is momentarily guiding an individual can be made in a crude way by asking the person to report on her or his thoughts. But this approach is just a beginning for understanding the internal processes. The fact that individuals will test and discard hypotheses in trying to determine the precise patterning, and that the recognition event comes with suddenness and is followed by nearly 100% correct responses, indicates that the operant conditioning description is inadequate even for this simple learning situation. Behaviorism does not emphasize the special nature of learning in higher organisms: the use of internal organization and internal processes in analysis and the importance of experience, that is, the individual's interpretation of events rather than the external stimuli themselves. Because we cannot define, today, precisely what is meant by internal processes or thoughts is not justification for minimizing or dismissing their role in producing behavior.

To admit the existence of an inner structure that is involved in human behavior and that is open to analysis through introspection and neurobiology is not to postulate demons, souls, or other nonphysical entities. Rather, it is to admit that behaviorism is but a first step in a complex program. To go beyond behaviorism is to go beyond artificial boundaries that may have been useful when constructed over fifty years ago, but that have become an obstruction for present-day psychologists and physiologists seeking new knowledge. To turn attention inward is not to turn away from a genetic and personal history, but to observe the organization and traces that were left by the history. The internal structure, properties, and states of the brain are the more immediate causes of behavior.

Of course, there are more than these two major schools in psychology and psychiatry, and various authors in this book reflect the modern interest in mental functions and consciousness largely from perspectives other than those of Freudian psychiatry and behaviorism. During our lifetimes we shall likely witness both the overthrow of Freudian psychiatry and Skinnerian behaviorism and their replacement with an understanding of mind that will require the coupling of behavioral observation, introspective insight, and deep knowledge of brain structure and function. Since there is little question of the importance of behavioral observations in understanding mental phenomena, in what follows I will emphasize the potential roles of introspection and of our knowledge of brain functions in leading us to an understanding of mind and consciousness.

The Identification of Mental Events with Brain Events

The speculations and conclusions reached below depend upon the accuracy of the claim that we directly experience some of our own brain processes. Philosophically, this assumption is a corollary of the identity theory of the relationship between mind and brain (Feigl, 1967; Place, 1956; Smart, 1963). These philosophers assert that the fact that we have one language for brain events and another for mental events does not mean that mental events are separate from brain events. This is the crux of the various versions of mind-brain identity. We are aware of some of the functionings of our brain. We are only indirectly aware of other aspects of brain functioning and totally unaware of yet other aspects. Perhaps the most difficult part of the identity concept is its expression in language. Philosophers continue to argue whether the mind-brain relationship is one of strict identity, and whether one can relate the term *mind* with the term *brain* when they belong to such different language frameworks (Borst, 1970). A full explanation of the meaning of an identification of mental processes with brain processes may require the development of a metalanguage, capable of encompassing both physical and mental terminologies. These technicalities aside, *scientifically* the identification of mental events with brain events is of the same kind as the identification of gene with DNA (Armstrong, 1968) or the identification of matter as a form of energy. Some variants of the identity theory have been developed and supported by neuroscientists (Globus, 1973a, 1973b, 1973c; Hubbard, 1975; Rose, 1976; Smith, 1969; Wilson, 1975, 1976). I am using identity in the sense of a theoretical identification of the referents of "mental functions" and "certain brain processes."

Other kinds of philosophic arguments that have been raised against any identity theory suggest that additional clarifications are needed. Structure-function identifications are not uncommon in biological science: DNA, a known chemical structure, has been identified as having the function of the hereditary material. Similarly, synaptic vesicles in neurons, which are structures seen with the electron microscope, have been identified as the holders of transmitter quanta. Both of these identifications are empirical and rely on observations or experiments for verification. The same is true of the identification of the brain as the structure some of whose functionings are mental processes.

Emergence

Consciousness is not something that can be said to be present in a single atom or even in a single neuron, for that matter. Just as one has different properties in a water molecule than were present in the two hydrogen and one oxygen atom that comprise the molecule, so the organized mass of neurons and glia in the brain can have different properties. It is the organization of the matter that gives rise to the ability to develop subjective experience and personal self.

Today many physicists feel relatively confident that the properties of a group of water molecules, such as boiling point and density, can be predicted or approximated from a knowledge of hydrogen and oxygen atoms by using quantum mechanics. This is a reductionist view of the water molecule. The reductionist view receives support from the demonstration that quantum mechanics can predict the properties of the hydrogen molecule (H_2) from a knowledge of hydrogen atoms (H) alone. For water and other molecules, the difficulties appear to arise more from complexity of calculations than from inadequacy of principles. We may someday be capable of a description of mental processes from a knowledge of neurons, glia, and brain structure. Such properties as consciousness may be new but that does not make them emergent, in the philosophical sense of the term (Meehl & Sellars, 1956).

An emergence hypothesis would consider mind and consciousness to be subject to scientific analysis but would consider the analysis to involve new laws and principles going beyond the laws that govern inanimate nature. Emergence does not necessarily entail violations in the laws of physics and chemistry, but does assert that such laws will be incomplete and incapable of accounting for higher brain functions. Without compelling evidence, the postulation of emergence unjustifiably precludes reductionist approaches to understanding mind. Similar postulates of emergence were made concerning genetic material and heredity earlier in this century (Morgan, 1923). Such postulates later proved to be unnecessary.

Sperry (1969, 1970, 1976a) appears to hold an emergent position in some of his writings:

> A full causal account of brain function is thus not possible in purely neurophysiological or biophysical terms that do not include these higher, yet-to-be-described mental processes with their subjective pattern properties different from the neural events per se. [Sperry, 1976a, p. 13]

And further:

> The subjective phenomena as emergent properties of brain activity are built of neural events and therefore always tied, as emergent properties, to the material brain with all its anatomical and physiological constraints. [1976a, p. 14]

However, Sperry's writings suggest that he accepts a holistic, apparently nonreductionist view for much of science:

> As high-level dynamic entities, the mental processes control their component biophysical, molecular, atomic, and other subelements in the same way, for example, that the organism as a whole controls the fate of its separate organs and cells or just as the molecule as an entity carries all its component atoms, electrons, and other subatomic parts through a distinctive time-space course in a chemical reaction. [1976a, p. 13]

Were emergent laws to be required for an explanation of consciousness, such laws would be expected to be of a more holistic nature. In modern science, thermodynamics is an example of a more holistic set of laws. Temperature and pressure cannot easily be said to exist in a single atom, but an ensemble of atoms has a definable temperature and can exert pressure. Although holistic, thermodynamic laws are not emergent, they are reducible to statistical mechanics. Thermodynamic laws are fully explainable on the basis of a knowledge of atoms and molecules.

It is possible that a holistic approach to mental functions may be more fruitful in the short run. Holistic generalizations may come before reductionist understanding. Such was the case with Darwin's holistic Theory of Evolution, which came a century before our understanding of his "variations" as changes in DNA. Similarly, thermodynamics was a fully developed holistic science before the advent of statistical mechanics. But with statistical mechanics, as with molecular biology, there came enlightenment concerning the scope of the holistic laws. Indeed, the Second Law of Thermodynamics was shown to be true only in a probabilistic sense. We may find it easier or more fruitful to approach mental functions first as special brain properties with holistic laws, but deeper insights should be forthcoming as reductionist links are forged.

Epiphenomenalism

Some arguments opposing the identification of mind with brain confuse the identity viewpoint with that of epiphenomenalism. A number of scientists have concluded that conscious processes are epiphenomena, that is, by-products of brain function, without causal roles in human behavior (Huxley, 1896; Skinner, 1971; Stent, 1975). However, this view is difficult to maintain in light of one's capability to describe verbally such inner processes as perceptions, thoughts, and self-awareness. If such processes were truly without a causal role in human behavior, how could the verbal expressions and descriptions of mental events come to be? How could a powerless by-product influence the physical events of speaking and writing? In other words, humans have evolved the language that allows for discourse concerning conscious experiences. These physical events, the verbal ones made possible by the evolution of language and culture within the human population, are crucial to the present argument. Persons speak about so-called private events that occur within themselves. The existence of this capability strongly suggests a causal role for mental processes in the human behavior. Otherwise, how could that knowledge of private events be made public? Muller (1955) has made a similar argument.

Mental Events and Physical Causation

From the viewpoint of identity theory, consciousness, or subjective experience, is not somehow tacked on to the physical process. Rather it has evolved with, and is an inseparable part of, the physical process. As Gray (1971, p. 253) correctly observes, one cannot ask, "What would happen if we suppressed the conscious events without altering the neuronal events normally accompanying these?" But the inability to ask this question is analogous to a neurophysiologist's inability to ask, "What would happen if we suppressed action potentials without altering the neuronal events normally accompanying these?" My point is that any theoretical identification in science similarly precludes the asking of such questions. Today, biologists cannot ask, "What would happen if we allow DNA synthesis, transcription, and so forth to occur as usual but suppress gene activity?"

According to the identity theory, consciousness is both a brain process and an active force in the behavior of higher organisms. That active force can be viewed from the personal side, as the experiencing self does, or can be viewed, in principle, by the neurophysiologist with implanted electrodes and so forth. This is not a dual-aspect position, but is merely two perspectives on the same brain events. Those who question why consciousness should have evolved and what survival value it has apart from brain events are assuming a dualistic view in order to attack a monistic position. Within an identity theory paradigm, to ask about the Darwinian survival value of consciousness is to ask about the survival value of the brain processes that *are* conscious events. Since these are likely the processes involved in situation-analysis and decision-making in the brain, their survival value is obvious. Furthermore, as the identification of mind with brain allows for a causal role of mental functions in human behavior, it allows for personal dignity, freedom of choice, and other humanistic attributes despite opinion to the contrary (Sperry, 1976b, p. 176).

I hope that the last few sections have served to clarify the usefulness of an identity theory. One can now view the capability for conscious experience as having evolved in organisms (Griffin, 1976) and as developing in each individual as a consequence of the complex interplay between heredity and environment. However, the identification of experienced events as particular brain events raises other more practical issues, some of which I discuss below.

Consciousness and Self

Undoubtedly there are processes in the brain that are not directly a part of one's self-consciousness. It is possible that some of these brain processes are themselves conscious (Wilson, 1976) but not directly accessible to the conscious "stream" that I term self$_1$. Self$_1$ refers to the series of brain processes experienced by the speaking and writing "I"; thus, self$_1$ refers to a set of processes, not to an entity. In this way, I avoid limiting conscious (or even self-conscious) processes in the brain only to those with access to the language-output apparatus. The need for such a distinction has become obvious after the experiments of Sperry (1968) on split-brain subjects, who appear to have two distinct domains of consciousness after section of the hemispheric commissures (Sperry, 1976b). Ultimately we may need to redefine a number of terms and concepts to deal with these complexities. As Sperry (1976b, p. 172) has said, "As knowledge of brain function and the mind-brain relation advances, one would anticipate that terms like 'mind' and 'person' will have to be redefined, or at least more precisely defined."[1] Already the data appear to require some distinction, such as that given above, between the general capability for being a conscious event in a brain and being a self$_1$-conscious event in the same brain.

1. In sharp contrast to Malcolm (1971), who writes, "People see, hear, think—not brains." Or again, "Our concepts of the mental are heavily based on the human form ... but not at all on happenings in the central nervous system." Scientists are always doing what philosophers don't consider possible. Scientific advances often involve changing concepts, and scientists often use the same word for the old and new concept. If there are multiple consciousnesses in the human brain, we might wish to preserve the use of the term "person" for the whole organism, including body and brain (Strawson, 1958). But there is difficulty in taking "person" as the central concept, as the ability to distinguish self from not-self appears to develop in infancy, and not to be innate (Piaget, 1967).

Introspection and Self

At its outset, psychology was considered the science of mind (Wundt, 1904), and introspection was considered a proper research method. At the turn of the century introspection was greatly used by prominent psychologists (James, 1890). Attempts to use introspection as a tool were not without their surprises. Introspection suggested that mental processes such as thoughts, intentions, and judgments were "unanalyzable," and their "content escapes further characterization altogether, or proves accessible to such characterization only with difficulty" (Humphrey, 1951, p. 36). As James (1890, Volume I, p. 251) has said of recalling a forgotten word: "The state of our consciousness is peculiar. There is a gap therein; but no mere gap. It is a gap that is intensely active.... There are innumerable consciousnesses of emptiness, no one of which taken in itself has a name, but all different from each other." Such unexplained limitations in the introspective approach perhaps contributed to the reduction of interest in this tool. Historically, this seeming lack of progress came when the competing school of behaviorism appeared to be making great strides toward psychological understanding (Watson, 1924).

Recently, some psychological experiments have led to the revival of introspection as a tool in psychological research (Warr, 1970). However, contemporary introspectionism has been evolving largely without a physiological or philosophical base. Introspection can be a dangerous tool without such foundations because there are severe limits to what can be ascertained through introspection alone. As will be discussed below, introspection gives an incomplete and misleading view of brain processes. Only through advances in neurobiology will we be able to gain the knowledge necessary to correct for such limited information. After such correction we may reach the point where introspective knowledge is able to contribute to advances in physiology. Introspection alone can be quite misleading, but to ignore it is to miss the opportunity for direct knowledge of mental (and physical) events. As Feigl (1967) has written: "Introspection may be regarded as an approach to neurophysiological knowledge, although by itself it yields only extremely crude and sketchy information about cerebral processes."

$Self_1$ probably has an even more narrow view of happenings in the brain than it does of happenings in the external world. We[2] have

2. The terms "we" and "us" are plurals of $self_1$.

come to realize and overcome some of the limitations inherent in our indirect, restricted view of the external world (Wilson, 1976). We have yet to do so as effectively for our inner world. Some of the seemingly (to self$_1$) direct information concerning our minds is demonstrably indirect. Proprioceptive feelings and pain localization offer two examples; they are perceived as occurring at particular points on or in the body, and such bodily locations of the feelings appear, to introspection, to be an integral part of the sensations. Clinical and physiological data on phenomena such as phantom limbs and direct electrical stimulation of neurons on sensory pathways indicate the indirect nature of such perceptions. The potential for mistakes is present if one is considering the external body and its actual state. The body and external world are perceived as being "outside." Perception involves reconstruction from sensory information and memory, and events are perceived as localized occurrences in the body or external world. Obviously such localizations have considerable survival value. For example, it is important for us to recognize what body area is giving rise to pain sensations in normal cases. We can live with the errors that arise thereby (such as hand and finger sensations after striking the elbow "funny-bone").

Introspection is limited not only by the potential for mistakes, as above, but because much of what occurs in our brains is not self$_1$-conscious. We can, self$_1$-consciously, direct some of the brain processes and be directly aware not of the processing but only of the output. In this way, self$_1$ resembles the conductor of an orchestra, who directs and is aware of the output from the musicians, but has no direct access to the events that produce each player's output. We are directly aware only of the consequences of a number of brain or cognitive processes.

Consider perception. We are not aware of the processing that gives rise to a perception. In vision, for example, we can view a Necker cube (Figure 1-1) and view first one face of the perceived cube as extending forward in space, then that same face extending backwards. We are not aware of the processing that is giving rise to the choice as the image flip-flops. Self$_1$ does not appear to have direct access to the events in the occipital lobe of the cortex where early processing of visual information is occurring. However, we do have control over what aspects of sensory inputs are attended to. At least a part of the actions of selective mechanisms can be governed by

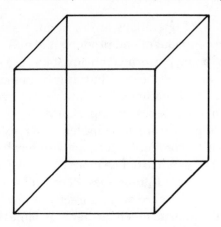

FIGURE 1-1. A Necker cube. The two-dimensional drawing is an ambiguous figure when perceived as a three-dimensional cube. One surface can alternately be perceived as protruding (being the front surface of the cube) or receding (being the back surface).

$self_1$. For example, at a cocktail party attention can be directed at one ongoing conversation while ignoring other conversations that are simultaneously taking place.

Again, if we compare thoughts with dreams, we can recognize that $self_1$ has more control over content and sequencing of thoughts than of dreams. $Self_1$ does not appear to have access to the processing that gives rise to dream sequencing. But even thoughts are far from complete in terms of $self_1$-awareness. The sudden eureka of insight upon understanding a new concept reflects a limited awareness of the procedure involved. And in the constant searching for a particular memory, we have some control ability in focusing upon particular associations or approaches to "finding" the memory, but aspects of the search itself are beyond $self_1$-awareness. A good example of this is the "tip of the tongue" phenomenon. We can have a feeling of being close to retrieving a particular memory without being aware of the process itself.

We naively consider ourselves to be consciously aware of much of what is happening in our brains. However, the above considerations suggest otherwise. We appear to be aware of the consequences of a number of brain processes without having access to the actual processing events that give rise to the $self_1$-conscious experiences. There is anything but continuity in $self_1$-consciousness if one refers thereby to the flow of operations in the brain. Instead, as activity progresses we are conscious of end products and only some intermediates. The rest, if being performed on any stage, are not on the one to which self$_1$ has any ready access. In this way, one can explain the "shadowy" (Ryle, 1949) nature of self-aware occurrences without having to deny their existence or importance.

Although it is premature to consider doing so now, we may ultimately be able to combine introspective knowledge with that from physiological research to define more tightly what brain regions actually are those where self$_1$ processes occur (and which regions are the locations of events that are only indirectly or not at all accessible to self$_1$). Today we cannot go much further than James (1890, Volume I, p. 66) could at the turn of the century: "Limiting the meaning of the word consciousness to the personal self of the individual, we can pretty confidently answer the question . . . by saying that the cortex is the sole organ of consciousness in man." We can perhaps eliminate primary sensory projection areas of the cortex as well, but that is about all. Of course this entire approach may be oversimplified: there is no known reason why different areas of the brain, even noncortical regions, could not participate in the generation of self$_1$ experiences at different times.

States of Consciousness and Freudian Concepts

Having reached this perspective on self$_1$, we can deal in a preliminary way with some clinical data. Consider altered states of consciousness. One common way of bringing about altered states of mental functioning is through drugs. Pharmacologists and physiologists are beginning to understand the effects of some of these drugs at neuronal and synaptic levels. Altered states of consciousness may tell us much that is useful in delineating the organ of self-awareness within the brain. Introspective data from the altered states of consciousness can be used in conjunction with the known physiological effects of the drugs and the known brain pathways of the cells affected by the drugs. A specific example of a drug that induces altered states of consciousness is LSD, which may act in the brain as a partial agonist of serotonin (a known synaptic transmitter). The serotonin-containing cells of the brain are located predominantly in the raphe nuclei of the pons and brain stem, which send processes through the hypothalamus to upper brain regions (Cooper, Bloom, & Roth, 1974). But our lack of knowledge of the precise effects of LSD on serotonin-associated cells and our lack of knowledge of the roles of the serotonin cells prevents the example from being extended at present. With greater future knowledge of drug effects, we may be able to establish a base for understanding modes of consciousness and thereby avoid establishing state-specific sciences (Tart, 1972). We may gain a unified understanding of occurrences in altered states from within our "normal" conscious state with an approach like that outlined above.

The postulate I am making is that altered states of consciousness are altered states of $self_1$. Some of the altered states probably involve a reordering of, or interference with, the roles of other brain regions in influencing $self_1$-awareness, perceptions, and the availability of particular memories.

Consciousness in other brain regions could have interesting implications and could eventually serve as a guide for better understanding of some clinical and psychological phenomena. Take dreams, for example. Are they the consequence, in part, of activities of other consciousnesses which are far from "asleep" when our self-consciousness is, and which may have a greater capability of controlling and sequencing experiences in the $self_1$ region during dreaming than during waking? Are some of the different stages of sleep due to different states of the other consciousnesses? If so, then some of the Freudian concepts that derive from dream analysis could be readily encompassed by this view. Attempts at understanding manifest dream content become attempts at understanding the mental processes occurring in brain regions to which $self_1$ does not have direct access. One could develop similar arguments for events occurring during hypnosis. While $self_1$ is mesmerized, other brain regions may utilize its mechanisms for verbal communication. In brief, Freud's unconscious could be conscious to itself.

It would be even more speculative to ascribe to such other consciousnesses the same capabilities of will and feelings we ascribe to $self_1$. In dealing with and redefining these psychiatric concepts, I have been building speculation on top of speculation. This is very risky, and the likelihood of accuracy in such derived postulates is correspondingly small. These speculations are meant only to indicate the way one can manipulate ideas concerning self$_1$ and to show that there may be room for Freudian concepts within a framework more firmly based in the neurosciences. We need verification of the initial hypotheses before building such a complex superstructure. Such verification experiments can come through approaches such as that described for altered states of consciousness. Globus (1973b) has proposed a different way of accounting for the unconscious under an identity theory.

Conclusion

Viewing introspective data as final statements concerning causes of human behavior was the mistake of some early psychologists. Viewing introspective data as unrelated to the causes of human behavior was the over-reactive response of the behaviorists. A position between these two extremes could be most useful in understanding the causes of human behavior.

Although behaviorism cannot serve as a base for the use of introspective data, there is justification for its use with an identity theory of mind and brain as a theoretical foundation. However, we must recognize the limited and sometimes misleading nature of introspective data. A coupling between introspective data and data from neurobiology may prove indispensable in understanding human beings and their behavior.

I hope that those who have read this far are not too disappointed by the present inability of the biological and physical sciences to describe the physical process that is consciousness or to indicate at what level of brain organization or complexity consciousness develops. Although answers are not available, a program that will allow us to gain the knowledge may be forthcoming. Such a program, to be most fruitful, must allow us to gain information from a number of different perspectives. Just as there was a great deal of knowledge concerning genes before they were identified with DNA, so we may learn much about consciousness before understanding the physical basis of consciousness. Indeed, such understanding may come only after we are armed with the additional information. But our philosophic foundation must be broad enough to allow data from such sources as behavioral psychology, physiology, and introspection to be unified.

We may be witnessing the end of the last bastion of human egocentricity. Earlier views of the earth as the center of the universe and of humans as products of special creation have become outdated in most scientific circles. In the near future, consciousness and mind may no longer be considered as uniquely human traits, unshared and unconnected with the rest of nature.

I recognize that the ideas presented here are difficult ones. But they are well worth struggling with. The hypothesis that mental events are brain events carries with it the corollary that our experiences are the personal side of physical processes and, therefore, that we directly experience some physical (brain) processes. This realization is probably as close as a Western intellectual can come to a Zen *satori*, which has been described by Suzuki (1955, 1962) as "a new view of life and things generally ... the unfolding of a new world hitherto imperceived in the confusion of a dualistically-trained mind ... there is perfect identity of Man and Nature" (1955, p. 188).

REFERENCES

Armstong, D. M. *A materialist theory of the mind.* London: Routledge & Kegan Paul, 1968.

Bolles, R. C. Reinforcement, expectancy and learning. *Psychological Review* 1972, *79:* 394–409.

Borst, C. F. (ed.) *The mind-brain identity theory.* London: Macmillan, 1970.

Cooper, J. R., Bloom, F. E., & Roth, R. H. *The biochemical basis of neuropharmacology.* 2nd edition. London: Oxford University Press, 1974.

Feigl, H. *The "mental" and the "physical."* Minneapolis: University of Minnesota Press, 1967.

Freud, S. *New introductory lectures on psychoanalysis.* New York: W. W. Norton, 1933.

———. *An outline of psychoanalysis.* New York: W. W. Norton, 1949. (Originally published in 1940.)

———. *The question of lay analysis.* New York: W. W. Norton, 1969. (Originally published in 1926.)

Globus, G. G. Consciousness and brain. I. The identity thesis. *Archives of General Psychiatry* 1973, *29:* 153–160. (a)

———. Consciousness and brain. II. Introspection, the qualia of experience, and the unconscious. *Archives of General Psychiatry* 1973, *29:* 167–176. (b)

————. Unexpected symmetries in the "world knot." *Science* 1973, *180:* 1129–1136. (c)

Gray, J. A. The mind-brain identity theory as a scientific hypothesis. *Philosophical Quarterly* 1971, *21:* 247–254.

Griffin, D. R. *The question of animal awareness.* New York: Rockefeller University Press, 1976.

Hubbard, J. I. *The biological basis of mental activity.* Reading, Mass.: Addison-Wesley, 1975.

Humphrey, G. *Thinking.* New York: Wiley, 1951.

Huxley, T. H. *Methods and results.* New York: W. W. Norton, 1896.

James, W. *Principles of psychology.* New York: H. Holt, 1890.

Kuhn, T. S. *The structure of scientific revolutions.* Chicago: University of Chicago Press, 1962.

Malcolm, N. *Problems of mind.* New York: Harper & Row, 1971.

Meehl, P. E., & Sellars, W. The concept of emergence. In H. Feigl & M. Scriven (eds.), *Minnesota studies in the philosophy of science 1.* Minneapolis: University of Minnesota Press, 1956.

Morgan, C. L. *Emergent evolution.* New York: Holt, 1923.

Muller, H. J. Life. *Science* 1955, *121:* 1–9.

Piaget, J. *Six psychological studies.* New York: Random House, 1967.

Place, U. T. Is consciousness a brain process? *British Journal of Psychology* 1956, *47:* 44–50.

Popper, K. *The logic of scientific discovery.* New York: Harper & Row, 1959.

————. *Conjectures and refutations.* New York: Basic Books, 1965.

Rose, S. *The conscious brain.* New York: Random House, 1976.

Ryle, G. *The concept of mind.* London: Hutchinson, 1949.

Sherrington, C. *Man on his nature.* 2nd edition. London: Cambridge University Press, 1951.

Skinner, B. F. *Beyond freedom and dignity.* New York: Knopf, 1971.

————. *About behaviorism.* New York: Knopf, 1974.

Smart, J. J. C. *Philosophy and scientific realism.* London: Routledge & Kegan Paul, 1963.

Smith, K. R. *Behavior and conscious experience.* Athens: Ohio University Press, 1969.

Sperry, R. W. Hemisphere deconnection and unity in conscious awareness. *American Psychologist* 1968, *23:* 723–733.

————. A modified concept of consciousness. *Psychological Review* 1969, *76:* 532–536.

————. An objective approach to subjective experience. *Psychological Review* 1970, *77:* 585–590.

————. Changing concepts of consciousness and free will. *Perspectives in Biology and Medicine* 1976, *20:* 9–19. (a)

————. Mental phenomena as causal determinants in brain function. In G. G. Globus, G. Maxwell, & I. Savodnik (eds.), *Consciousness and the brain.* New York: Plenum, 1976. (b)

Stent, G. Limits to the scientific understanding of man. *Science* 1975, *187:* 1052–1057.

Strawson, P. Persons. In H. Feigl, M. Scriven, & G. Maxwell (eds.), *Concepts, theories, and the mind-body problem.* Minneapolis: University of Minnesota Press, 1958.

Suzuki, D. T. *Studies in Zen.* London: Rider, 1955.

————. *The essentials of Zen Buddhism.* New York: E. P. Dutton, 1962.

Tart, C. T. States of consciousness and state-specific sciences. *Science* 1972, *176:* 1203–1210.

Thompson, R. R. *Foundations of physiological psychology.* New York: Harper & Row, 1967.

Warr, P. B. (ed.) *Thought and personality.* Harmondsworth, England: Penguin Books, 1970.

Watson, J. B. *Behaviorism.* Chicago: University of Chicago Press, 1924.

Wilson, D. L. Memory and retrieval. *Medical Hypotheses* 1975, *1:* 183–185.

————. On the nature of consciousness and of physical reality. *Perspectives in Biology and Medicine* 1976, *19:* 568–581.

Wundt, W. *Principles of physiological psychology.* London: Sonnenschein, 1904.

■ 2
Cartography of Conscious States: Integration of East and West

ROLAND FISCHER

> ... Arcane path
> Reveals blindfold;
> Horizons
> Bluff, angels scold.
>   (BBB, unpublished)

"The locus of all points equidistant from a given point" is a *state* description of the circle.

"To construct a circle, rotate a compass with one arm fixed until the other arm has returned to its starting point" is a *process* description of the circle.

These two modes of apprehending structure are the warp and woof of our experience. Pictures, blueprints, maps, and chemical formulas are state descriptions; recipes, differential equations, and playscripts represent processes (Scudder, 1975).

In these pages we intend to illuminate the *process* nature of the original version of our cartography of inner space (Fischer, 1971). Two voyages are charted on the map: The first is along the perception-hallucination continuum of increasing ergotropic arousal—an inner excitation, called central sympathetic or hyperarousal—and the second along the perception-meditation continuum of increasing trophotropic arousal—a tranquil relaxation, or central hypoarousal. A voyage along the path of hyperarousal is experienced by Western travelers as normal, creative, hyperphrenic (including manic and schizophrenic as well as cataleptic and ecstatic states); the voyage along the path of hypoarousal is a succession of meditative experiences referred to by Eastern travelers as *zazen, dhārnā, dhyān, savichār,* and *nirvichār samādhi* (Fischer, 1975a).

Inner space is meant to be a metaphor for the revolving stages of an experiential theater, and refers to states of consciousness based on archetypal (or stereotyped) scripts of particular knowledge. (Note the meaning of the Latin words *scio,* to cut, to make a distinction; *scientia,* knowledge; and *conscientia,* consciousness.) Each particular knowledge—scientific, artistic, literary, religious, or esoteric—is considered to be programmed, innate, or "already there" (Plato, 398 B.C.), and as the stage is set by a particular level of hyperarousal or hypoarousal, the pertaining scenario has to be reexperienced, or flashed back. Thus, the cognitive manifestation of experience is arousal-state-bound as well as (Western or Eastern) culture-bound (Fischer, 1976b).

Each revolving stage is set for a repertoire limited to a few plays or scripts. The theme of these archetypal repertoires consists of wish-fulfilling self-interpretations or stories that are constantly rewritten, repainted, and recomposed for each generation with but slight variations in style. Whenever the level of arousal is raised or lowered— when we ourselves become a moving experience—a new stage revolves to the fore and another type of knowledge appropriate to that particular state of consciousness becomes available. The real nature of fiction and the fictitious nature of reality are revealed through these transformations of consciousness. Accordingly, an essential criterion of masterful, and hence effective, art and literature is to induce state-bound flashbacks for archetypal human experiences of deep love, seething hate, overwhelming joy, loneliness, abject despair, ultimate dread, surging hope, and cosmic ecstasy. Hence, all art is good art insofar as it can reinduce an experiential "high" closely resembling that level of inspired, possessed, religious arousal that prevailed in the writer, painter, composer, filmmaker, or poet "once upon a time." It is not the quality of the artist's preceding feelings that determines the religious nature of his work but his ability to prove and to articulate the religious attitude in the creative process itself. Authentic art, literature, and ritual—at all times, including our own—retain a potentially sacred quality (Dupré, 1975).

Witness the continuous pattern of independent rediscovery of esoteric knowledge throughout the ages. The remarkable identity of doctrine and practice, irrespective of time and space, testifies to the arousal-state-bound nature of conscious knowledge. When Saint Teresa describes in her "Interior Castle" patterns of meditative prayer appropriate to specified states of consciousness, she does not realize that her outline closely parallels the levels of consciousness described in the Hindu Upanishads (Mackey, 1975). The rediscovery occurs by Saint Teresa simply achieving that religious state of arousal at which the pertinent knowledge is revealed. Note also the significant sameness in the descriptions of Saint Teresa, the Protestant Böhme, and the Muslim Gazzali, a sameness that would make it very difficult to distinguish one from another (Bälz, 1907).

Experience, however, is not only arousal-state-bound. The fact that scientific discoveries—the Mendelian laws of inheritance, to give just one example—are discovered independently by various researchers at about the same time testifies to the culture-bound nature of knowing *(zeitgeist),* and hence, consciousness. But culture-bound is just another term for cortical interpretations or "set and setting," or even better, stage set and setting. Hence we may say that experience is (arousal) state-bound and stage-bound.

Knowing-experiencing, then, is distributed over a variety of arousal states in such a manner that a certain scenario is bound to, and only retrievable at, a particular level of arousal. As already mentioned, there is no communication between disparate levels of arousal; to paraphrase Spencer-Brown (1969) and the Coptic Gospel according to Thomas (1968), what is revealed on one level (of arousal state) is concealed on the other, but what is concealed will again be revealed. The interpretation of particular levels of arousal can only be enacted in a restricted, stereotyped, or archetypal manner.

Whenever the stage is set by a particular level of arousal, the pertaining cortical interpretation or knowing, myth, narrative, script, role, or great story may be enacted, reexperienced, or flashed back. This is how scripts of an inner *Schauspiel* are enacted on stage in one's experiential magic theater (Fischer, 1976b).

But who are the role players or personas? The Romans conceived of persona as that which *per sonat* (sounds through the theatrical mask of the role player). According to our classification and terminology of depersonalization, the role player's sound is of a subcortical nature, while the interpretation of the role he plays appears to be his personal cortical or cultural creation. The cortical mask of the player may be equated with what we call set and setting.

The subcortical nature of that which *per sonat* seems to be borne out by Schaltenbrand's (1965) data. Through electrical stimulation of subcortical structures (the thalamic nuclei) he evoked speech, in contrast to Penfield and others, who could never do this when stimulating cortical structures, but obtained only unintelligible vocalizations (Schaltenbrand, Spuler, Wahren, & Rumler, 1971).

The word *mask,* according to Leuner (1974), is derived from the Langobardic *masca,* meaning the net in which a corpse was shrouded and then later, by extension, meaning the dead man himself on his return as an evil spirit. Among primitive peoples masks represent spirits, mainly the spirits of the dead in the broadest sense of the term. This ghostly community of ancestors assumes a great variety of forms and displays the greatest figural complexity in advanced demonology, where the resemblance to human features grows ever closer.

The inner matrix of these often broadly deployed symbolic structures—Leuner goes on to say—may be the figure of the wicked mother or of the aggressive and punitive father, as a regressive expression of the parental figures and the world the child misunderstood and distorted in its infancy. Originally perceived in terms of the magico-mythical experience and fantasy of childhood, subsequently distorted by affective enrichment, and contaminated by similar experiences, these archetypal figures are reexperienced during aroused states whether they are drug-induced or naturally occurring (Fischer, 1976c). Moreover, such masks and faces are repeatedly reexperienced during hyperphrenic or hypophrenic hallucinatory states irrespective of whether these states were initiated for religious and cultic ends (e.g., peyote rites), or were induced for therapeutic or research purposes.

"Memory is therefore not that which we remember, but that which remembers us." Memory, concludes Octavio Paz (1949), "is a present that never keeps passing."

The Perception-Hallucination Continuum

The circular model of inner space in Figure 2-1 is an updated version of the original cartography. In both instances varieties of conscious states are mapped on a perception-hallucination continuum of increasing ergotropic arousal, a central excitation or hyperarousal (Fischer, 1975b)—left half of Figure 2.1—and a perception-meditation continuum of increasing trophotropic arousal, a central relaxation or hypoarousal—right half of Figure 2.1 (Fischer, 1976a). These levels of subcortical arousal are cortically or cognitively interpreted by Western and Eastern man as normal, creative, hyperphrenic, cataleptic, and ecstatic states (left) and *zazen, dhārnā, dhyān,* and *samādhi* (right), respectively.

Perceptions restricted to normal levels of arousal are connected with daily routine activities. With rising levels of central sympathetic arousal, however, man's ability to verify with his hands and feet an experience as real is gradually inhibited and ultimately blocked. Evidently, reality is a touchy subject in that the proof of the sensory pudding is in the motor eating (Fischer, 1969a). Thus, when levels of arousal rise on the perception-hallucination continuum—such as during the hallucinogenic drug-induced waking dream state (as after the ingestion of mescaline, D-lysergic acid diethylamine [LSD] and psilocybin) or during dreaming (the rapid eye movement or REM sleep state)—voluntary motor (M) verification becomes increasingly irrelevent as well as difficult, and perceptions are transformed into intense "inner sensations" (S). Hence, hallucinations, whether drug-induced or natural, may be characterized as "inner sensations without action": by a high S/M ratio. We have measured high S/M ratios during hallucinogenic drug-induced states, specifically through an increase in handwriting area, reflecting the closing in of nearby visual space and a decrease in handwriting pressure over time (see Figures 2-2 and 2-3) (Fischer, Hill, Thatcher, & Scheib, 1970; Fischer, Kappeler,

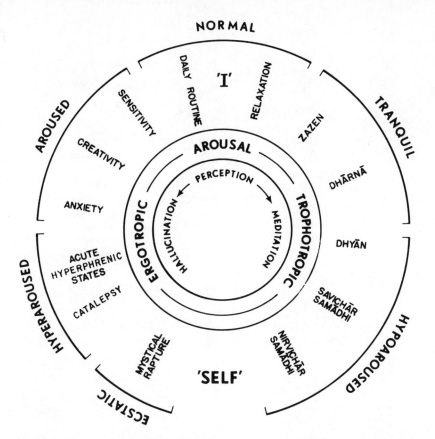

FIGURE 2-1. Varieties of conscious states are mapped on a perception-hallucination continuum of increasing ergotropic arousal or hyperarousal (left half) and a perception-meditation continuum of increasing trophotropic arousal or hypoarousal (right half). (From R. Fischer, "Transformations of consciousness. A cartography. I. The perception-hallucination continuum." *Confinia Psychiatrica* 1975, 18:221–244. Reproduced by permission of the journal and S. Karger AG, Basel, Switzerland. This figure also appeared in R. Fischer's chapter in Siegel, R. K. and West, L. J., eds., *Hallucinations*, New York: Wiley, 1975 and is reprinted with permission.)

Note that a labeling in terms of psychopathology has been omitted from this map. Hence it is perfectly normal to be hyperphrenic and ultimately ecstatic in response to increasing levels of ergotropic hyperarousal. Only when a person gets stuck in a particular state or role do we label him abnormal. The hyperaroused rapid eye movement (REM) stage of dreaming sleep may be placed between creativity and anxiety on the left side of the perception-hallucination continuum, whereas the delta or slow-wave EEG sleep is on the horizontally corresponding right side of the map, between *zazen* and *dhārnā*, on the hypoaroused perception-meditation continuum. Each night while asleep, we repeatedly travel to and from these states and experience in fast succession creative as well as psychopathological, or stereotyped, dialogues between the "I" and the "Self."

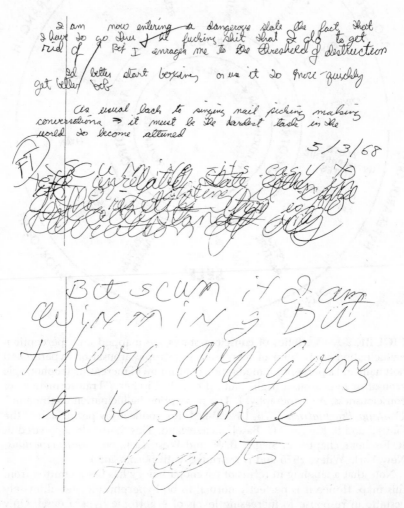

FIGURE 2-2. Entries in the diary of a 21-year-old college student while he gradually moves—without any drugs, i.e., naturally—into a hyperphrenic state. Note in the entry, at the bottom, the characteristic increase in handwriting area paralleled by a decrease in handwriting pressure (high S/M ratio). The illustration is 65% of original size. (From R. Fischer, "Transformations of consciousness. A cartography. I. The perception-hallucination continuum." *Confinia Psychiatrica* 1975, 18:221–244. Reproduced by permission of the journal and S. Karger AG, Basel, Switzerland.)

Wisecup, & Thatcher, 1970; Thatcher, Kappeler, Wisecup, & Fischer, 1970).

Figure 2-2 illustrates an increasingly high S/M ratio in the handwriting samples of a 21-year-old college student as he gradually moves—without any drugs—into a hyperphrenic state. The entry into his diary marked 5/3/68 may be labeled as a "jammed computer state"; the following sample (bottom of Figure 2-2) clearly displays the significant increase in writing area accompanied by a decrease in pressure.

Figure 2-3 depicts four attempts of a 22-year-old college student volunteer to copy a 28-word text at the peak of a brief hallucinogenic drug experience induced by the oral ingestion of only 6 mg. of psilo-

FIGURE 2-3. Illustration of an unusual hypersensitivity to a hallucinogenic drug. Attempts of a 22-year-old healthy college student to copy four times a 28-word text at the peak influence (90-100 minutes after the oral administration) of not more than 6 mg. psilocybin. The four handwriting samples clearly display a transient "jammed computer" state. The illustration is 40% of original size. (From R. Fischer, "Transformations of consciousness. A cartography. I. The perception-hallucination continuum." *Confinia Psychiatrica* 1975, 18:221–244. Reproduced by permission of the journal and S. Karger AG, Basel, Switzerland.)

cybin. Such hypersensitivity is rather rare, and we witnessed one out of about 1,000 cases during a 10-year period of experimentation with hallucinogenic drugs. The subject remained pretty much out of touch and in a "jammed computer" state for about 2.5 hours.

A high S/M ratio is also implicit in the recent findings of Goldstein and Stoltzfus (1973), who report that states of stimulation, excitation, anxiety, and hallucination correspond to a progressive narrowing of interhemispheric EEG amplitude differences with an eventual reversal of their relationship. In other words, data processing during hallucinations is preferentially shifted from the analytical-temporal, speech-dominant (dom), and motor-coordinating "major" side of the brain toward the nonverbal, spatial, symbol-laden, and nondominant (nondom) "minor" side of the cerebral cortex. To put it in our terms, the increase in interoceptive visuo-spatial imagery is paralleled by a decrease in willed motor activity reflecting a high S/M or high nondom/dom ratio.

During both increasing hyperarousal, which is characterized by EEG desynchronization, and increasing hypoarousal, characterized by EEG synchronization, there is a decrease in variability of the EEG amplitude (Goldstein, Murphree, Sugerman, Pfeiffer, & Jenney, 1963). We have interpreted this decrease in variability as an increase in stereotypy, borne out by the fact that Goldstein's coefficient of variation (C.V.) of the EEG amplitude is in the same low range during deep meditation as it is in catatonia: 7–8. It appears, however (at least during the psilocybin-induced travel on the perception-hallucination continuum), that the C.V. is personality-trait dependent (Thatcher, Wiederholt, & Fischer, 1971); in introverts the variability decreases with rising arousal whereas in extroverts it increases.

The perception-hallucination continuum of increasing ergotropic (i.e., central sympathetic) arousal is characterized by diffuse cortical excitation, as in awakening (Gellhorn & Kiely, 1972); EEG-desynchronization-hypersynchronization (Winters, Ferrar-Allado, Guzman-Flores, & Alcaraz, 1972); and an increase in noradrenergic, sympathetic discharge ascending from the *locus coeruleus.* Hofmann (1968) calls this state "the excitation syndrome" and does not fail to mention that motor activity during this state is "strangely damped." To put it in our terminology, the excitation syndrome is marked by a high S/M ratio (Fischer, 1971). There is also an increase in muscle tone and a decrease in skin resistance, the latter being a good index of increased ergotropic arousal, which again may be part of the "orienting reflex." One also observes fast habituation to alpha-blocking (Thatcher et al., 1971), mydriasis, hyperthermia, piloerection, reflexes (e.g., the knee jerk), and stimulation of synapses in the reticular formation. The latter results in an increased sensitivity to sensory stimuli in "minimizers" (Petrie's [1967] and Silverman's [1972] "reducers") and decreased sensitivity in "maximizers" (Petrie's [1967] and Silverman's [1972] "augmenters"). Minimizers are subjects displaying larger standard deviations on a variety of perceptual tasks; they are variable in that they possess a large cortical repertoire (variance being operationally identified with information, e.g., cortical interpretive ability [Panton & Fischer, 1973]). Maximizers, in contrast, display consistently small standard deviations on perceptual tasks; they are predictable, stable subjects.

The meaning of hyperphrenia (left side of Figure 2-1) includes the morbid and creative varieties of the schizophrenias, as well as the manic phase of manic-depressive psychosis. Catalepsy, or catatonia, is the next higher homeostatic step function on the perception-hallucination continuum, and it is generally accepted that while hyperphrenia is norepinephrinergically governed, catatonia is dopaminergically mediated through the nigro-striatal system.

Figure 2-4 displays the geometric-ornamental features in the writing of an acutely hyperphrenic person. The intense hallucinatory experience during high levels of central sympathetic arousal may be interpreted as threat and possession. The feeling of being overpowered by alien forces may be partially controlled by introducing a geometric-ornamental order (Fischer, 1969b). The ornamental reiteration of signs may also be regarded as a metalinguistic communication of the hallucinated writer about his quasi-cataleptic state.

It could be argued that the hyperaroused hallucinatory experience of being possessed or under a spell is, at least in part, comparable to the hyperaroused REM state. The low unit firing rate of the corpus callosum, for instance, during a cat's REM dream state, decreases interhemispheric integration (Rechtschaffen, 1973) and "one half hemisphere may not quite know what the other half is doing." This might account for the prevalence of strangers and strangeness in dreams; about 40% of characters in dreams are strangers, or people we do not recognize. Moreover, only stimuli such as light, sound,

"VAU- MA- VA- VŌVE -VÀ - MAṄ- MÀ-MAN-
NAM- HŌŌ?
MÀN- MAN-PAI-HŌZ - RAG- N'A'LIL-
QWA- SHA- SI ...
MA-SAA- AA- À- MI- MI- MẎ- MẎ- MINE-
MA- MÀN- ÀA-NAM- I- WAĊ - A- SAT-
IV- A- SHÀT- IṄ;
QᵥA- YIN- ÀMN- LA- HIN- VÀN- ÖL-É
WÀ- RAG-ĀNE- ŌM- NA- GIL.
VÉ- GA- RI- MŌ- SÀA- LA- LŪ- NÉ-PÉ-
YI- MA- NIN- YA-MA- RÀN- AĊ-AH-
RÀN- EE- RÀL RÀR'IN.
RÉ- GI- NAĊ - VAN- GAH- YÂW- MA-NA-LÉ
RA- CŪNE- VAN- RÀ- QŪR - ÀM -RAQ-
ITAḦ-RA -GRAG- RAHG- GRIN- GRAHG.

RÀ'-TIN-ROC- RHAI- NEI- VÀ- RIN -GRA-
SIN- RA- YIN-MALL-NÀN- PAṠ- HÀ-
VAS- TIN- BHAḊ- I- VAṀ- LÖ-LAH-GHA.

LHÀ - GHÀ- GHÀ- GI-VA- ṠA -SAN-SA-
RA- MAN- KAA- RAS- MŪS- KAND-Ō -EE.
Ū- NI- NI- NAN- AI- VAT- RAT- RI- RAT-
YA- ŌOE- LAN- LAN- LAN-LE -LA-LŌE.

RÀN- RÀN- RŨN- I- RÀN - DŌE- L'MA- SHA-
WHÉ- L'HA - WHÀ'L- É- NÉ- NÉ- NŬM.

GNÀ- GNA- GÀ- GNAT- À- MÀL- È - D'RA-
D'RA- DRÀT- DIN- DRÀ - DI- NAAM-
Ū- SEI- VÀNDRÀ- DIN. "

FIGURE 2-4. Handwriting sample of a young hyperphrenic male in a quasi-cataleptic state. The high S/M ratio (enlarged handwriting area and decreased pressure) that usually is a characteristic of hyperphrenic states apparently cannot be expressed in the "jammed computer" state, since at this point, the increasing loss of freedom was interpreted by the individual as possession. Note the stereotypy and ornamental reiteration as attempts to control the impact of high levels of arousal. The handwriting is 55% of original size. (The sample was obtained and is reproduced through the courtesy and with the permission of Marilyn Delphinium Rutgers. From R. Fischer, "Transformations of consciousness. A cartography. I. The perception-hallucination continuum." *Confinia Psychiatrica* 1975, 18:221–244. Reproduced by permission of the journal and S. Karger AG, Basel, Switzerland.)

scent, and so forth are incorporated into dreams that are associated with higher arousal thresholds (Bradley & Meddis, 1974). Thus, the hallucinatory waking dream state of being possessed may contain all, if not more, of the following factors: (1) reduced rate of interhemispheric integration, (2) selective incorporation of those outer stimuli that are paralleled by corresponding high levels of inner arousal, and (3) the preferential shift to the right hemisphere during transition from quiescent non-REM to REM state and from normal, routine levels of arousal to hyperaroused or hypoaroused states, respectively (Goldstein & Stolzfus, 1973).

Hence, being inspired, and on an even higher level of arousal, being possessed (Fischer, 1969a), may be varieties of self-possession or self-actualization depending on the intellectual and spiritual sophistication of the persona. Novalis, the eighteenth-century German writer, believed that indeed the greatest magician would be the one who could cast a spell on himself so that his own magic would appear to him strange and from without.

At the peak of ecstasy, alpha frequency increases but alpha amplitude decreases. Beta rhythms of increased amplitude (30–50 μV) are recorded from the Rolandic area with a frequency of 40–45 Hz. In ecstasy (as in *samādhi*) stimuli applied from without do not alter the EEG (Das & Gastaut, 1957); there is neither habituation (learning) nor alpha-blocking. During ecstasy in front of her church on a hot summer day, Saint Catherine of Siena was pricked with needles in many places, but apparently was unable to perceive it (Underhill, 1911). ". . . afterward when she came back to her senses, she felt the pain in her body and perceived that she had thus been wounded."

According to recent results obtained by Cohen, Rosen, & Goldstein (1976), a left to right hemispheric reversal of amplitude laterality—one that pertains when, for example, verbalization is followed by music or when NREM sleep changes into REM sleep (Goldstein & Stoltzfus, 1973)—is manifested at the peak of sexual ecstasy or orgasm. The left to right hemispheric switch observed in four of seven right-handed subjects of both sexes (in an eighth, left-handed subject the shift was in the opposite direction) is characterized by a 4/sec. frequency that is below theta and above delta activity, and a very high amplitude, 200μV. During this right hemispheric switch there is little change in left hemisphere, which displays a persistent preorgasmic alpha activity. It is intriguing to speculate about the nondominant or spatial quality of ecstatic experiences, especially today when the "container" concept of space, a nineteenth-century remnant, is undergoing a Leibnitzian-Chinese (gestalt-type or monadic, common to both Leibnitz and Chinese philosophical thoughts) transformation into a force-field. With due apologies to the reader for calling orgasm "a poor man's ecstasy," I submit that all ecstatic experiences may be characterized by a hallucinatory high S/M ratio and a very low coefficient of variation, at least in introverts.

Analogous to phantom limb sensations (Fischer, 1969a), ecstasies may be conceptualized as phanton universe experiences. Cut off—at the umbilical cord after birth—from a universal existence, the individual at the peak of ecstasy or orgasm incorporates again the universe into his body image as one indivisible gestalt. Such an experience may represent the ultimate interhemispheric integration with an ecstatic (not yet epileptic) focus in the right hemisphere. The similarity of specific EEG laterality data obtained by Goldstein and associates (Cohen et al., 1976; Goldstein & Stoltzfus, 1973; Goldstein, Sugerman, Marjerrison, & Stoltzfus, 1973) during hyperaroused and hypoaroused states prompts one to speculate about the orgasmic quality of the hypoaroused experience of the Void. The photograph of Ramakrishna in *samādhi* (Lemaitre, 1963) indeed may be interpreted as a phantom universe experience of the highest euphoric intensity.

Activation and Arousal

At this point, it may be useful to emphasize that activation and arousal denote different concepts. A novel and possibly meaningful stimulus brings about the orienting response, which implies dishabituation; repeated exposure to a frequently occurring stimulus results in habituation, that is, learning not to pay attention to an apparently meaningless stimulus.

Although activation and central sympathetic or ergotropic arousal denote two different phenomena, activation may develop into arousal (e.g., in response to a significant—particularly meaningful—stimulus that can trigger and evoke the flashing back of a past arousal-state-bound experience) (Fischer & Landon, 1972).

Activation, in contrast to arousal, is not a generalized hypermetabolic state; only a local increase in blood flow to the head at the expense of flow to the fingertips is noted. The EEG record obtained from the lateral surface of the cerebral hemispheres displays an increase in the low-amplitude, high-frequency components and a hypersynchrony from medial and basal brain structures (Pribram, 1971).

Arousal, or the "excitation syndrome," on the other hand, is a general hypermetabolic state. It proceeds from activation (low-voltage, fast EEG activity, or desynchronization) to arousal and hyperarousal, or hypersynchrony, that is, from "increased data content and increased rate of data processing" to the "jammed computer state" (Fischer, 1971). The former may correspond to a creative, the latter to a psychotic, state.

Desynchronization, as suggested by Lindsley (1961), is a functional independence of neuronal elements, with each available for separate information processing channels. Pribram (1971) sees this enhanced separation as an increase in organization, or in terms of information content, an increase in uncertainty. Apparently then, quantity changes into quality, information into meaning. Perhaps contacts of separate information channels produce the novel context for a creative text.

In conclusion, it is theorized that ergotropic mechanisms, either central sympathetic or hyperarousal, mediated via the brain stem reticular formation turn off the midline thalamic pacemaker, which in turn switches on the cortex and thus induces an alert focusing marked by very fast habituation. The ensuing desynchronization of cortical neurons, with a display of beta rhythm, is quite conducive to the creative elaboration of novel and original thoughts and images. On the other hand, in the hypoaroused state, trophotropic or central parasympathetic arousal mediated by the serotonergic mechanisms in the raphe nucleus turns the thalamic pacemaker on, thereby inducing an inhibitory cortical phasing of a 10/sec. frequency or alpha wave. During this synchronized, "decorticated," alert and inner-focused state, Zen masters show an alpha-blocking response to auditory clicks, but in contrast to normal controls, do not habituate to these stimuli. They report perceiving each stimulus more clearly than in ordinary waking states. "The world" apparently becomes "its own magic" (Suzuki, 1968). "He perceives the object, responds to it, and yet is never disturbed by it" write Kasamatsu and Hirai (1966). According to Pribram (1971), this "redundancy enhancement" refers to the brain mechanism by which the amount of redundancy in a system can be governed. This regulation seems not only to be effective over input, but also operates on motor activity. The Faustian, hyperaroused states on the left side of Figure 2-1 are thus conducive to that type of creativity the essence of which is novelty in concepts, images, and adventures. Western society, particularly since the Renaissance, has cultivated a consciousness biased and shaped by a hyperaroused, desynchronized, creative cortical activity. This can be seen in the discoveries of continents, science, technology, and the ever-evolving styles of primitive, classical, and baroque art.

The Perception-Meditation Continuum

A short historical introduction should assist in a clearer understanding of the Eastern hypoaroused meditative states and the Sanskrit terminology used in our cartography (Figure 2-1).

The spread of Buddhism from India to China between the first and fourth century of the Christian era ranks as one of the major events in the history of religion. Chinese equivalents were coined for Buddhist terms; thus, the Primal Nothingness of Taoism *(pên-wu)* prepared the way for understanding the Buddhist Void and *nirvāna*. Cosmic oneness with the All is felt differently by the Chinese, who live harmoniously with nature, than by the Indians, who tend to flee the world. Hence, Mahayana Buddhism found more congenial possibilities for development in the spiritual climate of China and Tibet than in its own country of origin, India. In any event, the Chinese received, along with the doctrine and cult of Buddhism, the knowledge of Buddhist meditation. They rendered the Sanskrit term *dhyān* as *ch'an* (archaic: *dian*), which in Japanese became *Zen,* a term denoting ceremonial renunciation or release (Dumoulin, 1963). Heiler (1933) regards Zen as a decadent form of Buddhist mysticism, an approximation to psychotherapy.

The *jhāna* of early Buddhism, however, was not yet identified with meditation, contemplation, or Yoga. *Jhāna* represented loneliness as a spiritual process not to be used for active thinking; its step by step evolution is described by Davids (1933).

According to Johnston (1971), the pattern described by people who have gone through the modern Zen experience may be subdivided into four stages: (1) initial stages and the *kōan,* or giving up the self (ego loss); (2) *sanmay,* a deep meditation; (3) *makyō,* a hallucinatory phase; and (4) enlightenment (*satori* or *kenshō*).

The initial stages are concerned with the emptying of self, the renouncing of the subject-object relationship, in short, with a spring cleaning of the mind that results in the creation of the Void. After breathing is regularized, and some facility for sitting in silent vacuity has been acquired, one may receive the *koān,* Mu (a character close to the English "nothing").

In a contemplative wrestling with Mu, one identifies with Mu and rejects one's ego. Fixing his eyes continuously on a point on the wall or on the ground, the disciple is then able to enter into a deep stage of meditation, called *sanmay* (from the Sanskrit *samādhi*). Kasamatsu and Hirai (1966) and Hirai (1974) note that from the electrophysiological point of view, this mental state will be shown as following several points. First, during *zazen* the level of the cerebral excitatory state is gradually lowered in a way that is different from sleep patterns. Second, the concentration of the mind in *zazen* is superficially similar to the hypnotic trance. But there are differences in electroencephalographic findings between the two. In the mental state during *zazen,* outer or inner stimuli are not neglected but precisely perceived. This is clearly shown in that there is alpha blocking but almost no habituation in EEG responses to stimulation. These findings seem to indicate that the mental state of Zen veterans is such that it cannot be affected by either an external or an internal stimulus beyond the mere response to it. One master described such a state of mind as that of noticing every person he sees on the street but of not looking back with emotional lingering.

As one progresses in the silent darkness, there may arise an hallucinatory phase known as *makyō,* which means literally "the world of devil." The *makyō* is generally explained as the rising of subconscious elements into the conscious mind. For certain people, a tampering with the subconscious—in our terms, the incommunicado between differing levels of arousal—may be delicate, even perilous. A skilled guru, however, may smoothly handle the uncovered body of knowing as one gradually and slowly travels through increasingly hypoaroused states.

Certainly the dangers of nervous collapse in Zen are not small, especially in the case of those who lack the strength to integrate the data rising from the unconscious or who are unable to face the basic anxiety that may be uncovered. For it seems probable that all the preparation I have described, especially the irrationality of the *kōan,* is calculated to create an artificial psychosis that may lead to the "Zen madness" that Japanese doctors know well enough, even though little has appeared about it in print in English (Johnston, 1971).

After this hallucinatory period, the great climax of *satori* or *kenshō* (the word more commonly used by the Japanese, meaning "seeing into the essence of things") is not far away (Johnston, 1971). It rarely comes when one is sitting silently in meditation:

> Master Hui-neng, for example, got enlightenment by listening to the chanting of the Diamond Sutra; Master Teshan got it by observing that Master Lung-t'an blew a candle flame out; Master Ling-yun got it by seeing a peach flower falling; Master Po-chang got it when his master, Ma-tsu, twisted his nose in his young days; Master Hakuin got it by hearing the sound of the temple gong.

About enlightenment little can be said that will even remotely express the reality. It is a great crash accompanied by joy and followed by deep peace. Or in the words of Dogen: "Now I have realized clearly that Mind is the mountain, the river, and the earth, the sun, the moon, and the stars."

But it should be recalled that there are other enlightenments that are more quietly spiritual, prompted by an esthetic experience penetrating deeply into the personality. It should also be noted that the Soto sect puts more stress on gradual enlightenment, insisting that the very squatting is part of the enlightenment, not just a preparatory phase.

Zazen, or the practice of Zen, with its aim of enlightenment may be labeled by some as a psychotechnique quite divorced from any system of thought. Nevertheless, it is a ritualized procedure using no words or letters but a right cerebral hemispheric gestalt-type perception-cognition with the aim of arriving at an Eastern "peak experience" or enlightenment: *satori.* The set, setting, and expectations (that is, the socially ritualized cortical interpretation of subcortical hypoarousal) are implicit in the atmosphere abounding with images of Shakya Muni (a form of Buddha) and of Buddhist saints, the smell of incense, the sound of the temple gong, the attire of the monks, and the reverent silence.

Thus, the essence of *zazen* and Zen is the submerging and disappearance of the ego. This is admirably expressed by the famous Rinzai monk, Hakuin Ekaku (1971): "It is like two mirrors mutually reflecting one another without even the shadow of an image between. Mind and object of mind are one and the same; things and oneself are not two." T. S. Eliot's "Four Quartets" expressed with rare intuition the same oneness:

Music heard so deeply
That it is not heard at all, but you are the music
While the music lasts . . .

Goldstein, Sugerman, Marjerrison, & Stoltzfus (1973) and Goldstein & Stoltzfus (1973) were the first to report that, in our terminology, both the hyperaroused hallucinatory and the hypoaroused meditative states correspond to a progressive narrowing of interhemispheric EEG amplitude differences with an eventual reversal of their relationship. Hence a characteristically high nondom/dom ratio marks the shift to nonverbal information processing and an experience of intense meaning. Bogen's (1973) interpretation of hemispheric specificity enables us to appreciate scientifically the esthetic quality of such internal "subjective" experiences. Bogen proposes "that each hemisphere represents the other and the world in complementary mappings, the left mapping the self as a subset of the world and the right mapping the world as a subset of the self."

But the Indian Yoga masters' attempts to go farther and flee the world completely is attested to by their more extensive lowering of the level of arousal. Note that during the deepest meditation of Yoga masters, in *samādhi,* the alpha rhythm is not altered or blocked by flashing lights, sounding gongs, or the touch of a hot test tube. (Recall in this context an analogous unresponsiveness to outside stimulation displayed by Saint Catherine of Siena during the most hyperaroused ecstatic state.) Yoga *samādhi* thus represents a lower hypometabolic (trophotropic) state, and expresses a greater inability to function in physical space time than *zazen* does (Anand, Chhina, & Singh, 1961). A corollary to this enstasis, a lowest metabolic and arousal state, is the experience of the Void. The Void is at the core of a philosophy of emptiness in general and Mahayana Buddhism in particular. *Sūnyatā* (from sūnya, "void or empty") may be translated as voidness or emptiness.[1] But *sūnya* also means cypher or zero in Sanskrit, and hence *sūnyatā* implies a philosophy of zero, which contains nothing in itself, but as a mathematical concept and symbol stands for a great many functions and possibilities (Chang, 1971). The mystical Self and the concept of zero thus share a common meaning that may be infinitely enlarged or diminished as a function of place value. Eliade (1967) and Jain and Jain (1973) concisely review Patanjali's five preparatory and four crucial steps that constitute the essential set and setting for the practice of Yoga and its aim of experiencing the Void in Nirvana. The preparatory steps are: *yama,* the principle of moral conduct; *niyam,* the sense of discipline; *āsan,* the habit of sitting in erect and relaxed posture; *prānāyām,* the practice of slow, rhythmic, deep breathing while in *āsan;* and *pratyāhār,* the detaching of the mind at will from the sense organs.

Within such a disciplined and ascetic set and setting after years of never-ceasing practice, the four crucial or cultic "operations" proceed as the ceremonial renunciation of the world and hence the dissolution of all thought processes.

Dhārnā is an uninterrupted concentration to hold the mind on a fixed center (such as a thought, an object, or any part or property of an object).

Dhyān is the maintaining of the meditation during the preceding step but at a constant rate of flow.

Savichār (sa-vichār: with thought) *samādhi* is the stage in which meditation deepens and the mind by projection may assume the form of (and thus become) the thought or the object itself on which it was meditating in the previous step. This complete union reveals to the Yogi the real and true nature of things. Just as there is no alternative but to taste an apple to know how an apple tastes or to bear a child and be a mother to know what motherhood is, so also there is no alternative to true being other than to experience what one already knows. In other words, to be equals to experience what you already know. That is why the Yogi claims direct and total knowl-

1. From the vantage point of our Faustian Western culture, a good life without content, even if it is spent in learning and mutual helpfulness with others—equally without content—is not a contented one. Evidently, values cannot be meaningfully translated or even discussed in terms of another culture. Meaning is "meaningful" only at that level of arousal at which it is experienced, and every experience has its state-bound meaning (Fischer, 1971). Meaning is state-bound as well as culture-bound to value whether that value pertains to paradigms or experiences.

edge and perception. Since at this stage the mind is still occupied, even though with only one thought process, it is called "substantive" (*sabeej, savikalpa, savichār,* or *savitark*) *samādhi.*

Nirvichār (nir-vichar: without thought) *samādhi* (union, totality, absorption) empties the Yogi completely, including a state which I would describe as pure self-reference without content, or a state of mind without content, unsubstantive, devoid of all desires, emotions, and thoughts. In other words, there is no cortical interpretation attached to a subcortical activity that proceeds at the lowest level of arousal and metabolic rate.

Patanjali and his commentators distinguish two kind of *samādhi:* One is obtained with the help of an object or idea (by fixing one's thought on a point in space or on an idea); the stasis is called *samprajñāta samādhi* (enstasis with support, or differentiated enstasis). When, on the other hand, *samādhi* is obtained apart from any "relation" (whether external or mental)—that is, when one obtains a "conjunction" into which no "otherness" enters but which is simply a full comprehension of being—one has realized *asamprajñāta samādhi* (undifferentiated stasis).

We are, then, confronted with two sharply differentiated classes of states. The first class is acquired through the Yogic technique of concentration *(dhārnā)* and the meditation *(dhyān);* the second class comprises only a single state, that is, unprovoked enstasis, raptus. No doubt, even this *asamprajñāta samādhi* is always owing to prolonged efforts on the Yogi's part. It is not a gift or a state of grace. One can hardly reach it before having sufficiently experienced the kinds of *samādhi* included in the first class. It is the crown of the innumerable concentrations and meditations that have preceded it. But it comes without being summoned, without being provoked, without special preparation for it. That is why it can be called a raptus (Eliade, 1967).

There is a state of emptiness between *nirvichār samādhi* and ecstasy (Figure 2-1) that is no longer experience and is called *nirodh*[2] (no prison) and is characterized by the lowest metabolic rate still compatible with life. It is the absolute cessation of consciousness, and may last for up to seven days although time—or, in our terms, data

2. *Nirodha* (cessation) *ni* denotes absence and *radha,* a prison. No prison or cessation of suffering "because it is a condition for the cessation of suffering consisting in non-arising" (Buddhaghosa, 1964).

processing (Fischer, 1967a, 1967b)—is suspended in this state (Goleman, 1972).

Very few individuals are able to enter this "self" state and stay in it for a predetermined period because of the "rebound" from ecstasy to *nirvichār samādhi*. We have referred to this rebound, which occurs in response to intense sympathetic excitation at ecstasy, the peak of ergotropic arousal or hyperarousal (Fischer, 1971). It is a rebound from a Faustian trip of creative-psychotic fragmentation or individuation (Campbell's [1949] mythological hero journey) into the cosmic-oceanic peace of unity. Such a rebound may be conceived as a physiological protective mechanism; while the rebound from *nirvichār samādhi* to ecstasy is called the Kundalini experience.

Rebounds are possible on all horizontal levels in Figure 2-1; in clinical psychiatry they are sometimes referred to as therapeutic abreactions. The capability to rebound is in any case an indication of health. Patients are those individuals who get stuck on either the left or right side of our continuum, thus incapable of rebounding or otherwise returning to levels of arousal that correspond to the normal state of daily routine. Such a return to the I, in-the-world state (top of Figure 2-1) is possible either by again using the path of travel or through horizontal rebound(s) in a zigzag manner. In any case, the Self of ecstasy and *samādhi* (bottom of Figure 2-1) are one and the same.

Trophotropic and ergotropic rebounds are directly related to the intensity of the preceding sympathetic and parasympathetic stimulation, respectively (Gellhorn, 1970). Since, however, each state of consciousness with its attendant behavior is both arousal-state-bound and culture-bound, we cannot say, for example, that a Western subject at the peak of a high, hallucinogenic, drug-induced ecstasy rebounds into *samādhi*. The rebound should be conceptualized in Western terms (that is, psychophysiologically) and called a peaceful, calm, hypometabolic state.

Let me illustrate this point with another example. Imagine a Western subject, and accompany him on his trip on the perception-hallucination continuum. The ergotropic stretch of the voyage up to hyperphrenia (Figure 2-1) may be said to be governed by norepinephrinergic mechanisms; the subject is expected now to continue to the next higher aroused state, the cataleptic, which is mainly under dopaminergic mediation. The progression, however, does not materialize, and the subject is sent to a psychiatrist, who has to decide whether the patient is manic or in an acute schizophrenic episode. The psychiatrist prescribes lithium, and the patient responds favorably to the drug. He is therefore diagnosed as being in the manic phase of a manic-depressive condition. This bipolar patient now may rebound after a certain amount of time, not into the *dhyān* state (Figure 2-1) but into the depressive phase of his illness. The *dhyān* state is certainly not a depression but a state experienced by an Eastern *sanyasi*. There are 17 million of these holy men in India (Klineberg, 1970) who live secluded in forests or mountains as religious medicants. They have left their families, after bringing up their children, and prefer to live the meditative life of a guru. Would one diagnose them as suffering from post-middle-age depression?

That the Eastern structure of consciousness does not fit the mental structure of our cortical interpretations—the Western set, setting, and expectations—has been impressively documented by Ram Dass (1973), who has repeatedly administered to an Eastern guru very high doses of the Western "medicine," LSD. The reaction of the guru to 1500 mcg. of the drug was remarkable:

> He laughed at me—and at the end of an hour just nothing has happened. And I was there all day and nothing had happened at all. At the end of the hour he says, "You got anything stronger?" I said no. "Oh."
> ... At the time, [the guru] used Christ as the saint he was talking about. He said [LSD] allows you to have the visit of Christ but you can't stay with him. ... He said love is a much stronger drug than LSD medicine. [Ram Dass, 1973]

It is to be remembered, then, that consciousness creates culture and culture creates consciousness.

Consciousness during Sleep, Drug-induced States, and a Healing State

Sleep experience (Jouvet, 1972) may be cartographed on the same map displayed in Figure 2-1. States of consciousness associated with the hyperaroused REM stage of sleep—noradrenergic regulation (locus coeruleus)—may be placed between creativity and anxiety on the left side of the perception-hallucination continuum, whereas the delta or slow-wave EEG sleep is maintained by serotonergic neurons (raphe nucleus) and may be located on the horizontally corresponding right side of the map, that is, between *zazen* and *dhārnā*, on the tranquil perception-meditation continuum. Thus, each night while asleep, we repeatedly move through a revolving trophotropic and ergotropic stage set of arousal states, and become actor and audience of creative or stereotyped scenarios, the dialogues between the I (or the world) and the Self (Fischer, 1971, 1976a).

A simultaneous association between REM and delta slow-wave states may be depicted by a horizontal line bridging these two states. Such a line may then represent a composite state, which in fact may be induced by marijuana ingestion; both a simultaneously increased heart rate and a slow-wave, EEG-patterned, relaxed meditative state characterize the marijuana-induced state (Fairchild, Jenden, & Mickey, 1971; Linton, Kuechenmeister, White, & Travis, 1975). Another line connecting the waking I and REM states may stand for the amphetamine-induced composite state of consciousness (Deniker, Boissier, Etevenon, Ginestet, Peron-Magnan, & Verdeaux, 1974).

But where on our map is the passive concentration (P.C.) stage of autogenic training (A.T., a relaxation therapy introduced by I. H. Schultz and used widely in Europe) as defined by Luthe (1970)?

The isopotential curves of the EEG power spectrum obtained by Degossely and Bostem (1975) during the P.C. state of A.T. assist us in answering this question, particularly when we compare their data with those obtained during states of vigilance and drowsiness as well as active and passive concentration, such as mental calculation without verbalization and execution of minor voluntary motor movements, respectively.

Interestingly, the P.C. stage of A.T. in Degossely and Bostem's Figure 5 (1975) is marked by an increased density of from 15 to at least 20 cycle/second frequencies and a concurrent slow-wave activity density. The intensity of the shading in the same figure also reveals that the A.T. is characterized by a more intense distribution of low, medium, and high EEG frequencies than any of the other conditions. We come, therefore, to the conclusion that the P.C. stage of A.T. represents both a state of arousal as well as a state of relaxation. The shaded areas in our Figure 2-5 accordingly model the P.C.

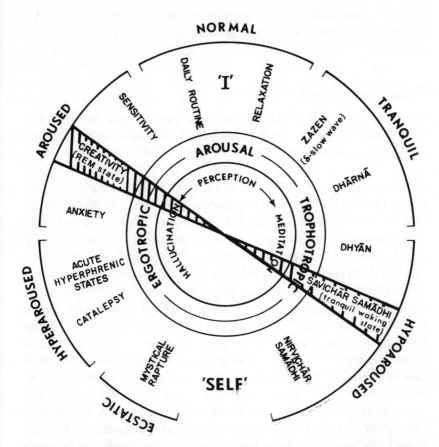

FIGURE 2-5. The passive concentration stage of autogenic training, a composite (healing) state of consciousness enabling detached (hypoaroused) inspection of exciting (hyperaroused) experiences. (From R. Fischer, "Healing as a state of consciousness." *Journal of Altered States of Consciousness.* Copyright © 1978 Baywood Publishing Company, Inc. Reprinted with permission.)

stage of A.T. as a composite dimension simultaneously embracing both the vigilant REM dreaming state and the diametrically opposite hypoaroused relaxed tranquil waking state.

Autogenic therapy has been compared with the Theravada Buddhist training (a form found in Ceylon and Southeast Asia) in general; the P.C. stage of A.T. has been compared with that of the Pali (sacred language and literature of Buddhism) access concentration in particular (Harris, 1976). Both processes integrate seemingly opposite states of consciousness in a therapeutic simultaneity that enables detached inspection of highly exciting (and sometimes traumatic) material.

Integration of East and West

Christian mysticism shares the most important features with the Eastern counterparts, and the correspondences have been described and analyzed in scholarly fashion by Otto (1932), Suzuki (1968), and others.

The Zen insight of "being" mind instead of "having it" is quite comparable to the Christian expression, "having the mind of Christ" (1 Cor. 2:16). Hui Neng calls this mind the "ultimate mind," the "unconscious" (*wu nien*, which is equivalent to the Sanskrit *prajna*, or wisdom), and contrasts it with the "conscious" empirical ego. Merton (1967) points out that the destiny of the conscious is to manifest itself the light of that being by which it subsists. It becomes one with God's own light, the "light which enlightens every man coming into this world" (John 1:9). And Saint John of the Cross teaches that the light of God shines in all emptiness where there is no natural subject to receive it. There is no definite method or technique that may lead the way to this emptiness. "To enter upon the way is to leave the way," for the way itself is emptiness. Western concentration and meditation may not be regarded so much as techniques; there is no clear-cut path to the end, and Christian mysticism became historically manifest along individualistic lines featuring journeys without maps. Johnston (1971) emphasizes that the Christian life of prayer normally begins, not passively like Zen, but with active meditation on the scriptures and on the life of Christ. This is the "discursive prayer" that tends to simplify while a right cerebral hemispheric shift takes place; reasoning decreases, and one comes closer to God without laborious intellectual efforts. This is the way the "affective prayer" begins, a being quietly and tranquilly with God. For those who go further, this simplification continues until there is only one aspiration repeated again and again, like that of Saint Francis Xavier, who spent whole nights repeating "My God and my All." Such prayer of simplicity has also been called acquired contemplation because it does not depend on God's grace, can be attained by one's own efforts, and is based on meditation of one thought or idea. The similarity between this prayer and the focused meditative states of *dhārnā* and *dhyān* is striking. The repeating of one aspiration closely resembles the repetitive utterance of the Zen *kōan;* both assist in the spring cleaning of the mind or renunciation of the ego.

Another shared feature of Christian prayer of simplicity, *zazen,* the *dhārnā-dhyān* states, and transcendental meditation is the repetitive utterance of one aspiration, the *kōan,* or mantra. Neurophysiological aspects of repetitive chanting, a form of meditation or prayer, were studied by Rogers (1973) using adherents of Nicheren Shoshu, a Buddhist group who chant *nam myo ho renge kyo* as part of their practice. EEGs recorded from electrode placement over both hemispheres all show evidence of synchrony (phase locking) with the rhythm of chant. The synchrony was found in one or more of the 1 Hz. analysis bands and was usually in the theta band (4–7 Hz.). The autospectrum of the chant voice amplitude signal usually showed peaks of intensity (power) in the frequency band in which synchrony was demonstrated. Rogers reported that although the chanters' enhanced EEG intensity was strongest in the frontal leads, there was an unrelated effect of enhanced "coordination" of activity in all leads. Such entrainment in response to rhythmic religious (or political) exercises is a way of cleaning the mind, or rephrased in Yogic terminology, the memory bank, *chitta,* is eventually filled with the mantra while thoughts gradually fade into the background (Rama, Ballentine, & Weinstock, 1976).

Being, seeing, and acting are synonymous and interchangeable in the Hui Neng school of Zen. Thus, there is in the Void of Hui Neng a surprising Trinitarian structure that reminds Merton (1967) of all that is most characteristic of the highest form of Christian contemplation. Historically speaking, the "void" of Christian mystics is another expression of their ambiguous opposition to the image.

Commonly, images (particularly in form of visions) are not admitted in mystical experience save in a preparatory role: They are exercises for debutants; for John of the Cross, images, forms, and meditations are suitable only for beginners. The goal of the experience is, on the contrary, the deprivation of images; it is to "mount with Jesus to the summit of our spirit, on the mountain of Nakedness, without image" (Ruysbroeck, 1552). John of the Cross notes that the soul "in an act of confused, amorous, peaceful, and fulfilled ideation" (successful in relinquishing distinct images) cannot without painful fatigue return to particular contemplations in which one discourses in images and forms. Theresa of Avila, although in this respect she occupies an intermediate position between John of the Cross and Ignatius Loyola, keeps aloof when it comes to the imagination (Barthes, 1971).

Ignatius of Loyola, however, initiates a new era by provoking, varying, and exploring imagery in a systematic fashion to constitute the field of image as a linguistic system of the mystical experience (Barthes, 1971). Images become products of the guided imagination: sights, representations, allegories, mysteries (of Gospel anecdotes) constantly created by the image-making senses, the constitutive units of meditation; Ignatius is, I submit, the so far unrecognized originator of guided affective imagery[3] using fantasy as "an imaginary scenario in which the subject is present and which embodies . . . the fulfillment of a desire" (Laplanche & Pontalis, 1967). Nevertheless, in the *Spiritual Exercises* St. Ignatius provides methods of procedure that are for all practical purposes identical with some of the Eastern meditation practices (to which he, in all likelihood, had no access).

For instance, by defining "the third method of prayer" as "a rhythmical recitation," he goes on to say:

> The third method of prayer is that, at each breath or respiration, he is to pray mentally as he says one word of the "Our Father" or any other prayer that is being recited, so that between one breath and another a single word is said. During this same space of time, he is to give his full attention to the meaning of the word, or to the person whom he is addressing, or to his own unworthiness, or to the difference between the greatness of this Person and his own lowliness. He will continue observing the same procedure and rule, through the other words of the "Our Father" and the other prayers, namely, the "Hail Mary," the "Anima Christi," the "Creed," and the "Hail Holy Queen." [St. Ignatius, 1522]

In the standard Greek Orthodox teaching, prayer is divided into three main stages: (1) oral or bodily prayer, (2) prayer of the mind, and (3) prayer of the heart. Those who use the Jesus Prayer also pass

3. Guided affective imagery was officially introduced as a psychotherapeutic method by Leuner (1970), who acknowledges E. Kretschmer's *Bildstreifendenken* (thinking in imagery strips) as a catalytic source. For related references, see Schultz (1970).

through these three degrees: (1) Initially, the Jesus Prayer is an oral prayer like any other, repeated with the lips, either aloud or silently. (2) In course of time it grows more inward, until eventually the mind repeats it secretly, without any outward movement. (3) Finally, the Prayer descends from the head into the heart, and from there it dominates the entire personality. Hence, orthodox spiritual tradition rejects the dualistic tendencies of Neoplatonism.

What parallels can be found for the Jesus Prayer in other cultures? In the first place, there are, as we should expect, Jewish parallels. But whereas the Byzantine mystic spent his whole time actually pronouncing the Name of God, for the Rabbinic Jew the *tetragrammaton* was a theme of meditation only: The syllables were too exalted to be framed with the lips and actually recited aloud.

Looking further afield, we may also discern parallels to the Jesus Prayer in the non-Christian East, in both Buddhism and Islam. Among the practices of Yoga there is *nembutsu* (the thought of Buddha), involving the incessant recitation of a formula. A still more striking similarity can be found in the Mohammedan *dhikr*, which occupies something of the same central position in Sufism that the Jesus Prayer holds in Byzantine mysticism. *Dhikr* involves the continual repetition of the Divine Name, Allah, either by itself or as part of some short phrase. Just as the Byzantines distinguish "prayer of the lips" and "prayer of the heart," so Sufism speaks of "*dhikr* of the tongue" and "*dhikr* of the heart."

Nor do the parallels between the Jesus Prayer and *dhikr* end here. There are references to the Invocation of the Name by fifth-century Greek writers such as Saint Diadochus of Photice and Saint Nilus of Ancyra, and clear evidence of the Prayer, in its developed form, from the sixth or seventh century onwards, whereas the earliest surviving description of the breathing technique dates probably from the fourteenth century (Ware, 1974). The decisive paragraph in this description reads as follows:

> Sit down in a quiet cell, alone in a corner, and do what I tell you. Close the door and raise your mind above all vain and passing things. Then rest your chin on your chest and turn your bodily eyes, together with your whole mind, towards the middle of your belly, that is, towards your navel. Compress the drawing in of breath through your nostrils, so that you do not breathe in and out freely, and search mentally in your inner

parts so as to find the place of the heart, where all the powers of the soul reside. At first you will find darkness and an impenetrable denseness, but if you persevere and practice this task day and night, you will find, o marvel! endless joy. For as soon as the mind discovers the place of the heart, it sees at once things which it never understood; for it sees the air that exists in the midst of the heart, and it beholds itself wholly radiant with light.

"It beholds itself wholly radiant with light"—this notion of transfiguration by light is a central theme of Greek Orthodox and Roman Catholic as well as Eastern spirituality. It is also described to occur during autogenic abreaction (Luthe, 1973).

The rare and unexpected onset of a "very Bright Light Phase" with "pure light" of "extraordinary intensity" and "almost blinding" quality tends to occur after prolonged and particularly demanding processes of neutralization of severely disturbing and dreaded material (e.g., accident, death, severely traumatizing childhood episodes, confrontation with one's own self), after repeated and prolonged crying spells, or after fulfillment of an ardently maintained wish (e.g., first orgasm after many years of frustrating experiences). The "enlightenment" is accompanied by feelings of liberation, of being unburdened from a very heavy load, and of "renewal of oneself" (Luthe, 1973).

The experience of blinding light implicates both lights, one perceptual, another "uncreated," metaphorical. Hence enlightenment, a state of being blinded through insight, reflects the double nature of man, a being partly divine (in his need) and partly animal (in the decoding of his program). Both may be complementary aspects of an unknown and unknowable reality, the signs of which may be *read between* the two aspects *(interlegere)*. Eckhart (1968) intuited it fairly precisely over five hundred years ago: "There is something in the soul which is uncreated and uncreatable.... This is the *Intellect.*" What appears, from the mundane perspective, as the intellect coming to know the absolute is in reality the intellect as absolute-in-man becoming perceptible to phenomenal awareness. Atman is Brahman: "Wonder of wonders, all things intrinsically are the Buddha-nature" (Smith, 1973). Or within the belief system of a circular self-referential and self-healing set and setting: The world is becoming conscious, therefore I am. And also: I am conscious, therefore the world is.

REFERENCES

Anand, B. K., Chhina, G. S., & Singh, B. Some aspects of electroencephalographic studies in Yogis. *Electroencephalography and Clinical Neurophysiology* 1961, *13:* 452–456.

Bälz, V. E., *Wiener medizinische Wochenschrift* 1907, *57:* 874, 926, 980, 1041, and 1090. In J. Zutt (ed.), *Ergriffenheit und Besessenheit.* Bern: Francke, 1972.

Barthes, R. *Sade, Fourier, Loyola.* Paris: Editions du Seuil, 1971.

BBB. The drawing room. Unpublished poem by Barbara Baily Bolton, Catonsville, Md.: 1974.

Bogen, J. E. Hemispheric specificity, complementarity, and self-referential mappings. *Proceedings of Society for Neurosciences* 1973, *3:* 413.

Bradley, C., & Meddis, R. Arousal threshold in dreaming sleep. *Physiological Psychology* 1974, *2:* 109–110.

Buddhaghosa, B. *The path of purification.* Translated from the Pali by B. Nyanamoli. Colombo, Ceylon: Gunasena, 1964.

Campbell, J. *The hero with a thousand faces.* New York: Pantheon Books, 1949.

Chang, G. C. C. *The Buddhist teaching of totality.* University Park: Pennsylvania State University Press, 1971.

Cohen, H. D., Rosen, R. C., & Goldstein, L. Electroencephalographic laterality changes during human sexual orgasm. *Archives of Sexual Behavior* 1976, *5:* 189–199.

Das, N. N., & Gastaut, H. Variations de l'activité électrique du cerveau, du coeur, et des muscles squelettiques au cours de la méditation et de l'extase yogique. *Electroencephalography and Clinical Neurophysiology* 1957, Suppl. *6:* 211–219.

Davids, C. A. F. Rhys. Religiöse Übungen in Indien und der religiöse Mensch. In O. Fröbe-Kapteyn (ed.), *Eranos-Jahrbuch 1, Yoga und Meditation im Osten und im Westen.* Zürich: Rhein-Verlag, 1933.

Degossely, M., & Bostem, F. AT and states of consciousness: a few methodological problems. Rome: *Proceedings of the Second International Symposium on AT,* Volume 4, 1975.

Deniker, P., Boissier, J. R., Etevenon, P., Ginestet, D., Peron-Magnan, P., & Verdeaux, G. Etude de pharmacologie clinique du delta 9 tétra-hydrocannabinol chez des sujets volontaires sains avec contrôle polygraphique. *Thérapie* 1974, *29:* 185–200.

Dumoulin, H. *A history of Zen Buddhism.* New York: Pantheon, 1963.

Dupré, L. The enigma of religious art. *Review of Metaphysics* 1975, *29:* 27–44.

Eckhart, M. As quoted by D. T. Suzuki, *On Indian Mahayana Buddhism.* New York: Harper & Row, 1968, p. 253.

Eliade, M. *From primitives to Zen.* New York: Harper & Row, 1967.

Fairchild, M. D., Jenden, D. J., & Mickey, M. R. Quantitative analysis of some drug effects on the EEG by long-term frequency analysis. *Proceedings of the Western Pharmacology Society* 1971, *14:* 135–140.

Fischer, R. Biological time. In J. Fraser (ed.), *The voices of time.* New York: George Braziller, 1966.

——. The biological fabric of time. *Annals of the New York Academy of Sciences* 1967, *138:* 440–488. (a)

——. Introductory address. *Annals of the New York Academy of Science* 1967, *138:* 371–373. (b)

——. The perception-hallucination continuum. *Diseases of the Nervous System* 1969, *30:* 161–171. (a)

——. On creative, psychotic, and ecstatic states. In I. Jakab (ed.), *Art interpretation and art therapy: Psychiatry and art,* Volume 2. Basel: Karger, 1969. (b)

——. A cartography of the ecstatic and meditative states. *Science* 1971, *174:* 897–904.

——. Cartography of inner space. In R. Siegel, & J. West (eds.), *Hallucinations: behavior, experience, theory.* New York: Wiley, 1975. (a)

——. Transformations of consciousness. A cartography. I. The perception-hallucination continuum. *Confinia Psychiatrica* 1975, *18:* 221–244. (b)

——. Transformations of consciousness. A cartography. II. The perception-meditation continuum. *Confinia Psychiatrica* 1976, *19:* 1–23. (a)

——. Consciousness as role and knowledge. In L. Allman & D. Jaffe (eds.), *Readings in abnormal psychology: Contemporary perspectives.* New York: Harper & Row, 1976. (b)

——. Hypnotic recall and flashback: The remembrance of things present. *Confinia Psychiatrica,* 1976, *19:* 149–173.

Fischer, R., Hill, R., Thatcher, K., & Scheib, J. Psilocybin-induced contraction of nearby visual space. *Agents and Actions* 1970, *1:* 190–198.

Fischer, R., Kappeler, T., Wisecup, P., & Thatcher, K. Personality trait-dependent performance under psilocybin. *Diseases of the Nervous System* 1970, *31:* 91–101.

Fischer, R., & Landon, G. M. On the arousal state-dependent recall of subconscious experience: Stateboundness. *British Journal of Psychiatry* 1972, *120:* 159–172.

Gellhorn, E. The emotions and the ergotropic and trophotropic systems. *Psychologische Forschung* 1970, *34:* 48–94.

Gellhorn, E., & Kiely, W. F. Mystical states of consciousness: neurophysiological and clinical aspects. *Journal of Nervous and Mental Disease* 1972, *154:* 399–405.

Goldstein, L., Murphree, H., Sugerman, A. A., Pfeiffer, C. C., & Jenney, E. H. Quantitative EEG analysis of naturally occurring (schizophrenic) and drug-induced psychotic states in human males. *Clinical Pharmacology and Therapeutics* 1963, *4:* 10–21.

Goldstein, L., & Stoltzfus, N. W. Psychoactive drug-induced changes of inter-hemispheric EEG amplitude relationships. *Agents and Actions* 1973, *3:* 124–132.

Goldstein, L., Sugerman, A. A., Marjerrison, G., & Stoltzfus, N. Interhemis-pheric EEG relationships in mental patients and normal subjects under modified behavioral states. Paper presented at the 28th Annual Meeting, Society of Biological Psychiatry, Montreal, June 8–10, 1973.

Goleman, D. The Buddha on meditation and states of consciousness, Part I: The teachings. *Journal of Transpersonal Psychology* 1972, *4:* 1–44.

Hakuin, E. Quoted by W. Johnson, *The still point.* New York: Perennial Library, Fordham University Press, Harper & Row, 1971.

Harris, J. Awareness and the process of relaxation East and West. Paper presented at the Innominate Society Meeting, November 29, 1976, Maryland Psychiatric Research Center, Catonsville, Md.

Heiler, F. Die Kontemplation in der christlichen Mystik. In O. Frobe-Kap-teyn (ed.), *Eranos-Jahrbuch 1, Yoga und Meditation im Osten und im Westen.* Zürich: Rhein-Verlag, 1933.

Hirai, T. *Psychophysiology of Zen.* Tokyo: Igaku Shoin, 1974.

Hofmann, A. Psychotomimetic agents. In A. Burger (ed.), *Drugs affecting the central nervous system, Volume II.* New York: Marcel Dekker, 1968.

Jain, M., & Jain, K. M. The science of Yoga: A study in perspective. *Perspectives in Biology and Medicine* 1973, *17:* 93–102.

Johnston, W. *The still point.* New York: Perennial Library, Fordham University Press, Harper & Row, 1971.

Jouvet, M. The role of monoamines and acetylcholine-containing neurons in the regulation of the sleep-waking cycle. In *Ergebnisse der Physiologie,* 64, Neurophysiology and neurochemistry in sleep and wakefulness. Berlin: Springer, 1972, pp. 166–308.

Kasamatsu, A., & Hirai, T. An electroencephalographic study on the Zen meditation (Zazen). *Folia Psychiatrica et Neurologica Japonica* 1966, *20:* 49–52.

Klineberg, O. An international view of mental health. *Totus Homo* 1970, *2:* 49–52.

Laplanche, J., & Pontalis, J. B. *Dictionnaire de psychoanalyse.* Paris: Presses Universitaires de France, 1967.

Lemaitre, S. *Ramakrishna.* R. Grimm (trans.). Hamburg: Rowhold, 1963.

Leuner, H. *Das katathyme Bilderleben.* Stuttgart: Thieme, 1970.

————. Masks and grotesque faces in toxic hallucinosis. In *Psychopathology and pictoral expression.* Series 21. Basel: Sandoz, 1974.

Lindsley, D. B. The reticular activation system and perceptual integration. In D. E. Sheer (ed.), *Electrical stimulation of the brain.* Austin: University of Texas Press, 1961, pp. 331–349.

Linton, P. H., Kuechenmeister, C. A., White, H. B., & Travis, R. P. Marijuana, heart rate, and EEG response. *Research Communications in Chemical Pathology and Pharmacology* 1975, *10:* 201–214.

Luthe, W. *Autogenic therapy. IV. Research and theory.* New York, London: Grune & Stratton, 1970.

————. *Autogenic therapy. VI. Treatment with autogenic neutralization.* New York, London: Grune & Stratton, 1973.

Mackey, J. B. Esoteric systems, nonconventional healing and meditation: generalizations for biofeedback specialists. Paper presented at the Innominate Society meeting, June, 1975, Maryland Psychiatric Research Center, Catonsville, Md.

Merton, T. *Mystics and Zen masters.* New York: Dell, 1967.

Novalis, F. *Werke und Briefe.* München: Winkler Verlag, 1968.

Otto, R. *Mysticism, East and West.* New York: Macmillan, 1932.

Panton, Y., & Fischer, R. Hallucinogenic drug-induced behavior under sensory attenuation. *Archives of General Psychiatry* 1973, *28:* 434–438.

Paz, O. *Aguila o sol?* (Eagle or sun?) E. Weinberger (trans.). New York: October House, 1949.

Petrie, A. *Individuality in pain and suffering.* Chicago: University of Chicago Press, 1967.

Plato. *Meno.* In *Protagoras and Meno* (398 B.C.). Baltimore: Penguin, 1972.

Pribram, K. *Languages of the brain.* Englewood Cliffs, N.J.: Prentice-Hall, 1971.

Rama, S., Ballentine, R., & Weinstock, A. *Yoga and psychotherapy—The evolution of consciousness.* Glenview, Ill.: Himalayan Institute, 1976.

Ram Dass, B. Lecture at the Maryland Psychiatric Research Center: Part I. *Journal of Transpersonal Psychology* 1973, *5:* 75–103.

Rechtschaffen, A. Discussing R. W. Sperry's chapter in F. J. McGuigan and R. S. Schoonover (eds.), *The psychophysiology of thinking.* New York: Academic Press, 1973.

Rogers, L. EEG correlates of chanting. Paper presented at the Transformations of Consciousness Conference, sponsored by the R. M. Bucke Memorial Society and McGill University, Montreal, October 1973.

Ruysbroeck, J. van. *Opera omnia.* Latin translation by L. Surius. Cologne: J. Quentel, 1552.

Saint Ignatius of Loyola. *The spiritual exercises.* R. W. Gleason (trans.) Garden City, N.Y.: Doubleday, 1964.

Schaltenbrand, G. The effects of stereotactic electrical stimulation in the depth of the brain. *Brain* 1965, *88:* 835–840.

Schaltenbrand, G., Spuler, H., Wahren, W., & Rumler, B. Electroanatomy of the thalamic ventro-oral nucleus based on stereotactic stimulation in man. *Zeitschrift für Neurologie* 1971, *199:* 259–276.

Schultz, I. H. *Das autogene Training.* Stuttgart: George Thieme Verlag, 1970.

Scudder, C. L. The mind: an evolving system of models. *Fields Within Fields* 1975, *14:* 49–58.

Silverman, J. Stimulus intensity modulation and psychological disease. *Psychopharmacologia* 1972, *24:* 42–80.

Smith, H. The relation between religions. *Main Currents* 1973, *30,* 52–57.

Spencer-Brown, G. *Laws of form.* London: Allen & Unwin, 1969.

Suzuki, D. T. *On Indian Mahayana Buddhism.* New York: Harper & Row, 1968.

Thatcher, K., Kappeler, T., Wisecup, P., & Fischer, R. Personality trait-dependent psychomotor performance under psilocybin. *Diseases of the Nervous System* 1970, *31:* 181–192.

Thatcher, K., Weiderholt, W., & Fischer, R. An electroencephalographic analysis of personality-dependent performance under psilocybin. *Agents and Actions* 1971, *2:* 21–26.

Thomas. The Coptic gospel according to Thomas. In R. Summers (ed.), *The secret sayings of the living Jesus.* Waco, Texas: Word Books, 1968.

Underhill, E. *Mysticism.* London: Lowe & Brydone, 1911.

Ware, K. T. The mystical tradition of the Christian East: Cultural varieties of mysticism. The R. M. Bucke Memorial Society *Newsletter Review* 1974, *7:* 3–26.

Winters, W. D., Ferrar-Allado, T., Guzman-Flores, C., & Alcaraz, M. The cataleptic state induced by ketamine: A review of the neuropharmacology of anesthesia. *Neuropharmacology* 1972, *11:* 303–316.

■3
Altered States of Consciousness: Putting the Pieces Together

CHARLES T. TART

I can summarize the overall scientific status of the field of altered states of consciousness very simply: Conceptually, it's a mess!

Hundreds of thousands of people in our culture are deliberately trying to achieve altered states of consciousness with such exotic techniques as meditation, so-called mind-control courses, and uncommon drugs. Millions more are doing it voluntarily with the more common drugs such as alcohol and marijuana. Millions more have involuntarily attained altered states, and some of them are institutionalized as a result. Altered states represent some of the most intense, exciting, dangerous, and potentially most valuable experiences that human beings can have. But what do we understand about them?

The current state of our scientific knowledge about states of consciousness is that we have thousands of fascinating observations, but in terms of how they relate to one another or what the whole picture is all about, there is a great deal of confusion. You can relate a few things here and a few things there, but by and large, our knowledge is just unrelated, mysterious fragments.

I have been studying various altered states of consciousness for twenty years, primarily as an experimentalist, and I am most comfortable in that role. A few years ago I began to look outside my narrow experimental specialities in order to get a grasp of the whole field, and I found the situation I have just described to you, thousands of unrelated facts. It looked as though my work were just going to contribute a few more unrelated facts to the thousands that already existed. While that was still an interesting thing to do and fitted in with my experimental bent, I saw it might not be of much value. I decided what was really needed was some kind of overview to put these facts together, some kind of theory that could, at the very least, perform what I call the "filing cabinet function" of a scientific theory: be a convenient way at least to organize our knowledge. Somewhat reluctantly, I forced myself into the role of theoretician; from those thousands of observations, some clearly remembered and many half forgotten, that have accumulated in my mind for years, I have developed a systems approach to states of consciousness (for more details of this approach, see Lee, Ornstein, Galin, Deikman, & Tart, 1975; Tart, 1975, 1976, 1977, in press a, b, c).

Ordinary Consciousness

In trying to make sense of various altered states of consciousness, I found myself more and more forced to examine our ordinary state of consciousness, and one of the most important things I have discovered is that there are a lot of tenacious and implicit assumptions about the nature of our ordinary state of consciousness that are rather questionable once they are made explicit. As long as they remain implicit, unconscious, they create a bias in the research we do and the way we look at this whole field. I have to start discussing altered states by mentioning the more important assumptions about ordinary consciousness.

The first assumption is that our ordinary state of consciousness is somewhat natural or given, that this is the natural way a mind or a brain organizes itself. This is a very tricky and dangerous assumption.

The naïve view of perception is the belief that somehow the world is out there, and there is a kind of straightforward transmission of information about the world into your mind so you receive a clear representation of what goes on in the world. With all that we know about sensory physiology at the present time, this obviously is nonsense. The process of perception is a highly complex process of abstraction and construction, and many of the steps may be somewhat arbitrary. Nevertheless, this naïve "realism" is the implicit and working assumption by which we almost always live. This kind of perceptual naïveté is analogous to the implicit operating assumption we make about our consciousness, namely, that consciousness is somehow a very straightforward process, simply and naturally given to us in the way we experience it. But our cognitive and emotional processes are also constructed in somewhat arbitrary ways in many of their most important aspects: They are not just "natural."

Coupled with this assumption of naturalness is an implicit value assumption that our ordinary state of consciousness is somehow the best or optimal or most rational state of consciousness there is. There is an implicit value dimension biasing a lot of our apparently objective research. At the top of this value continuum there is an adulation of a state of complete rationality, in which somehow you never make a mistake in your logic.

Now we recognize, primarily from looking at others, at our friends and patients, that there are occasional neurotic flaws in ordinary rationality. Our friends make lots of mistakes, especially when it comes to politics! Most people will recognize that even they personally may have a few minor, neurotic quirks, flaws in the otherwise complete rationality of our ordinary state. Those of us with insight will admit that much of our rationality is simply rationalization.

Somewhat lower in this implicit value continuum there is a kind of grudging and ambivalent valuing of creative states, unusual mental conditions that artists or perhaps a few scientists experience. Useful ideas sometimes come out of such states, but they are also threatening, so the valuing is ambivalent there. At the lower end of the orthodox value continuum we get down into some well-known altered states like marijuana intoxication or dreaming, which, by and large, are explicitly as well as implicitly considered much inferior to our ordinary state, as a toxic psychosis might be considered the ultimate deterioration of consciousness.

If the above continuum were an explicit value system, to be kept in mind when doing research on altered states, there would be no great problem with it, as one could try to compensate for the sake of objectivity. The trouble is that usually it is an implicit factor that makes for a biased view of the data that we gather about altered states.

The view I have been forced to accept in looking at altered states is that our ordinary state is a construction. It is not just given, it is built up through the socialization process, and in many ways, it is a somewhat arbitrary construction. Take a different cultural context, and there are many other ways of building up a so-called "ordinary" or "normal" state of consciousness.

Human Potentials

By virtue of being born human we have a certain kind of nervous system and a certain kind of body, suitable for dwelling in the environment of the Earth. There are many potentials we could develop if they are brought out in us. We could, for example, develop the ability to go into some kind of altered state of conciousness in which we would feel ourselves possessed by a friendly spirit who would teach us songs and dances, which we could then share with our friends, who would be very pleased. When lecturing, I often ask how many people were taught to do that in school, and I never see any hands go up! That is not a potential that is developed within our cultural setting: Indeed, it's looked upon as one that is quite pathological, yet it is highly developed among the Senoi of Malaysia, for example (Stewart, 1969).

None of us develop the full spectrum of human potentials. We do not grow up in isolation. We are born into a particular culture, and a culture, in this sense, can be looked upon as a group of people who, through historical processes, have a knowledge of part of the whole spectrum of human potentialities. Of the part they know, some of these parts have been judged to be good and worthwhile and healthy and to be developed, but other potentials have been judged pathological or evil. There is active suppression of these potentials if a child starts showing them; they are strongly repressed. There are also a large number of potentials that are simply unknown in any given culture. Some of them may remain latent and possibly may be developed at a later time. Some of them may disappear completely through lack of development at some critical period.

If we think about human potentials in terms of consciousness, as the kind of things we could experience, we can argue that the states of consciousness that are ordinary for different cultures (I use "state" very loosely so far) contain different selections of the kinds of things that could be experienced. If this is so, the ordinary states of consciousness of members of the two cultures can be quite different.

Similarly, an individual may tap different selections of potentials in different states of consciousness; if state of consciousness A is a person's ordinary state of consciousness, state of consciousness B might be a way of reorganizing the ordinary functioning of his consciousness to tap a different selection of human potentials, potentials that are not available in his ordinary state. This is the motivation behind most people's personal interest in experiencing altered states of consciousness, particularly if one doesn't like the way his life runs in his ordinary state of consciousness, when he does not externalize his unhappiness by blaming it on other people, but begins to ask the question whether there's something inherently wrong, or at least something not sufficient, in the way his ordinary consciousness is organized. Perhaps there's some way of reorganizing it that will turn some new potentials into functional, valued kinds of potentials. Of course, there is a great possibility of overreaction here. We have seen a good deal of it in our own culture, where people dissatisfied with life in their ordinary state of consciousness experience some drug-induced or meditative-induced altered state of consciousness and immediately jump to an opposite extreme in terms of values; so they say, "The altered state I experience is high, it's wonderful; the ordinary state is unenlightened, terrible, no good." That extreme is just as naïve an evaluation as the one that says, "The ordinary state is the optimal state of consciousness for every possible function." There are very real questions here about various altered states of consciousness: What are their values, their advantages? What are their costs, their disadvantages? How can you minimize the costs and dangers and maximize the advantages? By and large, I have to say we cannot scientifically answer those questions very accurately for any altered states of consciousness at the moment because of gaps in our basic knowledge and confusion of bias with data. Nevertheless, the appeal of seeking altered states of consciousness is this chance of tapping new potentials, especially if you are dissatisfied with your ordinary state.

Perception and Misperception

Going back to the perceptual aspect of consciousness, rather than the naïve view, it would be much more correct to say that we have had perceptual categories or concepts built up by enculturation, and they are a major aspect of our consciousness. When they are stimulated by something from the outside world that roughly matches the perceptual category, these internal structures respond with a sort of abstraction of the actual stimulus. That allows a very efficient, very rapid, automated response to the outside world. If you have prior knowledge of what squares are, and you're faced with squares, you can handle them very well. If my wife says to me, "Please bring home a loaf of rye bread from the store," I don't have to deal with all the complexities of the situation. There is a perceptual category, as it were, and once I recognize something that roughly matches that category, I can zero in on it and come home with the loaf of rye bread.

On the other hand, when you're faced with situations in the world that you're not prepared for, this automatization of perception is a drawback. Suppose an angel walked into the room right now. Because we have not been prepared to perceive that kind of thing by our cultural and especially our scientific training, we would have great difficulties in accurately perceiving it. Responses might be, "Oh, there's a little old lady in a white gown," or "There's an actor dressed up to look like an angel," or perhaps you would not even happen to look that way after initially seeing it with your peripheral vision. Now this is a fanciful example, but what I'm saying is that when we are faced with life situations, with perceptual situations, to which we have not been trained to respond, we are liable to engage automatically in a very distorted kind of perception; we're liable to see only the elements of the situation that already fit what we are prepared to see, and/or we are liable to repress or distort our perception of the situation.

Now, the focus here is on perceptual situations, but the same thing applies in a more general sense to dealing consciously with any kind of situations for which we have not been trained, to all our mental processes. Aldous Huxley put this very beautifully many years ago when he said that each of us is simultaneously the beneficiary and the victim of our culture. We are the beneficiaries in drawing on the stored knowledge of our culture, which is indeed adaptable to a wide variety of situations, but we are the victims in the sense that we all wear a set of cultural blinders that make it extremely difficult for us to deal with things outside the range of the already known.

As a scientist I am particularly concerned with implicit biases, whether perceptual, cognitive, or emotional. Science is supposed to start with observation, to give data priority over theory, but if the scientists in a given culture all share certain common cultural biases, it can mean that nobody looks for observations in a certain direction, and that makes for an incomplete kind of science. Carlos Castaneda (1968, 1971, 1973, 1974) reports that his mentor, don Juan, insisted that we are only alert about things we know. He also succinctly commented that it is stupid to believe the world is only as we think it is.

Altered States

With this background, bearing in mind that some of our implicit assumptions about ordinary consciousness need to be kept explicit and questioned, we can look at the concept of altered states of consciousness. To start with a problem, I must say that the way the term *altered state of consciousness* is commonly used is sloppy and confusing. I feel somewhat guilty about this as my book (Tart, 1969) helped to popularize the term, but people often use altered state of consciousness simply to mean any alteration in experience. If I tap the top of my head with my finger, am I in an altered state of consciousness, "tapping the top of my head state of consciousness," because my experience is different from what it was? Obviously this is such a general and sloppy use of the term that it does not mean anything. I have proposed a more precise term, a *discrete altered state of consciousness* (d-ASC), to indicate the radicalness of the changes usually associated with the altered states for scientific use, and I shall define the term below.

First, remember the kind of experiential basis for coming up with the concept of a state of consciousness in the first place. How do you know that you are right now reading this chapter, and not simply dreaming, and about to wake up in a minute? Reflect now. How do you know for sure? What did you do in order to answer that question?

I have found that what people do basically is one of two processes. They look at their ongoing experience. In one case, they look at some specific criterion aspect of it. Some people, for instance, would say, "Well, when I dream it is in black and white, but I'm obviously seeing color in my perceptual field right now, so this is not a dream." Or, "In a dream, I usually don't remember how I got to the present moment, but I distinctly remember getting here, there's continuity of experience, so this is my ordinary waking state." In the other case people don't look at specific experience so much as take a kind of holistic, gestalt look at the pattern of their experience and find it is obvious that their ongoing experience does not feel like a dreaming state. Some people do both.

Therefore, there are two kinds of basic experiential criteria that lie behind the concept of states of consciousness. One is whether or not certain distinct criterion experiences occur, and the other is the kind of gestalt feel of your pattern of consciousness. What this illustrates is that you not only have a certain number of human potentials available (you can tell people your name, do arithmetic, balance your checkbook, speak English, etc.) in your ordinary state, but you sense that these potentials are organized into a certain kind of pattern that you call your ordinary state of consciousness. Further, you find it useful to distinguish this pattern of your experience from other kinds of patterns. If you sensed, for instance, your experience as patterned in the configuration we call drunkenness, that would lead to a very practical decision that you shouldn't drive your car; whereas, if you sensed it was in the pattern of your ordinary state of consciousness, you wouldn't feel hesitant about driving your car. There are practical consequences of being able to classify your state of consciousness.

We are faced with external stimuli, we perceive the world selectively in ways that we have been trained to, and then the rest of our psychological potentials are organized into a pattern, a system that constitutes a state of consciousness. Basic awareness is only in one part of this pattern at any particular time. You are not experiencing everything you can experience in your normal waking state right now; you are only experiencing one or two of these possibilities, but by direction of your attention, you can experience other aspects of it. There are regularities among those experiences, connection, habitual routes of thinking, feeling, and so forth, that lead to a sense of shape or pattern of your consciousness.

This sense of pattern is what I mean by a discrete state of consciousness: There is a given selection of potentials available, and there is a definite pattern of organization. In practice, it is a lot of work to try to map out these qualities and relationships for an individual, but this mapping of qualities and relationships is the operation for defining a discrete state of consciousness.

A discrete state of consciousness is not a static entity. I can say, "Boo!", and I doubt that anybody will become enlightened or become drunk or go into a meditative state as a result of this change in experience, of hearing a sudden, loud noise. There is a range of experience, the particulars of which differ considerably but the feel of which is all within a certain kind of range. That is what we call our ordinary state. In any discrete altered state there is also a range of experiences, and they are related in a certain kind of pattern.

Subsystems

The kind of systems approach to consciousness I have been sketching here is very general. Specific parts or subsystems, human potentials, are organized into a specific, overall system, and the overall properties of this system, determined both by the nature of the subsystems and holistic properties arising from the gestalt of the system, are what we mean by a discrete state of consciousness.

The specification of particular subsystems, their individual and combinatorial properties, and the characteristics of the overall systems that are possible is the task of future research. Given the current state of psychological knowledge, I have so far specified ten subsystems, all of which show radical and important changes in various discrete altered states. These are our exteroceptors, interoceptors, input processing (learned perceptions), memory, our sense of identity (ego), evaluation and decision-making processes, subconscious processes, emotions, our space/time sense, and motor output. Basic awareness is not identical to any of these particular subsystems, nor do they include various latent human potentials of a quite different sort that might be activated and added to the overall system of consciousness in various discrete altered states.

Stabilization of States

A state of consciousness is not simply a collection of various human potentials that just happen to be laid out in some kind of pattern; it is a system that maintains its integrity in spite of environmental variation. That is, it is stabilized. In engineering terms, there are a lot of feedback, loading, and limiting stabilization processes that hold the system together. Again, if I said, "Boo!" very loudly, I doubt that anyone would become psychotic over that kind of thing, even though it is a sudden kind of change in the particulars of consciousness.

It is highly adaptive to keep your consciousness operating in the same kind of pattern in spite of change. Our state of consciousness, especially our normal state, is a tool for coping with our environment. If you are walking across the road, and a car is bearing down on you, about to run you over, and the sun glances off the chromed grill and throws you into an ecstatic state where we are all one and everything is right in the universe, colors are vibrant and beautiful, and you feel wonderful, and you are transfixed by this splendid vision, you're dead! It's much better to stay in your ordinary state in which you think, "Oh my God, I'm going to be killed. Run, jump, do something!" We can readily speculate on evolutionary pressures to develop highly stabilized states of consciousness for dealing with our ordinary environment.

The concept of degree of stabilization of our ordinary state, the tool for coping, can be applied for an understanding of some kinds of psychopathology. Some kinds of psychiatric syndromes may be deficiencies of stabilization processes, an inability to hold consciousness within an ordinary kind of pattern under environment stress in order to cope. Some people too readily alter their state of consciousness; with other people, stabilization is much too rigid—they can't alter their state when it might be adaptive.

You can roughly distinguish external kinds of stabilization processes and internal kinds. The external kinds derive from the fact that we live in a world that provides many pattern constancies. Even though the particulars of your sensory experience change, they stay within a known pattern, and you are usually getting so much sensory input that it helps to pattern your internal processes into the kind of things that keep your ordinary state stable. For instance, when I push on doors they usually open; when I act in certain ways the environment usually reacts in certain known ways.

There are also what I call consensus reality constancies, the implicit and explicit social contract. Other people will almost always act in "normal" ways. If you're feeling a little strange, you can keep company with people who act in acceptable kinds of ways and thus be bombarded by ordinary kinds of stimuli that pattern and reinforce your ordinary internal processes. If you're wondering whether things are real, you can turn to the person next to you and ask, "Is this real?" Usually he will reassure you and say, "Yes, this is real." Our social interaction patterns, in spite of changing particulars, stay within a known range, and because we're constantly bombarded with them, they help to stabilize our internal processes.

We also get a tremendous amount of sensory input from our bodies, from our kinesthetic receptors. We experience a known, familiar body that reacts in known ways. As with social input, this is a massive amount of stimulation that helps to pattern our consciousness within ordinary ways.

Further, there are many internal processes in which we are constantly thinking, emoting, and acting in accordance with ordinary social standards. If we look at our own internal activity we usually find that we are constantly thinking, fantasizing, planning, and/or having emotions resulting from these activities; our minds are extremely active systems, constantly carrying out internal mental activities that run along lines that again help to stabilize the systems.

I should also add that our state of consciousness is multiply stabilized; it is not as if there were just one process that held our ordinary state of consciousness together. In engineering terms, our ordinary state is a well-engineered system. Usually several stabilization processes are going on simultaneously, so we are not likely to have our ordinary state of consciousness break down unexpectedly. It would be very poor engineering if there were only one bolt holding the entire mechanism together, so that if one bolt failed, the whole thing fell apart! As a side reflection on psychopathology, however, in some people there seems to be a lack of stabilization, insufficient multiple stabilization of their ordinary state, so they are liable to lose it under stress and be unable to cope.

Altered States

Now that I have outlined the idea of a discrete state of consciousness (d-SC) and the ways it is stabilized, we can look at the concept of a discrete altered state of consciousness (d-ASC) in more detail. Note the term d-SC is the more general of the two: d-ASC means that, with reference to some d-SC we take as a standard of comparison, usually our ordinary state, we have a different d-SC, a d-ASC.

Earlier, I presented a way of conceptualizing a d-SC as an organizational pattern of a particular selection of human potentials. We could take this pattern as our ordinary state, our reference d-SC. A d-ASC is a different selection of human potentials organized into a different pattern, a different system. We have some new potentials functioning in the d-ASC (you might feel new kinds of emotions, perceive in different ways, think in a different logic) as well as continuing function of some potentials that were available in the baseline state. The organizational pattern of the system is discretely different.

As for the altered states of consciousness we know something about—sleep, for instance, especially stage-one dreaming, rapid eye movement sleep—they are a discrete state of consciousness, a quite drastic kind of organizational change, on a psychological as well as a physiological level. I should make it clear that the systems approach I'm outlining here is primarily a psychological approach. Its usefulness does not depend on finding physiological correlates of d-ASCs. Indeed, for many of the d-ASCs we know about, there are no obvious basic physiological changes at all, although we might expect such changes to exist in deep brain structures. Stage-one dreaming is, in a sense, a mistaken example of a d-ASC because it involves a clear-cut physiological state change. This systems approach can be started from the physiological side of things and lead to similar kinds of conclusions, but at this stage of our knowledge, this is a psychological approach.

If ordinary consciousness is the most frequent d-SC in our culture, sleep would be the second most frequent. Stage-one dreaming, which takes up about twenty percent of sleep, would be the third most frequent; drunkenness on alcohol would probably be the fourth. You would probably find marijuana intoxication the fifth most frequent d-SC in our culture, and then the more exotic d-SCs like lucid dreaming (van Eeden, 1913), in which your consciousness seems to have its ordinary pattern even though perceptually you are in a dreamworld.

I suspect that other very common states, which have not been looked at as d-ASCs, are extreme emotions. In terms of this systems approach, you can take an ordinary state of consciousness, and if you are experiencing some emotion to a mild degree, there isn't much change in the rest of your mental processes. You can get a little angry at being shortchanged at the grocery store, but you can still count, your identity remains the same, and so forth. But suppose you were enraged by it. Now you might literally be seeing red, a real perceptual process change. You might lose your sense of who you are, what your social responsibilities are. When you take almost any emotion and push it to an extreme intensity, I suspect there is a change in all the rest of psychological functions, an unrecognized induction process, and you're actually dealing with d-ASCs. This is a new line of thinking for me, so I can't detail this concept yet, but I think it is going to be very profitable to look at strong emotions as often leading to d-ASCs.

Inducing Altered States

The opposite of the process of stabilizing a state of consciousness is inducing an altered state. In order to induce a d-ASC, you first have to disrupt the stabilization of a person's ordinary state. You may disrupt it with psychological techniques, physiological techniques, drugs, and so forth. If the induction procedure is successful, there is a point at which these disruptive forces will break up the organization of the baseline d-SC; then what become important are what I call patterning forces, the physiological or psychological factors that push this transitional period toward a specific new kind of organization, toward a specific d-ASC. This is where expectations about the outcome of the induction process become very important. If induction is successful, consciousness will be reorganized into a different shape of consciousness, a different system pattern as well as a different selection of potentials.

Let me concretize this discussion of induction with a common instance of d-ASC induction: going to sleep.

The first thing you do is lie down in a quiet room, someplace where no one is talking to you. That action removes the stabilizing forces of social interaction. It is a dark, quiet room: You don't have a physical environment to deal with, so you are not engaging in those known kinds of physical coping actions that ordinarily pattern your psychological energies into an ordinary d-SC pattern.

You lie down on a soft, comfortable bed, and you relax. That has a very interesting effect. Most of our kinesthetic receptors respond to change: If you lie still for a while, the receptors literally stop firing, and in an experiential sense, your body literally disappears. Almost all that massive known pattern of stimulation stops coming in; another major factor that ordinarily helps you stabilize your consciousness in a certain way is removed. Tossing and turning is one of the worst ways to go to sleep!

Further, you take a mental attitude that you could best characterize as not trying to go to sleep. If you lie there and grit your teeth and say, "I'm going to relax and go to sleep," you know how far you're going to get—nowhere. That attitude of pushing, of actively trying, works very well for quite a few things in our ordinary d-SC and helps to stabilize that state, but it won't help the induction to the desired d-ASC of sleep. Instead, you adopt an attitude of, "I've decided to go to sleep, but now I'm not going to worry about it. I'm going to forget about it." That attitude destabilizes all sorts of feedback stabilization processes that are common in the ordinary state.

Now these induction procedures by themselves may or may not put you to sleep. They are all disrupting forces that destabilize the ordinary state, but they interact with the poorly understood factor we rather loosely call "tiredness," the physiological need to sleep. If that is there to a reasonable degree, there will come a transitional period we call the hypnogogic "state." For most people this hypnogogic experience doesn't look like a d-SC, because it doesn't really seem organized, so I prefer to call it the hypnogogic period. It looks to most people like a fragmentation of consciousness for a few minutes; then the state of sleep occurs. That patterning force of tiredness is simultaneously a disruptive force that helps to break up your ordinary d-SC and a patterning force. If it is not present, if you're not at all tired, you may lie down in your dark, quiet room and decide, "I'm going to go to sleep," but nothing happens. On the other hand, if it's there to an extreme degree, you may fall asleep on your feet; you don't need to go through the other steps of the induction procedure.

Problem Areas for Research

This has been a brief outline of my systems approach to d-SCs. Now let's consider some major research problems about d-SCs from this perspective. I started out by saying that our knowledge of states is a mess. While I hope that this systems approach I have briefly outlined will help to organize and extend our knowledge, the application of this systems approach still has to be done. My graduate students and I are beginning to apply it to the existing literature and are trying to make sense of it, seeing where this approach works, where it has to be modified, and so forth.

Still, our present knowledge is very poor; we really lack basic descriptive knowledge about d-ASCs to a surprising degree. Let me give you an example that will probably surprise you. Some years ago I did a study of marijuana intoxication (Tart, 1970, 1971) that was really a basic mapping of what veteran users say they experience when they are high. When I was writing up the results of that study, I thought that, for comparison purposes, I'd better go over to the library and find out what people experienced when they were intoxicated with alcohol. I found out that there are many books about how demon rum is the cause of all our ills, and many more about how a little drink never hurt anybody, but there is practically no straightforward descriptive literature at all on what people experience when they are intoxicated with alcohol! Here we have a tremendous lack of basic, descriptive knowledge on one of the most frequent d-ASCs around; when you try to study even more exotic d-ASCs like those produced by meditation, hypnosis, drugs, and so on, the lack of basic descriptive data makes precise scientific work almost impossible. We very badly need basic, descriptive mapping of the experiential, behavioral, and physiological correlates of various d-ASCs if we want to understand these phenomena scientifically.

The second thing that is really important if we are going to make progress in this area is that we must start recognizing our cultural limits. We must start making explicit our implicit value judgments. If we make them explicit, we can turn them into formal scientific hypotheses and test how well they work. Is dreaming an inferior state of consciousness, or are there certain ways in which it might be superior? If so, what are the ways? I've come to the view that there are no free lunches in the universe; everything may have its use and everything has a price. But if you try to state in detail just what are the disadvantages or dangers of certain d-ASCs, and just what are their advantages, you find that, by and large, we have strong biases one way or the other, "That's awful" or "That's wonderful," but almost no scientific, solid knowledge about real advantages and disadvantages.

A third major line of research is an adequate study of individual differences. I have become convinced that there are enormous differences in our so-called ordinary state of consciousness. If we could see all the different patterns in which our minds work in their ordinary states, we might think each other really weird!

Most of the time we do not notice these differences. The English language is excellent for dealing with external events, but it is not very good at describing internal events, so that makes it hard to see some of the differences. Also, our social conventions call for a lot of ignorance. It is easier to say, "You and I are alike, and we like each other, and everything is wonderful," and not really look very closely to see what differences really exist. But we have to do that. For instance, what is a d-ASC that can be gotten into only by special procedures for some people is for others a part of their ordinary state. You cannot deliberately hallucinate something with full sensory reality in your ordinary state of consciousness? You have to take drugs to do it? How defective! It is just part of my ordinary power of visualization. I am not claiming I can do that: My visualization abilities are not very good, but there are some people who can do just that as part of their ordinary state. The well-adapted ones have learned to keep quiet about it, of course, because they have become aware of some of the negative cultural value judgments attached to the idea of hallucinations.

Fourth, the transitional period between two d-SCs needs thorough investigation. Experimentally, these seem to be fragmentary periods; they are difficult to collect data on, because if you try to question somebody about the transition from one state to another, what you frequently find is that they will say, "Yes, I definitely recognize when I'm in my ordinary state, and I definitely recognize when I'm in the altered state, but it's very hard to describe the transition." This makes sense from the systems point of view because the organization, this state of consciousness, is the observer, who provides the experiential data. If that observer is fragmented, who is there to give you the kind of reports we would like to have about mental functioning? What I frequently find is that some people say, "There was a blank space, I don't know how long it lasted, but I know there was a blank space, and then I was in this altered state of consciousness," or others will say, "Well it was like a dream that I never can quite remember properly; it doesn't hold together." I suspect, however, that some training in meditation techniques may make more complete observation possible. Judging from some self-report data, it seems to be possible for people with certain kinds of meditative training to establish an "observing self" that phenomenologically is partially or wholly detached from the ongoing operations of consciousness. They can describe in much better detail what happens in one of these transitional periods.

State-Specific Sciences

The last thing I want to talk about is an idea I proposed several years ago (Tart, 1972), which hasn't been put into practice yet, although it has caught on in theory. One of the things you often see in d-ASCs is a different style of thinking. Investigators who are not aware of the implicit value orientation that says our ordinary state is logical—that it is the ultimate logic—often say, "There's a deterioration of logic," or "People show nonsensical thinking."

If you look at the nature of logic, you see that any logic is actually arbitrary. You make certain assumptions; you can assume anything you want. Given that, you then develop a set of rules for information processing: a grammar. If things follow that grammar, you are being logical. What you seem to get in some d-ASCs is a different logic that is specific to that particular d-ASC. The assumptions and rules for thinking, as well as for perceiving (perceptual logic) have changed to another pattern.

Now that offers very interesting possibilities. Some people will say that it enables them, for instance, to get insights into their own personal functioning or into external situations that are quite different in nature from their ordinary understandings, insights they find very valuable. But while they're in a d-ASC, they cannot adequately explain to someone in an ordinary state just what these insights are or why they make sense. When they return to their ordinary state, they themselves often cannot adequately understand what it was that they found so insightful or why it seemed logical. However, the next time they go back into that d-ASC, the line of reasoning is immediately available again, it is remembered and can be further developed.

What you seem to get, at least for some d-ASCs, is one or more state-specific logics. These may operate in conjunction with state-specific memory. Phenomena happen that are stored in memory in such a way that the memory only partially, or perhaps not at all, transfers to the ordinary state, but when the d-ASC is reinduced, the memory is accessible once more. This is embodied in a bit of folklore that has been experimentally demonstrated now (Goodwin & Powell, 1969): that if you lose something while you're drunk and can't find it the next day, if you get drunk again you may be able to find it.

Coupled with the construction of state-specific perceptions, this has intriguing implications. In a d-ASC, you can perceive and think in a different logic, and you store the information in a way that is not otherwise accessible. This led me to propose an idea (Tart, 1972) for the creation of state-specific sciences. I am greatly enamored of scientific method as a way of refining our knowledge, the method of committing yourself to good observation and constantly trying to refine that observation, of theorizing about your observations logically, of fully communicating your observations and theories to your colleagues, and of testing the implications—the predictions of your theories—to see whether they work. I think this process can work on experiential data as well as it works on external, physical-world data. It is easier to get agreement, interobserver reliability, on external data, but if we ever want a complete psychology, we cannot ignore important phenomena just because they happen only inside a person's mind. I think we can develop sciences of experience, with which we describe experiences we have had to colleagues who have also worked on examining these experiences in themselves. We can come up with hypotheses about them, test them experimentally, and so forth.

Now this same scheme can be applied to d-ASCs. You establish a group of scientists who can get into a particular d-ASC, who, after exchanging reports while in the d-ASC, agree that it's a similar mental pattern that they are dealing with. They can develop a science of what goes on in that d-ASC, what kind of theories seem best to explain it, and so forth. But what you will have is a state-specific science, a science that makes full sense only to a person who is in that d-ASC. You could have the rather amusing result of the scientist coming home from his laboratory, back in his ordinary d-SC, responding to his wife's "What did you do at the lab today?" with "I don't know now, but I vaguely recall it was brilliant, and I've written an article on it." (Now that may sound very exotic, but actually it is not, because most of us could go into, say, a physicist's laboratory, ask him what he is doing, and he will babble the most arcane sort of nonsense we couldn't understand at all. You have to go through a seven-year induction procedure called "getting a Ph.D. in physics" to repattern your mind in that direction before it begins to make any sense at all.)

The state-specific-sciences proposal is very exciting to me. When it was published it drew some interesting comments that illustrated the value assumptions I discussed earlier. There were forty or fifty letters to the editor written in response to the proposal. About two-thirds of them came from older scientists, all of whom said more or less that our ordinary state of consciousness is the best possible, most wonderful state of consciousness ever, and anything you do in a d-ASC is done in a deteriorated mental state, so how could you possibly do science in an altered state? The remainder of the letters, usually from younger scientists, said the proposal made excellent sense, and they wanted to get started on developing state-specific sciences. The most amusing letter, or rather pair of letters, came from a psychiatrist who succinctly illustrated the basic reason for the proposal. Unfortunately, the editor chose not to print that particular pair of letters, but what he said was this: In his first letter, he was like the majority of writers; he said our ordinary state is wonderful and logical, and everything else is a deterioration, so why waste our time on such mystical mumbo jumbo? His second letter, written three days later, said that he was rather embarrassed to write this second letter, but his commitment to observation and good reporting in science required him to write it. The previous night he had gotten into an altered state of consciousness and thought about the proposal, and it was obviously perfectly appropriate! No matter how much he tried in the morning to talk himself out of it, while he was in an altered state it was perfectly obvious to him that there were certain kinds of knowledge that could only be known in that altered state.

I am proposing that if we ever want a complete understanding of the many d-SCs humans can experience, we're going to have to train investigators to experience various d-ASCs and give us the kind of data and engage in the kind of theorizing that will give us these various state-specific views. Not that this will replace our ordinary lines of investigation; we obviously need to pursue our ordinary approaches to gathering and theorizing as much as possible. The development of various state-specific sciences will provide what, in physics, is termed a complementary set of views, views based on different sets of assumptions, different sets of mental operations, views that will be evaluated for their usefulness. They will neither validate nor invalidate the ordinary state of consciousness view.

This is a long-term vision, a direction in which I hope to see this field move. It is not going to move that way rapidly, and we are going to have many problems with our implicit value assumptions. I will close by reminding you again of Aldous Huxley's statement that we are simultaneously the beneficiaries and the victims of our culture. Insofar as we are committed to effectiveness as therapists, to completeness as scientists, we have to learn somehow what these cultural blinders are that limit our observations and theorizing, so that we can do something about them. An implicit assumption is something you are controlled by totally. Once you make it explicit, you do have the possibility of testing it, and discarding it if it is a hindrance.

REFERENCES

Castaneda, C. *The teachings of don Juan: A Yaqui way of knowledge.* Berkeley: University of California Press, 1968.

————. *A separate reality: Further conversations with don Juan.* New York: Simon & Schuster, 1971.

————. *Journey to Ixtlan: The lessons of don Juan.* New York: Simon & Schuster, 1973.

————. *Tales of power.* New York: Simon & Schuster, 1974.

Goodwin, D., & Powell, B. Alcohol and recall: State-dependent effects in man. *Science* 1969, *163:* 1358–1360.

Lee, P., Ornstein, R., Galin, D., Deikman, A., & Tart, C. *Symposium on consciousness.* New York: Viking, 1975.

Stewart, K. Dream theory in Malaya. In C. Tart (ed.), *Altered states of consciousness: A book of readings.* New York: John Wiley & Sons, 1969.

Tart, C. (ed.) *Altered states of consciousness: A book of readings.* New York: John Wiley & Sons, 1969.

————. Marijuana intoxication: Common experiences. *Nature* 1970, *226:* 701–704.

————. *On being stoned: A psychological study of marijuana intoxication.* Palo Alto, Cal.: Science & Behavior Books, 1971.

————. States of consciousness and state-specific science. *Science* 1972, *176:* 1203–1210.

————. *States of Consciousness.* New York: Dutton, 1975.

————. The basic nature of altered states of consciousness: A systems approach. *Journal of Transpersonal Psychology* 1976, *8:* No. 1, 45–64.

————. Putting the pieces together: A conceptual framework for understanding discrete states of consciousness. In N. Zinberg (ed.), *Alternate states of consciousness.* New York: Free Press, 1977.

————. Drug-induced states of consciousness. In B. Wolman (ed.), *Handbook of parapsychology.* New York: Van Nostrand/Rheinhold, in press. (a)

————. Sex and drugs as altered states of consciousness. In K. Blum (ed.), *Social meaning of drugs (Principles of social pharmacology).* New York: Harper & Row, in press. (b)

————. A systems approach to altered states of consciousness. In J. Davidson, R. Davidson & G. Schwartz (eds.), *Human consciousness and its transformations: A psychobiological perspective.* New York: Plenum, in press. (c)

van Eeden, F. A study of dreams. *Proceedings of the Society for Psychical Research* 1913, *26:* 431–461. (Reprinted in C. Tart [ed.], *Altered states of consciousness: A book of readings.* New York: John Wiley & Sons, 1969).

■ two
INDUCTION
OF ALTERED
STATES OF
CONSCIOUSNESS

4
The Uses of Meditation in Psychotherapy
PATRICIA CARRINGTON

Despite the fact that the art of meditation represents a new area of interest for the Western scientific establishment, it is an ancient one. Its techniques have been refined over the ages through a trial and error process stretching out over thousands of years. While much has been learned about meditation in a practical sense, systematic testing of its postulates is relatively new, and its clinical application to the field of psychotherapy has only begun to be explored.

It is this wedding of meditative techniques with psychotherapeutic approaches that, in my opinion, promises to be one of the most exciting and potentially fruitful of meditation's applications to modern life. It would seem particularly appropriate that an ancient technique devised to foster human growth should be combined with new techniques that assist human growth.

While traditional meditation was used almost exclusively to achieve spiritual goals, forms of meditation have recently come upon the scene that are of a strictly secular nature. These I have termed practical meditation. They are well suited for clinical use, and are the ones that are discussed here.

Modern Meditation

Westernized forms of meditation suitable for use with psychotherapy are simple and relatively undemanding in nature. They are exceptionally easy to learn, and are sufficiently pleasant so that the dropout problem is no greater for practical meditation than it is for any other major self-help program. Some people, of course, discontinue participation in any self-help program—even when it may be benefiting them. This is true for Weight Watchers, Alcoholics Anonymous, physical exercises, autosuggestion, relaxation techniques, or the taking of medicine, as well as for meditation. Keeping up with any activity, even a pleasant one, is difficult.

The attrition rate for the simpler forms of meditation is encouragingly less, however, than it is with other relaxation techniques. Several studies have shown, for example, that subjects tend to stay with meditation more tenaciously than they do with Jacobson's Progressive Relaxation or with alpha-biofeedback (Carrington, 1977). Because of its inherent appeal and its simplicity of procedure, as well as for other reasons to be described later, practical meditation seems, therefore, to be one of the most promising self-help methods yet devised for reducing stress.

Recent laboratory studies on meditation have for the most part been conducted on only one form of practical meditation—transcendental meditation (TM). While this is a limitation, useful information is emerging from current experiments, and research evidence on other Westernized forms of meditation is beginning to accumulate.

TM is a form of mantra meditation (meditation on a resonant sound repeated mentally or aloud to focus attention). Derived from an ancient Indian technique, it is taught commercially in many areas of the world by the International Meditation Society and is readily available in a standardized form to those willing and able to pay the fee for learning it ($165 for adults as of January 1978). Because TM is the first standardized form of meditation to be widely disseminated in the West and is also the only form to be backed by an active organization with any considerable energy and money to promote it, it has received a good deal of attention from the press as well as from the scientific community.

TM is not, however, the only effective form of Westernized meditation. Boston cardiologist Herbert Benson, for example, has devised a standardized form of breathing meditation, known simply as Benson's Method, which combines both Zen and Yoga techniques in a simplified form. This method has been used successfully to lower blood pressure in hypertensive patients and as a treatment for heart arrhythmias (Benson, 1975).

Another form of practical meditation is the one I have developed. It is a standardized form of mantra meditation used specifically for clinical and research purposes, called clinically standardized meditation (CSM). CSM is similar to TM in its permissiveness and ease of learning, but differs from it in that it is not based on the teachings of Hindu cosmology, does not require a *puja* (Hindu religious ceremony) for its instruction, and does not assign mantras by a secret process. In CSM each trainee chooses his or her own mantra from a list of sixteen Sanskrit mantras (Carrington, 1977). Other researchers, such as Woolfolk, Carr-Kaffashan, Lehrer, and McNulty (1976) and Fehmi (1975), have also developed new standardized forms of meditation. Without doubt, other useful forms will soon be appearing on the scene.

There is a distinct advantage for psychotherapists in using a form of meditation they themselves can teach. The TM organization, for example, does not allow a psychotherapist to teach TM unless the clinician has spent six months in residence and has become a certified TM teacher. They also disapprove of any psychotherapist suggesting alterations in the TM meditation technique to assist a meditating patient. The official position of their organization is that TM should never be regulated to suit a meditator's personality, but rather that all that is necessary for it to work satisfactorily in any given instance is for a qualified TM teacher to determine that the meditation is being done entirely effortlessly.

A number of clinicians, myself included, have noticed undesirable side effects from TM in certain meditating patients, however (Lazarus, 1976), and the TM organization's negative attitude with respect to regulation of their technique is causing an increasing number of psychotherapists to be concerned about recommending this form of meditation to their patients. Many of us in the field of psychotherapy are, therefore, finding it useful to recommend, or to teach, standardized forms of meditation other than TM. This not only eliminates undue expense to the patient, but permits clinical adjustment of the technique to suit the personality and requirements of each trainee. This is a distinct advantage when dealing with emotionally disturbed patients undergoing psychotherapy.

TM is also undesirable as a research strategy because the members of the organization refuse to modify their technique to meet requirements of many types of research. They will not, for example, dispense with the *puja* through which individuals are initiated into TM; will not waive the requirement that the initiates bring fruits, flowers, and white handkerchiefs to their initiation; and will not reveal the particular mantra assigned to any subject so that researchers might know the experimental variable they are dealing with. With other standardized meditation techniques, however, researchers can readily break down the technique into its component parts and thereby isolate experimental variables, and no procedure need be kept secret.

Physiology of Meditation

While some of the original TM research is holding up well over time and is being replicated in a number of laboratories, other findings have been contradicted by later evidence in the typical manner of science. Despite such minor inconsistencies, however, some basic facts seem well established.

As a physiological state, meditation appears to exhibit qualities of both sleep and wakefulness, yet to be distinct from each of these. While it resembles the hypnogogic (i.e., falling asleep) state, it is, at the very least, an artificial prolongation of the presleep condition. Research suggests that during meditation the body tends to be in a profound state of rest, with oxygen consumption lowered as much as (or more than) in deep NREM (quiescent) sleep. Heart rate also tends to be slowed down at this time, blood flow to be augmented in forearms and head, skin resistance to be heightened, and blood lactate levels to be reduced (Wallace, 1970; Wallace, Benson, & Wilson, 1971).

EEGs show predominant alpha waves during meditation, occasional theta waves, and a tendency in certain subjects for an unusual synchrony to be seen in all leads at once (Banquet, 1972). Because these regular, rhythmic EEG patterns occur in a state of relative wakefulness (sleep occurring during meditation is usually transient), meditation has been termed by Wallace et al. (1971, p. 795) a "wakeful hypometabolic state" and by Gellhorn and Kiely (1972, p. 399) a "state of trophotropic dominance compatible with full awareness."

Effects of Meditation

Meditation can affect personality both in an immediate sense and in terms of its ability to alter character traits. The former outcome might be expected—it is not surprising, for example, that deep relaxation reduces stress—but the latter is somewhat more difficult to understand at first glance. If we consider the practice of meditation in light of its meaning to the practitioner, however, we can see how its regular practice may actually exert considerable influence on personality.

Persons regularly practicing one of the popular forms of meditation such as TM, Benson's Method, or CSM usually spend two twenty-minute periods (or forty minutes a day) in meditation, plus a few additional minutes coming out of meditation. This brings the total time spent in meditation per day close to the forty-five- or fifty-minute psychoanalytic hour. The meditators, however, spend this time with themselves seven days a week instead of three or five days as in psychoanalysis. Considering the intensity of the exposure to it, we can begin to see how regular meditation may become a potent agent for personality change.

Clinical and research evidence suggests that a number of personality changes take place in people who meditate regularly and that these changes are repeated in large numbers of meditators. The most prominent changes I have noted in my patients who have learned meditation, and in trainees of CSM on whom we have kept systematic records, are the following.

Tension Level

Sharp, and sometimes even dramatic reductions in overall tension have occurred in many people after they started to meditate. The drop in tension level is variously manifested in a lessening of the person's anxiety; in the disappearance of inappropriate startle responses; in increased frustration tolerance; in the improvement of psychosomatic conditions, such as tension headaches, asthma, and hypertension; in improved sleep; and in a reduced need for psychotropic medication (Carrington, 1977).

Energy Level

Some people, after they start meditating regularly, experience an unaccustomed surge of energy, which may manifest itself in a lessened need for daytime naps; in increased physical stamina; in greater productivity and/or ideational fluency; in the dissolution of writer's or artist's "block"; in the release of hitherto unsuspected creative potential; or in a combination of any of these. Patients undergoing psychotherapy may free-associate with greater ease or discover that they have reached innovative solutions to problems almost effortlessly. Sometimes these solutions may pop into their minds spontaneously during the meditative state itself.

Self-Esteem

Self-recrimination seems to be markedly lessened in a number of people after they start to meditate. Obviously of advantage to psychotherapy, this permits formerly unacceptable or repressed material to be faced openly by the patient and handled with comparative ease. Concomitant with this lessened self-blame is a decrease in paranoid tendencies in certain meditating patients and a general increase in spontaneity and openness.

Mood

Meditating patients with depressive tendencies may experience elevation and stabilization of mood after commencing meditation. Frequently, such people become steadier, more optimistic, and more willing to engage fully and energetically in the work of psychotherapy. Patients with acute depressive reactions do not, however, respond as well, on the whole, to meditation as do patients with subacute neurotically determined depressions, or mild, chronic, low-grade depressions. Acute depressive patients seem likely to discontinue practicing meditation even though it may have markedly elevated their moods. In my opinion, this tendency to flee from meditation is due to the complex role that the depressive symptoms play in the psychic economy, often reflecting a strong unconscious reluctance on the part of the patients to relinquish the maladaptive pattern.

Affect Availability

After they have started meditating, patients frequently report that they experience strong feelings of pleasure, sadness, anger, love, or other emotions that were previously suppressed. They may experience this emotional release during a meditative session or outside of it.

Because meditation seems to have this facilitating effect on the expression of emotion, I find it useful to ask certain patients to meditate immediately prior to their psychotherapy sessions. If a session in progress is blocked, and the patient seems unable to deal genuinely and meaningfully with the content of the session, I sometimes meditate together with the patient during the psychotherapeutic hour. I have always found this to be a helpful maneuver. After we have meditated together, the rapport between myself and the patient is excellent; patients tend to be relaxed, thoughtful, and in touch with their own feelings.

Bernard Glueck (1973, p. 7) has noted that the reduced level of anxiety resulting from meditation also seems to "facilitate entry into consciousness of previously repressed anxiety-laden material."* I have even seen several dramatic instances in which traumatic repressed memories were recovered during meditative sessions (Carrington, 1977). It is important to note, however, that had these same memories occurred during meditation in patients who were not in psychotherapy at the time, the chances are that the patients in question would have abandoned the practice of meditation because of anxiety experienced over having to face hitherto unrecognized and potentially threatening aspects of themselves. More often than not, a combination of psychotherapy and meditation seems to be more effective than either of these interventions used alone.

*[See also Chapter 5 of this volume, pp. 109–110. Eds.]

Side Effects of Tension-Release

The stress-release component of meditation is important to consider when managing this technique in a therapeutically effective manner. The TM organization refers to this as "normalizing"; I have termed the resulting temporary symptoms "tension-release side effects." What is referred to by both terms is the tendency for psychological and/or physiological symptoms of a temporary nature to appear during or following a meditation session. Their appearance is usually therapeutically useful, and these side effects appear to be caused by the release of deep-seated tensions on a nonverbal level (Carrington, 1977, Chapter 6).

Certain precautions are necessary, however, with respect to these side effects. If tension-release during or following meditation is too rapid, this can cause a person to back off from meditation or perhaps abandon the practice of it altogether. Careful adjustment of meditation time and other details of the technique will usually eliminate any serious problems from tension-release, however. Adjusting meditation to suit individual needs is therefore central to the teaching of CSM.

Increased Sense of Identity

A very common result of meditation is an increase of a sense of separate identity in the meditator. This is particularly apparent in people who have only a tenuous sense of their own identity to begin with. For patients with this problem, experiencing a new and convincing sense of self during meditation may establish a base of self-awareness that can then be built upon productively in psychotherapy.

Archimedes, the ancient Greek mathematician and physicist, is reputed to have said, "Give me a place to stand and I will move the world." This advice seems to apply to the process of psychotherapy as well. Many patients are unable to make progress in psychotherapy because they seem to lack a base of self from which therapeutic change may be effected. If this is the case, even penetrating insight into their own problems may build on quicksand, as it were. I have found that meditation often makes a significant contribution to psychotherapy by fostering an indefinable, convincing, nonverbal experience of self that is regularly reinforced.

Meditating patients in psychotherapy often report that they are becoming more aware of their own opinions, that they are no longer as easily influenced by others as they were previously, and that they can arrive at decisions more quickly and easily. They may also be better able to sense their own needs, more outspoken and self-assertive, and more able to stand up for their own rights in an effective manner.

Such changes can pose difficulties for certain patients, however. If they are not prepared to assimilate the independence and self-assertion that meditation brings about, they will usually abandon the practice rather than suffer a crisis in terms of self-image. This is particularly likely to occur if the patient has been clinging to a self-effacing role for a long period of time and if such a role has played an important part in his psychopathology. If the threat that the growing sense of individuation and separateness poses for him is not dealt with successfully in psychotherapy, the patient may stop meditating rather than experience the acute conflict that is engendered.

Antiaddictive Effects

Several large-scale studies (Benson & Wallace, 1971; Shafii, Lavely, & Jaffe, 1974; Winquist, 1969) have shown that in those persons who continue meditating for long periods of time (usually for a year or more) there is a marked decrease in abuse of nonprescription drugs such as marijuana, amphetamines and barbiturates, and of psychedelic substances such as LSD. It even appears that many long-term meditators have discontinued use of such drugs entirely.

Antiaddictive trends are also seen in cigarette smokers and abusers of alcohol. In one study, measures of reduction in cigarette smoking (in persons who had practiced meditation more than two years) showed that 71% of these meditators had significantly decreased their use of cigarettes, and 57% had stopped smoking altogether, while cigarette usage figures for a control group of nonmeditators remained nearly the same over a two-year period (Shafii, 1973).

The only available surveys on attrition rates of the popular forms of meditation such as TM (Davies, 1976; Otis, 1974; Shelly, 1976), however, show that about half of the adults in a typical community who learn to meditate discontinue the practice within three years of having learned it, and an even larger number cut down to once instead of twice a day. Current figures on attrition rates are difficult to obtain since the TM organization, which has by far the largest number of practitioners among the general public, does not release data on this. The best available current figures are reported elsewhere (Carrington, 1977).

The dropout factor must be taken into account when considering the antiaddictive effects that occur when meditation is continued over time. The effectiveness of long-term meditation in combating the above-mentioned forms of addiction is, however, impressive enough to warrant its adjunctive use with patients showing these types of addictive problems.

On a clinical level, I have observed several of my patients, after commencing meditation, to stop heavy use of marijuana. Two patients brought incipient drinking problems under control, two patients stopped smoking, and two (nonobese) patients spontaneously regulated their need for food intake. The patients with severe obesity problems, however, showed no lessening of their compulsive eating after starting meditation, and no weight loss, although they seemed to have benefited from the practice in other respects.

Why Does Meditation Work?

Why does meditation have the effect it does on a sizable number of people who practice it? There is no clear-cut answer to this question. Obviously the process is a complex one. Meditation seems to "work," when it does, for a number of different reasons.

First, there is the similarity between the situation that occurs during meditation and that which occurs during systematic desensitization as used in behavior therapy. In systematic desensitization, increasingly greater increments of anxiety (prepared in a graded hierarchy) are "counter-conditioned" by being paired with an induced state of deep relaxation. If the treatment is successful, presentation of the originally disturbing stimuli will no longer produce anxiety.

In meditation the situation is somewhat analogous, since the meditative "focus" (a mantra, one's breathing, a candle flame, or whatever) becomes a signal for turning attention inward and bringing about a state of deep relaxation. At the same time, the meditators practicing a modern technique of meditation are maintaining a permissive attitude with respect to thoughts, images, or sensations experienced during meditation. They neither reject nor unduly hold onto them, but merely let these thoughts flow through their minds. The thoughts appear either simultaneously with their focus of meditation, or they may alternate with this focus.

The subjective state that is set up pairs a state of deep relaxation (brought about by attention to the meditative focus) with a rapid, automatic review of an exceedingly wide variety of mental contents, both verbal and nonverbal. As these thoughts, images, sensations, and impressions drift by during meditation, the meditative focus seems to neutralize them. The result is that no matter how unsettling a meditation session may be subjectively (occasionally, meditation can be a stressful experience), a frequent response of meditators is that they find themselves emerging from meditation with the "charge" taken off their current concerns or problems. This almost invariably enables them to cope with these problems more effectively.

But practical meditation does not appear to be just another form of behavior modification. While there are resemblances between the two, there are important differences. In systematic desensitization, a therapist and patient work together to identify areas of anxiety. They then proceed to deal with single isolated problems in a step-by-step, organized fashion. In meditation, the areas of anxiety to be "desensitized" are selected automatically by the responding organism itself (the meditating person).

In many respects the brain appears to behave during meditation as though it were a computer programmed to run certain materials through demagnetizing circuits that are set up to handle large amounts of data at one time. We might even conceptualize subsystems within the brain scanning vast memory stores during the meditative state. This process would go on at lightning speed, the brain being programmed to select the contents of the mind that are (1) most pressing emotionally, (2) most likely to be tolerated without undue anxiety, and (3) best able to be handled at the present time. A decision to surface certain mental contents rather than others for "demagnetizing" would then need to be made. This would presumably be done by automatically weighing such considerations as the above and arriving at an optimal compromise. Meditation, then, seems to possess considerably more scope than the behavior therapies, although it possibly lacks the precision of the latter.

Another aspect of meditation makes it a state particularly likely to bring about personality change. During meditation, the meditator's conventional mental set is freed from its usual constraints. This can alter the meditator's view of self and environment radically, while at the same time he remains alert and wakeful. Meditators often emerge from their sessions feeling freed from the overrestraint of programmed ways of thinking and perceiving. It is, therefore, not surprising that creativity is frequently fostered by meditation and habitual self-blame lessened by it.

Still another explanation for the effects of meditation, although it is admittedly highly speculative, should be mentioned. It is conceivable that meditation enables the meditating person to benefit from an exchange of energy with an as yet unidentified source of energy, similar to the pervading energy fields which the Indians refer to as *prana.*

Perhaps, in the quiet of meditation, meditating persons are able to tune in to some cosmic source of energy capable of replenishing and renewing them. Such a concept may seem at this point more mystical in nature than scientific, but it cannot be entirely dismissed by serious researchers, since the concepts of modern quantum physics suggest the presence of large underlying force-fields, more fundamental than the matter that we perceive with our senses. The relationship of the organism to a larger energy flow is, in fact, beginning to be studied in such disciplines as biometeorology.

On a clinical level, I have noticed that meditators frequently report an indefinable sense of harmony with the world and even with the universe, during meditation, and the concept of fusion with a fundamental life-force during this alert yet quiet state is an interesting working hypothesis.

Meditation's Relationship to Psychotherapy

Meditation is clearly different from conventional forms of psychotherapy. The therapeutic process usually seeks to pinpoint conflicts and problem areas, often of an unconscious nature, and to bring into play the conscious integrative functions of the ego. Meditation, on the other hand, provides no conceptual handle for use in reorganizing one's cognitions of self. In fact, the rational elements of the psychodynamic psychotherapies are conspicuously absent in meditation. The interpersonal elements of the former are also dispensed with; during meditation, one is alone with oneself.

In my opinion, the changes brought about by meditation seem to be of a more global nature than those resulting from psychotherapy. Meditation would appear to affect broad field-tension states, to bring about complex but nonspecific adjustments. Therefore, it may leave intact specific inner conflicts and psychopathological solutions to them while at the same time fostering positive personality traits on a more general level.

I have seen long-term meditators who, through meditation, became more emotionally responsive, tranquil, personally insightful, energetic, and sensitive to the world around them. But these people continued to carry emotional burdens centering on unresolved conflicts concerning sexual adjustments, social maturity, marriage, career, and so forth.

I have also known people who had recently learned to meditate and were benefiting considerably from it, who entered psychotherapy (after commencing meditation) specifically for the purpose of working out their personality problems. According to these people, meditation had reduced their anxiety level to a point where they could contemplate exploring their emotional problems in depth. Often this was the first time they could do so without experiencing so much anxiety that they were forced to shy away from the therapeutic process.

In my opinion, the complementarity of these two processes, meditation and psychotherapy, is impressive. I have not seen any occasions where meditation has been used by patients as a resistance to psychotherapy or where it has caused patients to terminate their psychotherapy prematurely. Nor have I seen any instance (provided their therapists had a thorough knowledge of and positive attitude toward meditation) where patients' psychotherapy has interfered with their practice of meditation.

Limitations

Meditation clearly has limitations, as do all other techniques used to effect personality change. I have mentioned the inevitable drop-out rate. This is scarcely grounds for concern, however, since some patients will drop out of all programs designed to assist them, psychotherapy included. A more pressing problem that arises with the therapeutic use of meditation is the rapidity with which certain personality changes may occur in meditators and the way in which meditation frequently effects changes incompatible with the pathological life-style (or defensive system) of a patient (Carrington, 1977).

Even positive changes from meditation, if they occur at the wrong time, that is, before the groundwork for them has been laid by readjusting the patient's value system, can cause an impasse that can only be resolved in one of two ways: (1) The pathological value system may be altered to incorporate the new attitude brought about by the meditation, or (2) the practice of meditation may be abandoned. Whether or not meditators reaching such an impasse have recourse to psychotherapy to help them work through this impasse may determine whether or not they will continue with their meditation and whether they will be able to use it to effect a basic change in life-style.

Meditation may threaten a patient's pathological life-style in any of the following ways:

1. By fostering a new and spontaneous self-assertion that clashes with a habitual neurotic "solution" of self-effacement.
2. By fostering a feeling of well-being and optimism that runs counter to the playing out of a depressive or martyred role serving a function such as unconscious revenge. A patient may be so reluctant to relinquish such a role that he prefers to give up meditation instead.
3. By bringing about pleasurable feelings that cause guilt and anxiety. Patients with severe masturbation guilt often view meditation (an experience where one is alone giving oneself pleasure) as forbidden, and may discontinue that practice if this conflict is not worked through in therapy.
4. By bringing about an easing of life-pace that threatens a fast-paced, high-pressure life-style that is being used neurotically as a defense or in the service of drives for power, achievement, or control.

In all of the above instances, patients sensing these potential conflicts may refuse to learn meditation. Or if they do learn it, they may quickly discontinue their meditation practice unless the conflict it has engendered is handled in psychotherapy. With psychotherapeutic intervention, however, patients' negative reactions to meditation may be fruitful material for therapy, with discussion of them often unmasking important self-defeating aspects of the personality.

Still another form of resistance to meditation might be classified as a type of negative transference to the meditation process itself or to the meditational object of focus, such as a mantra. This can occur when meditators come to view meditation unconsciously as an ideal parent. When such people eventually discover that in reality the technique varies in its effectiveness according to external circumstances, or changes with their own mood or physiological state, they may become irrationally angry at the meditation process and "counter-reject" it by quitting the practice.

Such complications do not occur, of course, in all meditating patients. Meditation may assist the course of psychotherapy in such a straightforward fashion that there is no necessity to analyze the patient's reactions to it. A number of healthy persons certainly appear to benefit from meditation without difficulty of any sort, and the same is true of some patients undergoing psychotherapy.

Meditation, then, seems to be clearly promising as an adjunct to psychotherapy, provided it is accompanied by assistance in handling any resistances to it that may arise as a function of a patient's psychopathology.

Meditation for Psychotherapists

Aside from the personal benefits I have derived from my own practice of meditation (which no doubt has contributed to my work with patients), I have noticed a number of beneficial changes in my professional approach since I commenced meditating, and similar changes are reported by meditating colleagues. These are as follows:

1. Several of us have found ourselves more receptive to our own spontaneous perceptions of unconscious conflicts since we commenced meditating. Ease in communicating these perceptions to patients has also increased. One analytically oriented psychotherapist discovered that during meditation he frequently visualized vivid scenes of a symbolic nature that, on postmeditation analysis, proved to be valuable insights into one or another of his patients' psychodynamics.

2. Ability to handle dreams and other primary process material is often sharpened. We seem to handle such symbols more easily and with greater insight, and a number of us have reported that we are able to communicate dream interpretations to our patients more effectively than before.

3. We find that we have more staying power when patients' single hours follow one another in long succession, and less of a tendency toward drowsiness from work-stress.

4. A patient's sudden negative reaction, catching us off guard, is experienced as less startling and as less threatening. This appears to be part of a generally increased tolerance to all noxious stimuli (interpersonal or other) that frequently develops after commencing the practice of meditation.

5. As meditating psychotherapists, we are sensitive to the difficulties our meditating patients may be experiencing with this technique, and are frequently able to help our patients meditate more effectively.

Since meditation is proving personally and professionally valuable to us as psychotherapists, it may be a worthwhile aid in teaching certain therapeutic skills such as empathy, not readily conveyed by more formal methods. In an attempt to investigate this problem, Lesh (1970) studied the effects of meditation on the development of empathy in psychological counselor-trainees. The result was a significant improvement in empathic ability in those counselors who regularly practiced meditation during the course of the study, as compared to two control groups of counselor-trainees who did not practice meditation.

Meditation may, in fact, foster the "evenly suspended attention" to patients' comments that Freud considered essential in the practice of psychoanalysis. Freud (1912) advised the analyst to "simply listen and not bother about whether he is keeping anything in mind. . . . he must turn his own unconscious like a receptive organ towards the transmitting unconscious of the patient" (p. 112). Meditation might be considered an exercise designed to strengthen the precise "psychic muscles" necessary to achieve Freud's state of "evenly suspended attention." The experiences reported by myself and other meditating psychotherapists also suggest that meditation may help to strengthen the ability for adaptive regression, another valuable attribute for the psychotherapist.

Conclusions

Experience gleaned from teaching a form of practical meditation (CSM), work with meditating patients, and the available research on meditation all suggest that meditation can be a valuable adjunct to psychotherapy, but only if any resistances to meditation are worked through in psychotherapy by insight into the patient's psychodynamics. It also appears that meditation is effective in sharpening the professional skills of the meditating psychotherapist.

Clearly, more extensive research on the use of meditation as an adjunct to psychotherapy is needed at this point. Creative pilot programs using meditation in therapeutic settings, and programs incorporating meditation as part of training programs for psychotherapists, will give us much-needed information about its value to this field. Let us hope that such developments will be forthcoming in the near future.

REFERENCES

Banquet, J. P. EEG and meditation. *Journal of Electroencephalography and Clinical Neurophysiology* 1972, *33:* 449–458.

Benson, H. *The relaxation response.* New York: Morrow, 1975.

Benson, H., & Wallace, R. K. Decreased drug abuse with transcendental meditation: A study of 1862 subjects. *Congressional Record,* 92nd Congress, 1st session. June 1971, Serial No. 92–1.

Carrington, P. *Freedom in meditation.* New York: Anchor Press/Doubleday, 1977; Doubleday paperback edition, 1978.

Davies, P. Personal communication. Lawrence, Kansas: Kansas University, 1976.

Fehmi, L. *Open focus training.* Paper presented at the Sixth Annual Meeting of the Biofeedback Research Society, Monterey, Calif., February 5, 1975.

Freud, S. Recommendations to physicians practicing psychoanalysis (1912). In J. Strachey (ed.), *Standard Edition of the Complete Psychological Works of Sigmund Freud* (Vol. 12). London: Hogarth Press, 1958.

Gellhorn, E., & Kiely, W. F. Mystical states of consciousness: Neurophysiology and clinical aspects. *Journal of Nervous and Mental Disease* 1972, *154:* 399–405.

Glueck, B., as quoted in the *Hartford Courant,* May 27, 1973, p. 6.

Lazarus, A. A. Psychiatric problems precipitated by transcendental meditation (TM). *Psychological Reports* 1976, *39:* 601–602.

Lesh, T. V. Zen meditation and the development of empathy in counselors. *Journal of Humanistic Psychology* 1970, *10:* 39–74.

Otis, L. S. TM and sleep. Paper presented at the 82nd Annual Meeting of the American Psychological Association, New Orleans, La., Aug. 30–Sept. 3, 1974.

Shafii, M. *Smoking following meditation.* Unpublished paper, Ann Arbor, Mich.: University of Michigan Medical Center, 1973.

Shafii, M., Lavely, R., & Jaffe, R. Meditation and marijuana. *American Journal of Psychiatry* 1974, *113:* 60–63.

Shelly, M. Personal communication. Lawrence, Kansas: Kansas University, 1976.

Wallace, R. K. Physiological effects of transcendental meditation. *Science* 1970, *167:* 1751–1754.

Wallace, R. K., Benson, H., & Wilson, A. F. A wakeful hypometabolic physiologic state. *American Journal of Physiology* 1971, *221:* 795–799.

Winquist, W. T. *The effect of the regular practice of transcendental meditation on students involved in the regular use of hallucinogenic and "hard" drugs.* Unpublished paper, Department of Sociology, University of California at Los Angeles, 1969.

Woolfolk, R. L., Carr-Kaffashan, L., Lehrer, P. M., & McNulty, T. F. Meditation training as a treatment for insomnia. *Behavior Therapy* 1976, *7:* 359–365.

5
Psychophysiological Correlates of Relaxation

BERNARD C. GLUECK and CHARLES F. STROEBEL

In the past six years we have been studying, both in the research laboratory and in clinical settings, techniques directed toward the general goal of inducing a more relaxed state in research subjects and in patients with a variety of illnesses. We have tended to subsume all of these efforts under the general heading of "relaxation" in the very specific way that Dr. Herbert Benson (1975) does, since not everyone agrees with his contention that humans have both an emergency response and a relaxation response system. Benson argues that the built-in response systems that are designed to produce a more relaxed state within the organism are triggered by all of the relaxation techniques, be they his particular technique, Transcendental Meditation, other forms of Yoga, or the increasingly sophisticated electronic approaches using various biofeedback techniques that are proliferating rapidly.

Interestingly, Benson's argument that there is a natural tendency within the organism to produce a more relaxed state that can

The support of the Fannie E. Rippel Foundation in creating the computer programs used in this study is gratefully acknowledged.

be triggered by a variety of techniques is quite similar to the contention of one of the leading exponents of the meditational approaches, Maharishi Mahesh Yogi (1966), that the organism moves naturally toward a state of lessened tension and greater pleasure. This also is the thesis of one of the foremost psychoanalytic thinkers of recent times, Sandor Rado (1969), who states that for a healthy adaptation man must be motivated by the experience of, and desire for, pleasurable gratification, as well as seeking to avoid or escape from painful situations. Whether the pleasure response capabilities are inherent in the organism or need to be learned or can be evoked by specific techniques is still open to debate. There seems to be little doubt, however, that the various techniques used to produce relaxation all have an impact on the emergency response systems. This may be perceived by the individual as a reduction in the subjective feelings of anxiety, or it may be measured by the observer as a drop in pulse rate, a fall in blood pressure, an increase in the galvanic skin response (GSR), or in significant changes in the patterns of electrical activity of the brain.

We began investigating the patterns of brain wave activity using scalp electrodes and the traditional electroencephalographic (EEG) recordings six years ago, starting at a time when alpha wave EEG biofeedback was the primary biofeedback technique. Our first two studies used volunteer subjects who were interested in enhancing relaxation in order to relieve some of the tensions and stresses that they felt were interfering with their daily patterns of living. In these experiments, we utilized the EEG signals coming from the occipital cortex, analyzed by a computer, and fed back to the individual as either a tone or a light. Changes in the amount of alpha waves produced would cause corresponding changes in the loudness of the sound or the intensity of the light.

The brain waves in the 8–12 Hz. frequency band, the alpha waves, were utilized in these early experiments because of the observations made by some of the early investigators (Green, Green, & Walters, 1972; Kamiya, 1969) who were able to study individuals who had spent their lives learning and practicing various yogic and meditational techniques. They found that these men, who appeared to be very well integrated, calm, relaxed individuals, were able to produce alpha waves and the even slower theta wave forms almost at will. The argument was made that alpha wave production was somehow directly associated with the relatively calm and relaxed state in these individuals. Therefore, if we could teach our subjects to increase the amount of alpha that they were producing, they would feel a greater degree of calmness and tranquility.

These expectations were met only partially, in general by subjects who were good spontaneous alpha producers initially and who seemed to be fairly well integrated, healthy people. Other subjects, who showed a greater degree of anxiety and tension, ranging in two cases to fairly severe overt psychiatric symptoms, showed little or no spontaneous alpha wave production and seemed to have considerable difficulty in learning to enhance their alpha wave production. There was enough enhancement of the alpha density in most of our subjects, however, accompanied by a drop in skin conductance, in pulse rate, and in the respiratory rate (all presumed to be indicators of a more relaxed psychophysiologic internal steady state and described subjectively as an awareness of a reduction in inner tensions), for a decision to continue the studies with our psychiatric inpatient population. Our general hypothesis was that if we could teach the patient techniques that he could employ on his own and that would reduce tension and anxiety and improve the patient's general level of adaptation, it would be a useful addition to the other treatments being utilized in the hospital setting.

To briefly summarize our results, which have been reported elsewhere (Glueck & Stroebel, 1975a, b), two of our patient groups —those doing a general relaxation exercise modeled on Luthe's techniques (1965) and those doing alpha biofeedback training—soon dropped out of the experiment because of their inability to subjectively perceive any significant changes in their tension and anxiety levels. This was reflected in our objective measures, such as changes in the EEG patterns, in the GSR, blood pressure, pulse rate, and so on. By contrast, patients who were practicing the passive type of meditation known as Transcendental Meditation (TM) seemed to be subjectively aware of a drop in their inner tensions and anxieties following the very first meditation. Initially, this tended to be of fairly short duration, but as they continued to meditate, the feeling of reduced tension seemed to persist for longer and longer periods.

Because we had lost our two comparison groups of patients, we selected a group of patients from the remainder of the hospital population to compare with patients doing TM. The comparison group was matched for sex, age within three years, and level and kind of psychopathology as reported by the patient using the Minnesota

Multiphasic Personality Inventory (MMPI) at the time of admission to the Institute of Living. The mean MMPI profiles for the male and female TM patients, and the matched comparison groups are shown in Figures 5-1 and 5-2. From these profiles it would appear that, at least on their self-appraisal, the groups were well matched at the time of admission.

By contrast, it is interesting to note that only 18% of the pairs were diagnosed identically on admission; 26% were diagnosed within the same general group, for example, schizophrenia or neurosis; and 56% carried quite different diagnoses. This same general

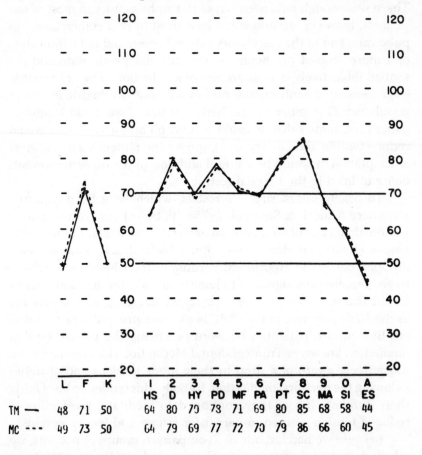

	L	F	K		1 HS	2 D	3 HY	4 PD	5 MF	6 PA	7 PT	8 SC	9 MA	0 SI	A ES
TM —	48	71	50		64	80	70	73	71	69	80	85	68	58	44
MC ---	49	73	50		64	79	69	77	72	70	79	86	66	60	45

FIGURE 5-1. Comparison of mean admission MMPI profiles for male patients doing TM and the matched comparison group (males: N=68 for both groups).

discrepancy in diagnostic classification existed at the time of discharge, with 18% of the pairs having identical diagnoses, 24% being within the same general group, and 58% having quite different diagnoses. Since the treating psychiatrist's assessment of his patient (summed up in the shorthand of the diagnostic label) determined the treatment of all patients in the study except for the addition of TM for the experimental group, the sizable discrepancy in the diagnoses on admission to the hospital explains, at least in part, the rather wide variation in treatment patterns observed in the two groups.

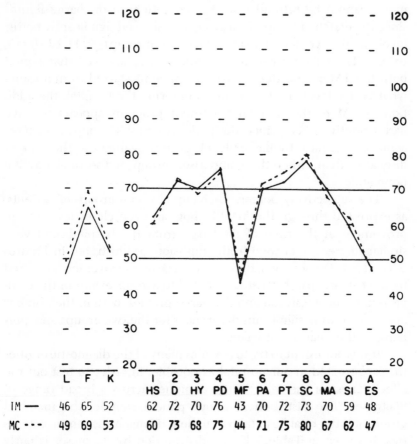

	L	F	K		1 HS	2 D	3 HY	4 PD	5 MF	6 PA	7 PT	8 SC	9 MA	0 SI	A ES
IM —	46	65	52		62	72	70	76	43	70	72	73	70	59	48
MC - - -	49	69	53		60	73	68	75	44	71	75	80	67	62	47

FIGURE 5-2. Comparison of mean admission MMPI profiles for female patients doing TM and the matched comparison group (females: N=41 for both groups).

While condition on discharge is an admittedly crude measure of change in a patient, it does represent a global judgment on the part of the treating psychiatrist that can be used for comparison purposes. Patients doing TM showed statistically a significantly greater degree of improvement than was seen for the hospital in general ($\chi^2=37.75$, $df=2$, p<.0001). They also showed a significantly higher level of improvement than their comparisons twins ($\chi^2=13.93$, $df=2$, p<.001). That both groups of patients, the TMers and the comparison group, may have been somewhat different from the total group of hospital patients, that is, better candidates for any sort of treatment, cannot be refuted from the condition on discharge figures since the matched comparison group also showed significantly better levels of improvement than the total hospital group ($\chi^2=11.13, df=2$, p<.01). These figures would seem to indicate, however, that even if both the TMers and the comparison patients started from a somewhat better level of adjustment on entering the hospital, the addition of TM to the hospital treatment program appears to have had a positive effect, since the patients doing TM appear to have achieved significantly higher levels of improvement at the time of discharge than either the comparison group or the total hospital population.

The subjectively perceived changes in both groups of patients, as expressed through the MMPI, show an even closer level of improvement at the time of discharge from the hospital, and very similar degrees of change from admission, as illustrated in Figures 5-3 and 5-4. The somewhat greater degree of improvement reported by the treating psychiatrist is reflected to a lesser extent in the comparison of the admission and discharge profiles, both in the number of scales showing significant differences for the two groups and, perhaps, in the quantity of change.

It was our intent to try to cover as many of the diagnostic entities that are treated in our hospital as possible, in order to test out the effectiveness of the relaxation techniques across a broad range of diagnoses. The distribution of our patient sample, the matched group, and the total hospital population, by major diagnostic categories, is shown in Table 5-1. The distribution by diagnoses is fairly similar for the TM group and the total hospital population. There is a sizable discrepancy, however, mainly in the number of patients diagnosed as suffering from a schizophrenic illness, between the TM patients and the comparison group.

The different diagnostic distributions may have influenced the outcome figures for the TM group and the comparison group shown in Table 5-2 by diagnosis and by level of improvement. Comparing the outcome figures for the schizophrenic patients shows a significant difference in level of improvement in favor of the patients doing TM

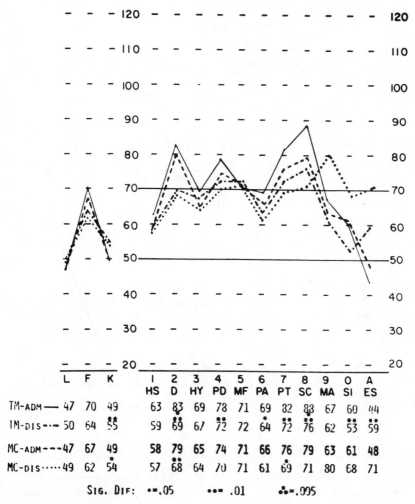

	L	F	K	1 HS	2 D	3 HY	4 PD	5 MF	6 PA	7 PT	8 SC	9 MA	0 SI	A ES
TM-ADM —	47	70	49	63	83	69	78	71	69	82	83	67	60	44
TM-DIS -·-	50	64	55	59	69	67	72	72	64	72	76	62	53	59
MC-ADM ---	47	67	49	58	79	65	74	71	66	76	79	63	61	48
MC-DIS·····	49	62	54	57	68	64	70	71	61	69	71	80	68	71

SIG. DIF: •=.05   •••.01   •••=.005

FIGURE 5-3. The admission and discharge profiles for male TM patients and the matched comparison group (males: TM–N=36, MC–N=35). Eight scales show significant differences for the TM patients between admission and discharge; only three scales show significant differences for the comparison group.

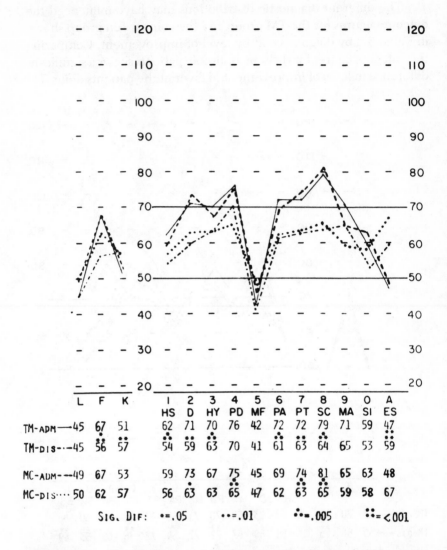

FIGURE 5-4. The admission and discharge profiles for female TM patients and the matched comparison group (females: TM–N=23, MC–N=22). Nine scales show significant differences for the TM patients between admission and discharge; five scales show significant differences for the comparison patients.

TABLE 5-1. Diagnostic Distribution by
Research Category

Diagnosis	TM		MC		HP*	
	N	*%*	*N*	*%*	*N*	*%*
Schizophrenia	43	39%	69	62%	240	38%
Neuroses	26	24%	11	10%	129	20%
Personality Disorders	18	16%	12	11%	64	10%
Alcoholism	4	4%	5	5%	44	7%
Drug Dependence	11	10%	4	4%	21	3%
Adjustment Reactions	8	7%	9	8%	39	6%
Other	—	—	—	—	100	16%
Totals	110	100%	110	100%	637	100%

*Hospital percentage, 1973-1974.

($\chi^2=15.184$, $df=2$, p<.0002). By comparison, the remainder of the sample, comprising the other diagnostic groupings, shows no significant difference in the outcome levels between the two groups ($\chi^2=1.638$, $df=2$).

The fact that 40% of our sample had a diagnosis of a schizophrenic illness demonstrates, we believe, that even quite seriously ill hospitalized psychiatric patients can learn the meditation technique if they are able to comprehend the instructions. Because of the immediate awareness of a drop in the levels of anxiety and tension, most of our patients were willing to continue practicing the technique on a regular basis twice daily. We experienced the greatest difficulty in getting patients to meditate regularly in those individuals with a significant amount of depression, and in our younger, teen-aged patients. Even in these individuals, it was more a matter of needing to be reminded to practice the meditation regularly than any resistance or unwillingness to do so. In fact, less than 10% of the total number of patients taught to meditate stopped meditating within the first six weeks of learning the technique.

While the patients remained in the hospital, most attempted to meditate quite regularly during the period of time that they were in the research project. After termination of their participation in the project, there was a gradual attrition in the regularity of meditation

TABLE 5-2. TM Versus Matched Comparison (MC)
Group Condition on Discharge by Diagnosis (N = 220;
TM = 110, MC = 110)

	Group I		Group II		Group III		Total	
	TM	*MC*	*TM*	*MC*	*TM*	*MC*	*TM*	*MC*
Schizophrenia	20	18	22	28	1	23	43	69
Neuroses	17	5	5	4	4	2	26	11
Personality Disorders	5	3	9	8	4	1	18	12
Alcoholism	1	2	3	1	0	1	4	5
Drug Dependence	4	1	6	3	1	0	11	4
Adjustment Reaction Adolescence	5	2	3	6	0	1	8	9
Total	52	31	48	51	10	28	110	110

Group I = recovered or much improved.
Group II = moderately improved.
Group III = slightly improved or unimproved.

that continued after discharge from the hospital. At the time of our first follow-up inquiry, approximately three months after discharge, 42% of the respondents were continuing regular meditation twice a day. Another 22% were meditating somewhat irregularly, and 36% had stopped entirely for one reason or another. Many of these patients indicated that they planned to resume meditating at some point in the future. In a somewhat smaller sample, followed up at one year, 43% of the respondents were continuing to meditate regularly, but the number of patients who had stopped had risen to 42%, with the remainder reporting irregular or infrequent meditation.

There are no precise figures available from the TM organization as to the number of individuals in the general community who stop meditating after going through the learning process. Estimates from several sources seem to agree on about a 50% attrition rate. If this is correct, then our patients are continuing to meditate in about the same percentage as individuals in the general population who are learning the TM technique.

It is interesting that Benson reports that the major difficulty with the use of his technique is the failure of individuals taught the technique to continue to use it regularly. This is true in spite of the fact that most of the individuals with whom he deals have significant problems with their blood pressure, coronary artery disease, and so forth. We have seen the same phenomenon in the patients in our Biofeedback Clinic, where we are teaching people to trigger a general relaxation through vasodilation of the vessels in the hand and through relaxation of the striated muscle. These patients have seriously incapacitating, painful headaches (vascular and tension headaches) or Raynaud's disease of the fingers and sometimes the toes. In spite of the extreme pain that these conditions can cause, pain that is either completely relieved or significantly improved through the use of the relaxation techniques, approximately 50% of these individuals complain of a recurrence of symptoms at four to six months. In addition to whatever else may have changed, the universal finding is that they have stopped doing their daily relaxation exercises entirely or do them only very sporadically. Usually, if they come back into the clinic for a refresher course in the relaxation techniques, their symptoms are again brought under control.

Over and above the general human tendency to become careless or sloppy about doing anything regularly and consistently that takes some time and effort, we are concerned with the possibility of significant psychodynamic factors in these individuals that may make it very difficult or impossible for them to lead comfortable, pain-free lives. One can construe this as a reflection of the puritan ethic (life should be hard, difficult, uncomfortable), or one can label these individuals masochistic or, in a more recent terminology, pain-dependent. Unfortunately, due to the limitations of personnel time, we have not been able to investigate the detailed psychodynamic patterns in these patients in sufficient detail to arrive at any conclusions on these points.

An additional factor in individuals learning TM may be the very common experience that the initial relief of tension and anxiety feelings, which may be quite dramatic, tends to become less and less noticeable as the individual continues to meditate over the first two or three months. Since it is extremely difficult for us to remember, with any precision, exactly how tense and anxious we may have been at some previous point in time, even fairly recently, the degrees of difference from day to day as the general levels of tension subside become increasingly difficult to distinguish. It is at this point, we feel, that many individuals, if they are not reinforced in some way to continue the daily meditation or relaxation techniques, may conclude that nothing of significance is occurring and that the sessions are really a waste of time.

In addition, at about this time for many people the meditation process appears to release memories that have previously been quite thoroughly repressed. For persons, and this includes some of our psychiatric patients, who have had little or no contact with their unconscious processes this can be quite a disturbing experience. The appearance in a fully conscious, alert state, of intense affects and ideation that are usually quite completely repressed can be a very disturbing experience, especially if there is no one to help the individual to understand what is happening. Even though the TM teachers try to deal with this experience by stating that these thoughts represent stress being released from the nervous system, that this is a good experience, and that the thoughts should simply be allowed to float through the mind and disappear, this may not be sufficiently convincing or reassuring for many individuals who become troubled by both the content and the intensity of the ideation. We are convinced that many individuals stop meditating at this point because of their conviction that meditation is harming them and may perhaps be causing some sort of mental disturbance.

While we had some awareness of this phenomenon when we began our research project, we were not prepared for the intensity and rapidity with which these repressed memories can arise. We are quite certain that several of the patients who stopped meditating within their first two to three weeks early in the project did so because we were not dealing with the ideation adequately. Once we became aware of the significance of the above events and alerted the psychotherapist to this possibility, we found that we could turn the experience to a distinct advantage for our patients. We feel that there is little question that meditation can speed up the entire psychotherapeutic process by virtue of the release of previously completely repressed material. This has been the experience of other therapists using TM with their patients, as reported by Carrington and Ephron (1975), Carrington (1977),* and Bloomfield and Kory (1976).

*[See also Chapter 4 in this volume. Eds.]

If one does attempt to use techniques like TM in an effort to mobilize the release of material that has been previously repressed, it is extremely important that the patient understand and carefully follow the instructions about how to deal with the thoughts as they arise in meditation. We gave patients very specific instructions to follow the meditation rules while they are meditating. In general, these rules state that one should not attempt to understand, associate to, or otherwise deal with ideas that come up while meditating; that one should simply let the ideas pass through the mind and if they seem to be too bothersome, to return to the mantra. We believe this is an essential instruction since the meditation would be seriously interfered with otherwise. We also instructed our patients, however, that following the meditation, if they could recall specific ideas, events, or situations that came into their minds while meditating, to utilize these in their psychotherapeutic activity. Once we understood this general process and conveyed the information to the therapists in the hospital, many of them utilized this phenomenon to great advantage in the treatment of their patients. Carrington carries this process several steps further by timing the meditation to occur just before the therapeutic session or, at times, having the patient meditate during the session, so that any ideation that comes up will be quite fresh and available for the psychotherapeutic process. While we do not understand how this phenomenon occurs, we do have some ideas about what may be involved in the central nervous system. This will be discussed later in the chapter in talking about the electrophysiologic phenomena that accompany the meditation process.

Up to this point we have been reporting primarily subjective responses to these relaxation techniques. To be sure, a change in symptoms, such as the loss of intense tension and anxiety feelings, the disappearance of migraine headaches, the normalization of the blood supply in the fingers in Raynaud's disease, are all fairly important indicators that something significant may be happening. We are fortunate, however, in that there is accumulating a wealth of more objective evidence, primarily psychophysiologic data, that tends to support the subjective, anecdotal type of reports. It was the finding of significant changes in such basic psychophysiologic mechanisms as GSR, EEG wave forms, changes in heart rate, and in blood pressure that first excited the interest of psychophysiologists in exploring these various relaxation techniques. Since there is such a wide variety of relaxation techniques—including all of the various forms of yoga, the meditational techniques, such as TM and Zen meditation, similar derivations of these, such as Carrington's Clinically Standardized Meditation and Benson's Relaxation Response technique—one must ask what the similarities are in these various techniques, and do they, in fact, produce the same end point, as their proponents insist. Competition in this area is very keen; the adherents of each technique insist that theirs is the best technique to use in the attempt to achieve the results desired. In the oriental yogic and meditation techniques, this usually is the state of exaltation or bliss, given various names, such as *nirvāna, samādhi,* and so forth. With Western variations, the endpoint tends to be more specifically targeted; for example, relief of psychic tension and symptoms; relief of specific psychophysiologic difficulties, such as hypertension, migraine, and Raynaud's disease; and achieving a general state of relaxation. At this time, with an incomplete understanding of the specific details of the impact of all of these various approaches, we are inclined to think that all of these techniques represent different paths toward the same general end. We are also quite certain that they vary in effectiveness with different individuals, perhaps different basic personality types, and also vary in their impact on specific pathologic processes. One good example is the generally acknowledged failure of TM to significantly affect migraine headaches and Raynaud's disease. We add the caution here that the individuals we have studied have been practicing TM for six months to several years. It is entirely possible that with long-term use of the TM technique, significant improvement might occur in these somatic illnesses. By contrast, however, the same individuals, after three to six hours of training in the specific biofeedback techniques of vasodilation and muscle relaxation, obtain either complete relief or marked improvement in their somatic complaints in approximately 80% of cases.

In looking at the various psychophysiologic parameters, we found that patients doing TM were showing the same physiological changes described by Wallace (1970a, b), that is, slowing of the heart rate, slowing of respiration, and increasing the GSR. The most consistent finding was a universal increase in the GSR in all subjects (up to 30% increase over baseline) although we never saw the extreme changes described by Wallace in his original studies (up to 400%). The same types of changes have been observed in subjects utilizing Benson's Relaxation Response and in patients using the specifically targeted biofeedback procedures.

In addition, each of the relaxation techniques we have studied produces augmentation of alpha density in subjects with significant alpha rhythm in the "eyes closed" baseline condition. While subjects with minimal baseline alpha rhythm achieve very little EEG augmentation, they do report a comparable subjective "alpha state." We recognize that alpha density per se was probably only a portion of the physiologic variance that was needed to clarify the possible psychophysiological differences among these techniques. However, more recent evaluations of EEG records in patients and subjects using these relaxation techniques reveal remarkable periods of intrahemispheric alpha and theta synchrony at times, even for inexperienced subjects. This observation has been confirmed by Banquet (1973) and Levine, Herbert, Haynes, and Strobel (1975) in their studies of intra- and interhemispheric synchrony in experienced meditators. We are currently using machine and Fortran language programs for our PDP-12, PDP-15, and 15-Graphics terminal configuration for analyzing monopolar and/or bipolar eight-lead EEGs* for isometric power spectra using the fast Fourier transform, and associated measures of coherence and phase angle (for each cycle, 1–31 Hz.), and also a measure of synchronicity expressed as a percentage of time that two electrode placements had a coherence greater than 0.8 and a phase angle within ± 10° for whatever frequency is being measured.**

Figures 5-5 through 5-10 show the displays generated by the above programs in a TM meditator who had been meditating for more than four years. The appearance of synchronous alpha activity upon closing the eyes, even before starting to meditate, is shown nicely in Figures 5-5, 5-6, and 5-7 for the temporal, central, and occipital cortical areas. The increased amount of synchronization

*International electrode placements: Fp1, left frontal; Fp2, right frontal; T3, left mid-temporal; T4, right mid-temporal; O1, left occipital; O2, right occipital; C3, left central; C4, right central. Reference electrodes are placed on the mastoid bone behind each ear, A1 and A2. The left ear is used for ground.

**Documentation and calibration techniques for these programs may be obtained at reproduction cost from the authors.

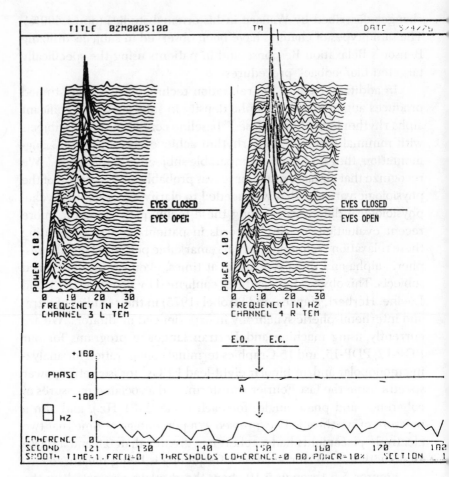

FIGURE 5-5. The isometric display of one minute of EEG data from the left (channel 3) and right (channel 4) temporal areas. Each line in the upper part of the display shows the distribution of the energy in each frequency from 1 to 31 Hz. for one second of EEG recording. The bottom half of the display (24 seconds) is during the initial "eyes open," resting state. With eye closure, there is a prompt organization of high amplitude alpha waves in the 8 to 10 Hz. range. The bottom lines of the display show the phase angle and coherence between the two temporal leads for the same minute of the EEG recording. Phase angle (the intermittent lines, e.g., "A") is shown only when the coherence exceeds 0.8.

114

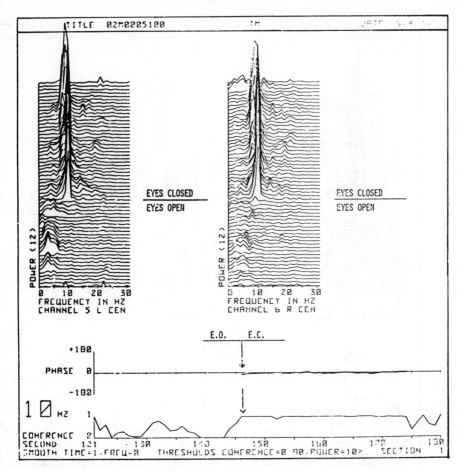

FIGURE 5-6.   This is the same minute of EEG data as shown in Figure 5-5, now showing the pattern from the left and right central areas. With the mere closing of the eyes, coherence jumps above the 0.9 threshold in this instance, with phase angle being essentially zero for most of the same 30 seconds.

upon meditating is shown for the temporal and central areas in Figures 5-8 and 5-9. Figure 5-10 is an example of the numeric information that also is available from these programs. It shows the numerical data for the same minute of meditation as Figure 5-9. This program is proving particularly useful in evaluating subjects who utilize different relaxation techniques and in evaluating our patients because of its ability to give a precise analysis of the amount of energy in each frequency from 1–31 Hz., as well as giving averages for the

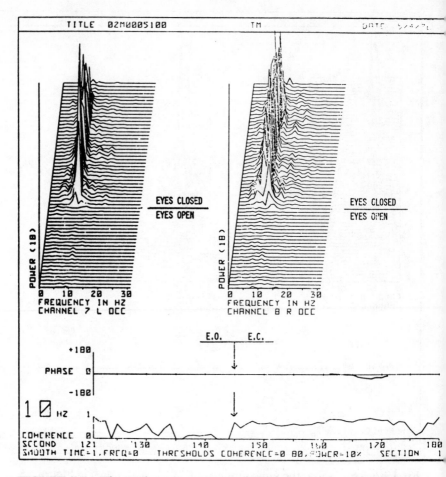

FIGURE 5-7. This is the same minute of EEG data as shown in the two previous figures, displayed here as coming from the left and right occipital areas. Coherence immediately increases with the closure of the eyes, but there is less synchronization, approximately 10 seconds, than in the central leads. There is a considerable increase in the amount of alpha activity, which can be judged by the figures in parentheses following the vertical word "power." These figures indicate the amount of reduction required to produce approximately the same size elevations on the graphic displays and increase progressively from the temporal, to the central, to the occipital areas.

116

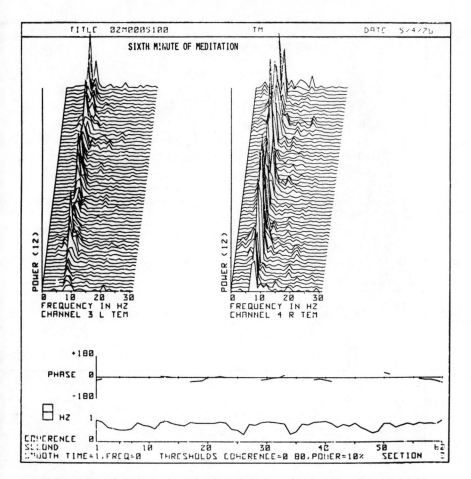

FIGURE 5-8. The increase in the amount of synchronization during meditation is visible here in the increased amount of time that the phase angle relationships remain within the ± 10° criterion. The left and right temporal areas are being compared during the sixth minute of meditation in an experienced (four years) meditator.

various bands, such as theta and alpha. Other authors have referred to synchrony primarily in terms of the amount of coherence between any two leads. We believe that adding in the phase angle relationship after coherence exceeds a certain threshold, in this example a coherence of 0.9, provides a much truer estimate of the amount of synchronization between any two cortical areas being analyzed. The high percentage of synchrony seen in the temporal and central corti-

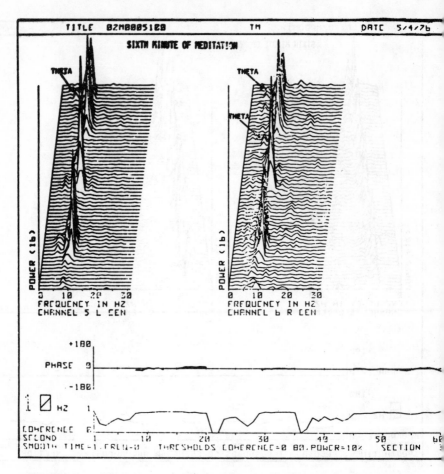

FIGURE 5-9. The sixth minute of meditation displayed for the two central areas. There is a high degree of synchrony at the 10 Hz. alpha frequency with periods in between when relatively little activity is present. The appearance of low voltage theta activity is indicated by arrows on the display.

cal areas is more characteristic of the synchronization-relaxation effect produced by TM, as compared to the other techniques we have studied.

Figures 5-11 and 5-12 show the amount of synchronization in the temporal and occipital cortex produced even quite early in the use of the TM technique. These are from a meditator who had been meditating just four weeks at the time we ran his EEG patterns.

Although it is obvious that he does not show the marked degree of synchronization exhibited by the more experienced meditator, it is also obvious that he is showing a considerable degree of synchronization early on, more so than we see in naïve subjects or in our psychiatric patients. Figure 5-13 is an example of the energy distribution, coherence, and synchrony in this subject for the same minute as shown in Figure 5-12.

Using these techniques, we are beginning to see some very interesting similarities and differences in the degree of synchronization produced by the various relaxation techniques. Figure 5-14 is an early estimate of the percentage of time synchrony in individuals using TM, the Benson Relaxation Response (RR), and thermal and EMG biofeedback (BF). Interhemispheric synchrony is shown in the upper panel, and intrahemispheric synchrony (dominant side only) in the lower panel for representative individuals in these three groups. Though sample sizes are still small, interesting differences in synchrony are emerging. The percentage of time that the synchrony measure was above criterion was obtained from a 20-minute sample of each technique with each subject sitting with eyes closed in a comfortable chair under dim ambient light. Both TM and RR subjects demonstrate significant interhemispheric synchrony between the temporal placements, while BF subjects demonstrate virtually none. Compared to TM and BF conditions, RR subjects have virtually no occipital synchrony. The BF subjects demonstrate a greater amount of intrahemispheric synchrony than do the meditating subjects. While none of the three techniques can be differentiated as yet on the basis of simple enhancement of the dominant alpha frequency, these data suggest that significant differences do exist for measures of synchrony (high coherence and low phase angle).

Current studies with the Carrington technique, in which the beginning meditator selects a mantra most pleasing for him, may illuminate the issue of mantra uniqueness that is a central claim of the TM organization. Will certain mantras produce greater degrees of synchrony than others? Can multiple pattern biofeedback of synchrony, per se, be used to replicate exactly the synchrony patterns that develop with the meditation modalities (Fehmi, 1975)?* Pend-

---

*[See also Chapter 7 in this volume. Eds.]

ing outcome of these studies, we have developed speculative hypotheses for interpreting the development of synchrony between the various cortical areas as described above.

1. THE MANTRA AS A BORING HABITUATION STIMULUS. This hypothesis suggests that the language-logic functions of the dominant left temporal cortex predominate mental activity under conditions of beta rhythm activation (desynchronization) with a tendency for symbolic activation of the emergency response; that normalization of viscero-autonomic homeostasis, regulated by the normally unconscious right temporal cortex-limbic system, predominates under conditions of alpha-theta synchronous activity (schematically represented in Figure 5-15); that "Type A" persons feel so much time pressure from depending on left cortical beta activation that they are in a state of relative deprivation of right cortical alpha

```
FILE:
TITLE: 02M0005100                    , TM              DATE: 5/4/76
CHANNELS : 5, L CEN        &     6, R CEN
SECTION :    3
SECONDS :    1 10   60
TIME SMOOTHING          =  1
FREQUENCY SMOOTHING     =  0
COHERENCE THRESHOLD     =  0.80
POWER THRESHOLD         =  10 PERCENT
PHASE LIMIT             =  10 DEGREES
```

| | POWER
CH.5 L CEN | | POWER
CH.6 R CEN | | | | |
HZ	(AVG)	(MAX)	(AVG)	(MAX)	AVG COH	XCOH	%SYNC
1	5	23	21	76	0.10	2	2
2	13	35	46	128	0.32	7	5
3	24	77	51	161	0.38	12	2
4	24	109	60	200	0.43	9	3
DELTA AVGS:	17	60	45	139	0.31	8	3
5	73	258	66	227	0.58	33	12
6	52	245	83	291	0.52	10	0
7	49	130	183	299	0.60	24	14 ←
8	301	913	347	1180	0.82	67	28
THETA AVGS:	119	387	155	499	0.63	34	14
9	206	719	238	1027	0.79	53	28
10	1222	4070	1006	3931	0.78	60	47 ←
11	212	1106	197	1106	0.62	47	29
12	42	134	73	239	0.63	31	17
ALPHA AVGS:	421	1659	399	1576	0.74	40	30

FIGURE 5-10. A sample computer printout. Continued on p. 121.

activation; that the mantra is a boring stimulus leading to habituation of beta activation and augmentation of alpha-theta synchrony.

2. THE MANTRA AS A CRITICAL DRIVER OF SYNCHRONIZATION. If the mantra is a key factor in achieving the kinds of psychophysiologic changes observed, it may represent an input stimulus to the central nervous system, most likely the limbic circuitry. We have been informed that analysis of the resonance frequencies of a number of mantras shows that they have a value of 6–7 Hz., which is in the high theta EEG range and also approximates the optimal processing of the basic language unit, the phoneme, by the auditory system (Lenneberg, 1967). Our current speculation is as follows: Since the mantra is a series of sounds, the formation of the thought mantra (for example, Oom, which is a common, well-known mantra) probably takes place where most neurophysiologists think it does:

13	21	55	42	112	0.35	10	9
14	37	150	48	181	0.47	14	2
16	36	99	59	147	0.51	33	9
16	24	96	48	194	0.43	19	7
17	19	60	60	184	0.43	17	5
18	17	50	64	185	0.42	17	8
19	16	67	38	112	0.38	10	3
20	22	74	49	151	0.49	17	2
21	24	91	56	231	0.45	19	5
22	14	40	25	71	0.35	10	3
23	28	65	38	96	0.43	16	18
24	17	59	24	56	0.21	3	8
26	9	28	28	108	0.21	3	2
26	11	49	21	62	0.12	0	8
27	8	25	19	58	0.18	0	8
28	7	17	28	66	0.11	0	8
29	5	19	20	58	0.06	0	8
30	7	18	24	64	0.15	0	8
31	5	20	28	58	0.06	3	8
BETA AVGS:	13	44	31	95	0.25	7	2

FIGURE 5-10. A sample of the computer printout giving the average and maximum power for each lead across the 1–31 Hz. frequency range, with averages for the four major bands (delta, theta, alpha, beta). The average coherence between the two leads, the percent of time during the one minute sample that coherence exceeds the 0.8 threshold, and the percent of time that synchrony (coherence greater than 0.8, phase angle ± 10°) occurs are shown in the three right-hand columns. The arrow at "A" shows the beginning synchronization of theta activity. The arrow at "B" shows the high percentage of synchrony at the dominant alpha rhythm. This is the same minute of data that is shown graphically in Figure 5-9.

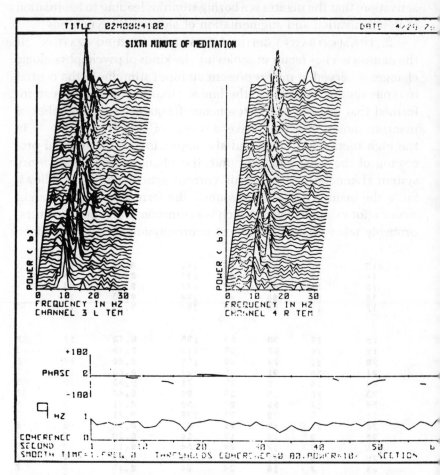

FIGURE 5-11. Beginning synchronization of the left and right temporal lobes during the sixth minute of meditation in a meditator of four weeks' experience.

in the ideational speech area in the temporal lobe. Penfield and Roberts (1959) have mapped three areas involved in the ideational elaboration of speech—a large area in the posterior temporal lobe, an area in the posterior-inferior parietal region, and a small area in the posterior part of the third frontal convolution anterior to the motor-voice control area. They claim that the second two areas both can be destroyed and speech will return, so that the posterior temporal speech area is the fundamental locus for the formation of words.

They state that the ideational mechanism of speech is organized for function in one hemisphere only; usually the dominant hemisphere. Therefore, in thinking a mantra, a significant stimulus is introduced in the temporal lobe and probably directly into the series of cell clusters and fiber tracts that have come to be known as the limbic system. Since limbic system activity is fairly well accepted today as the origin of much emotionally based behavior, and since an increasing excitation in the limbic system through a series of feedback stimulatory mechanisms has been postulated to explain dis-

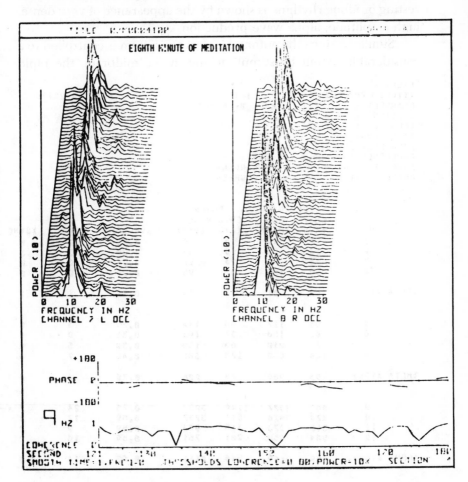

FIGURE 5-12. Synchronization of the occipital lobes during the eighth minute of meditation in a meditator of four weeks' experience.

turbed behavior (Monroe, 1970), we theorize that introducing a driving mechanism with a dominant frequency of 6–7 Hz. may act, with considerable rapidity, to dampen the limbic system activity and produce a relative quiescence in this critical subcortical area.

Since there are extensive connections running from the thalamic structures to the cortex, quieting the limbic system activity might allow for the inhibition of cortical activation with the disappearance of the usual range of frequencies and amplitudes ordinarily seen coming from the cortex and with the imposition of the basic resting or idling rhythms as shown by the appearance of very dense, high amplitude, alpha wave production.

Similarly, since the autonomic nervous system is controlled to a considerable extent by stimuli arising in the midbrain, the rapid

```
FILE:
TITLE: E2N0900190             ; 1H              DATE: 4/26/76
CHANNELS : 7, L OCC     &     8, R OCC
SECTION  :  4
SECONDS  :  121 10  186
TIME SMOOTHING          =  1
FREQUENCY SMOOTHING     =  0
COHERENCE THRESHOLD     =  0.90
POWER THRESHOLD         = 10 PERCENT
PHASE LIMIT             = 10 DEGREES
```

| | POWER | | POWER | | | | |
HZ	CH.7 L OCC (AVG)	(MAX)	CH.8 R OCC (AVG)	(MAX)	AVG COH	%COH	%SYNC
1	7	49	5	29	0.01	0	0
2	14	53	13	35	0.28	3	3
3	26	98	23	97	0.21	0	0
4	59	124	32	98	0.25	0	0
DELTA AVGS:	27	81	18	65	0.17	1	1
5	53	117	48	144	0.35	3	0
6	62	150	37	103	0.31	0	0
7	71	210	65	150	0.39	5	0
8	104	660	178	506	0.46	7	0
THETA AVGS:	93	296	78	226	0.38	4	0
9	860	2677	1144	3054	0.75	24	7 ←
10	478	3476	517	3737	0.59	12	2
11	512	1873	315	903	0.59	9	2
12	264	950	201	751	0.56	10	2
ALPHA AVGS:	529	2169	544	2111	0.62	14	3

FIGURE 5–13. Computer output. Continued on p. 125.

changes observed in the peripheral autonomic nervous system (such as the changes in the GSR, respiratory rate, heart rate, and so on) could be explained by the quieting of the limbic system activity.

Presumably, in sleep limbic system activity diminishes, mediated perhaps by the reticular activating system. One of the theories about the appearance of dreams, especially about the ideational content in dreams, has to do with an increasing access to the nondominant hemisphere, where presumably repressed memories are stored. The weakening of the repression barrier that occurs in sleep and in other altered states of consciousness, such as free association during the process of psychoanalytic therapy, may be produced in a relatively simple fashion during TM meditation. This would offer an explanation of a phenomenon that has been seen repeatedly in our patients. During meditation, thoughts and ideas may appear that are ordinarily repressed, such as intense hostile-aggressive drives, murderous impulses, and, occasionally, libidinal ideation. An impressive aspect of this phenomenon is that, during the meditation, the intense emotional affect that would ordinarily accompany this ideation, that is, when obtained by free association, seems to be markedly reduced or almost absent.

13	135	336	113	541	0.39	2	A
14	58	209	53	325	0.37	0	A
15	52	213	33	187	0.38	7	5
16	41	95	39	150	0.48	2	A
17	57	191	32	81	0.33	0	A
18	64	241	56	197	0.44	3	A
19	51	137	54	169	0.36	3	A
20	68	325	51	180	0.42	2	A
21	54	137	41	124	0.49	5	A
22	33	118	26	116	0.32	0	A
23	22	67	23	65	0.34	2	A
24	19	59	23	65	0.15	0	A
25	28	73	19	66	0.21	2	A
26	21	62	16	75	0.16	2	A
27	17	27	10	35	0.18	0	A
28	17	73	15	67	0.12	0	A
29	10	37	7	26	0.01	0	A
30	6	20	5	13	0.01	0	A
31	6	14	3	14	0.03	0	A
BETA AVGS:	29	99	25	87	0.22	1	A

FIGURE 5-13. The computer output for the same minute of meditation, and the same leads, as graphed in Figure 5-12. The beginning increase in synchronization at 9 Hz. is indicated by the arrow at "A."

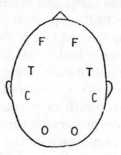

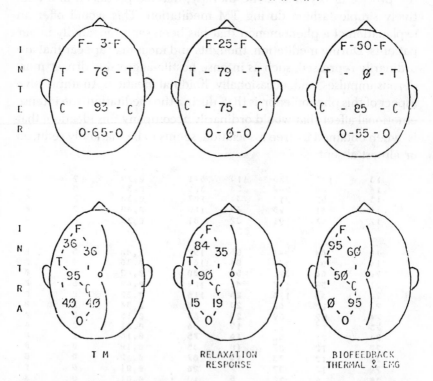

FIGURE 5-14. A schematic display of the differences in synchrony percentages seen in three different relaxation techniques. The positions do not represent actual electrode placements. The interhemispheric synchrony is presented in the top three displays; the intrahemispheric synchrony for the dominant hemisphere is shown in the three bottom displays.

126

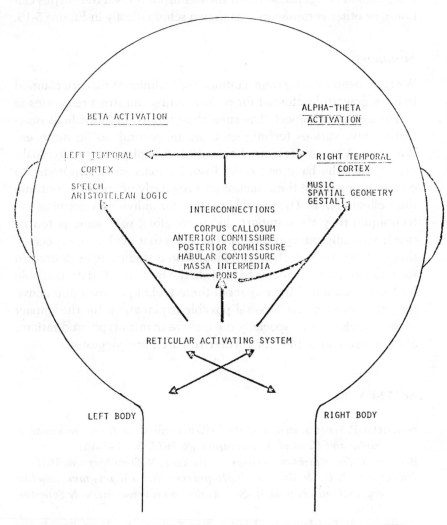

FIGURE 5-15. A schematic representation of the functions usually attributed to the left and right temporal cortices, with some of the interconnecting pathways between them. Our speculations about the effect of relaxation techniques upon these systems is discussed in the text.

127

Our speculation is that, during passive meditation, the usual affective outflow from limbic structures is diminished with enhanced transmission of signals between the hemispheres, via the corpus callosum or other commissures, as shown schematically in Figure 5-15.

Summary

We have been investigating a number of techniques that are claimed to have powerful potential for counteracting the stress responses to which we all are subject. The subjective reports of individuals practicing these various techniques tend, in general, to be quite enthusiastic. A major problem, however, is that of getting individuals, even those who have had relief from incapacitating symptoms, to continue practicing these techniques regularly in order to continue their effectiveness. The possible reasons for individuals stopping the techniques they are using are discussed, along with some potential psychodynamic interpretations. The objective evidence, especially that coming from electroencephalographic studies, is presented in some detail since this seems to provide the best "hard" data available for the evaluation of the impact of these techniques over and above the subjective reports. Several possible explanations for the impact of these techniques, especially the passive mantra-type meditations, are discussed, and lines for further research are suggested.

REFERENCES

Banquet, J. P. Spectral analysis of the EEG in meditation. *Electroencephalography and Clinical Neurophysiology* 1973, *35:* 143–151.
Benson, H. *The relaxation response.* New York: William Morrow, 1975.
Bloomfield, H. H., & Kory, R. B. *Happiness: The TM program, psychiatry, and enlightenment.* New York: Dawn Press/Simon & Schuster, 1976.
Carrington, P. *Freedom in meditation.* New York: Anchor Press/Doubleday, 1977.
Carrington, P., & Ephron, H. S. Meditation as an adjunct to psychotherapy. In S. Arieti & G. Chrzanowski (eds.), *New dimensions in psychiatry: A world view.* New York: John Wiley & Sons, 1975.
Fehmi, L. Abstract. *Proceedings of the Biofeedback Research Society.* Denver, Colorado, 1975.

Glueck, B. C., & Stroebel, C. F. Biofeedback and meditation in the treatment of psychiatric illnesses. *Comprehensive Psychiatry* 1975, *16:* 303–321. (a)

Glueck, B. C., & Stroebel, C. F. Biofeedback and meditation in the treatment of psychiatric illnesses. In J. Masserman (ed.), *Current psychiatric therapies* (Vol. 15), New York: Grune & Stratton, 1975. (b)

Green, E. E., Green, A. M., & Walters, E. D. Voluntary control of internal states: Psychological and physiological. *Journal of Transpersonal Psychology* 1972, *1:* 1–26.

Kamiya, J. Operant control of EEG alpha rhythm and some of its reported effects on consciousness. In C. T. Tart (ed.), *Altered states of consciousness.* New York: John Wiley & Sons, 1969.

Lenneberg, E. H. *Biological foundation of language.* New York; John Wiley & Sons, 1967.

Levine, P. H., Hebert, J. R., Haynes, C. T. & Strobel, U. *EEG coherence during the Transcendental Meditation Technique.* Weggis, Switzerland: MERU Press, 1975.

Luthe, W. *Autogenic training.* New York: Grune & Stratton, 1965.

Maharishi Mahesh Yogi. *The science of being and the art of living.* London: SRM Publications, 1966.

Monroe, R. R. *Episodic behavioral disorders.* Cambridge, Mass.: Harvard University Press, 1970.

Penfield, W. & Roberts, L. *Speech and brain mechanisms.* Princeton, N.J.: Princeton University Press, 1959.

Rado, S. *Adaptational psychodynamics: Motivation and control.* New York: Science House, 1969.

Wallace, R. K. *Physiological effects of Transcendental Meditation: A proposed fourth state of consciousness.* Ph.D. Thesis, Physiology Dept., University of California, Los Angeles, 1970. (a)

Wallace, R. K. Physiological effects of Transcendental Meditation. *Science* 1970, *167:* 1751–1754. (b)

■6
The Biofeedback Hypothesis: An Idea in Search of a Theory and Method

ANDREW M. ELMORE and BERNARD TURSKY

During the last decade there has been a remarkable proliferation of biofeedback research projects (Kamiya, Barber, DiCara, Miller, Shapiro, & Stoyva, 1971–1976). Hundreds of published laboratory studies demonstrate the consistency of a learning effect in individual response systems as a result of reinforcing a response in that system. Attempts have also been made in the laboratory to utilize biofeedback training techniques to alter the physiological functions that relate to a number of psychological, psychosomatic, and physiological disorders. Although the majority of these studies have not shown a consistent or long-term therapeutic result, they have triggered in

This research was supported by NIMH Grant # MH-22296-04 and NSF Grant # S041125. We are indebted to Dr. Harry I. Kalish for his thoughtful discussion and suggestion, which helped clarify our ideas. We would like to express our gratitude to Dr. David Shapiro and Dr. Gary Schwartz for their helpful comments, and we thank the staff of the Laboratory for Behavioral Research, State University of New York at Stony Brook, for providing the facilities and encouragement to produce this work.

130

the public media a positive, though possibly undeserved, exposure of biofeedback applications as a therapeutic technique. Partly as a result of this publicity, biofeedback techniques are currently being used by physicians, psychiatrists, clinical psychologists, and in some instances, by lay people to treat disorders that range from simple nervous tension to serious cardiac arrhythmias. This expansion of the clinical applications of biofeedback may be premature since the recent reviews of clinical studies (Blanchard & Young, 1974; Shapiro, Mainardi, & Surwit, in press) indicate that the number of successful studies is very small relative to the number of reports that have failed to demonstrate the efficacy of biofeedback as a treatment procedure.

The purposes of this chapter are, first, to outline the evolution of the concept of biofeedback, and in particular, its rationale for application as a therapeutic tool; second, to overview briefly some representative experimental and clinical studies with an eye for differentiating biofeedback's success from its failures to demonstrate therapeutic usefulness; third, to argue that the traditional biofeedback paradigm has repeatedly employed a single type of operant methodology that is not sensitive to the recent finding that certain external response consequences produce more meaningful associations with certain classes of responses (Garcia & Koelling, 1966; Hinde & Hinde, 1973; Seligman & Hager, 1972); fourth, to draw from specific concepts in neurophysiology support for the theory that systematic strategies exist that may be used in the selection of experimentally arranged feedback stimuli, and that the application of such strategies defines some alterations in current biofeedback techniques that may produce a more consistent and longer-lasting therapeutic effect.

The Biofeedback Hypothesis

The early research that immediately preceded the concept of biofeedback emerged from a reaction against the idea that instrumental learning in the autonomic nervous system was impossible (Kimble, 1961). The theory that autonomically mediated physiological responses could not be instrumentally conditioned rested on the assumption that the autonomic nervous system was not subject to environmental manipulation because it did not interact in any direct way with the external environment (as may be said for functioning in the skeletal nervous system). This notion was reinforced by two separate studies—one by O. H. Mowrer (1938), who reported that he had not been able to operantly condition the galvanic skin response, and the other by B. F. Skinner (1938), who failed to show learning in the peripheral vasculature. The failure of these studies led to the conclusion, strongly stated by Skinner (1953), that autonomically mediated responses could be modified only by the use of classical conditioning.

These conclusions were supported by the findings of Mandler, Preven, and Kuhlman (1962) as late as 1962. This conception of autonomic responses went unchallenged until a series of successful physiological operant conditioning studies by Fowler and Kimmel (1962), Kimmel and Kimmel (1963), Shapiro, Crider, and Tursky (1964), and Shearn (1962) demonstrated that both frequency and level of responsivity in many autonomically controlled functions could be altered temporarily by the application of basic instrumental conditioning procedures. The implications of this early research are summarized in Kimmel (1967, p. 344). "At the present time it would appear that Skinner's assumption that autonomically mediated responses cannot be modified instrumentally was both premature and probably incorrect."

The instrumental response in the operant conditioning paradigm used in biofeedback research is a naturally occurring change or fluctuation in some autonomic behavior that produces a consequent stimulus in the external environment. In most of the early physiological operant conditioning studies, the response-consequent signal (reinforcer) was the onset of a brief sensory stimulus such as a flash of light, a short burst of sound, or the fluctuation of a meter.

The terminology of operant conditioning states that the response-consequent stimulus comes to control the operant behavior. Experimental designation of the response consequence as a reinforcing event usually produces an observed increase in the frequency of the physiological response. Thus, early operant conditioning research produced a demonstration of learning in the autonomic nervous system that appeared to follow the basic principles of instrumental conditioning (i.e., shaping and extinction). "Biofeedback," however, is a term that, out of some implications of this literature, evolved to encompass a quite different and more complex meaning.

The proof that operant conditioning was possible in peripheral physiological measures controlled by the autonomic nervous system led to the broader and highly theoretical concept that an individual may establish novel and nontransient control over specific aspects of his autonomic physiology as a result of reinforcing spontaneous alterations in a specific response system (Brown, 1974; Miller, 1969).

The conceptual transition from a theoretical formulation that established control by the response-consequent signal (operant conditioning) to one that entailed control exerted by the individual was facilitated by a series of studies conducted by Trowill (1967), Miller and DiCara (1967), and Miller and Banuazizi (1968) using animals whose skeletal musculature had been paralyzed by curare. These experiments presented evidence that operant conditioning could produce extremely large autonomic response effects that were apparently independent of mediating influences. The curarized condition of the animals seemed to insure that any possible somatic mediation was eliminated. Also presented was conclusive evidence regarding generalized transfer of training when the reinforcement was withdrawn. Such transfer effects are necessary if it may be said that biofeedback training can result in establishing long-term control by the individual that would persist outside the laboratory environment. There is little doubt that primarily on the basis of these results biofeedback came to mean that individuals could learn sustained control over the behavior of functions controlled by the autonomic nervous system.

In an early review article, Katkin and Murray (1968) raised the issue of the possible role of somatic mediation in instrumental learning of autonomic responses. These authors accepted the results of the curarized rat experiments as the only evidence that demonstrated instrumental autonomic responding in the absence of such potential influence. In a bold stroke to address this issue with respect to the human studies, Birk, Crider, Shapiro, and Tursky (1966) undertook a demonstration of instrumental autonomic conditioning in a partially curarized human subject—the senior author. These authors successfully demonstrated operant conditioning of the galvanic skin response, apparently in the absence of somatic influences. Only very recently have researchers (McCanne & Sandman, 1976) again raised serious questions concerning possible mediating influences in biofeedback learning.

The concept that biofeedback training would result in long-term control similar to the persistent transfer effects found in the curarized rat experiments has survived and flourished despite the repeated failure of the Miller Laboratory group to replicate the dramatic results originally reported (Miller & Dworkin, 1974).

A strictly operant definition of biofeedback requires that the presentation of the response consequence alone is responsible for controlling the subject's behavior. However, the current conception of biofeedback consists of two assertions that relate to the establishment of control by the subjects over their own behavior and not exclusive control by the response-contingent feedback signal. The first of these assertions is that the "information" provided by the response-consequent signal is prima facie associable with the internal response being manipulated. This implies that a light flash contingent upon a predetermined fluctuation in blood pressure is providing the individual with information that is meaningfully associable with changes in blood pressure. The second assertion is that such response-consequent information can be utilized by the organism directly to control or modify the level of functioning of a specific response system. These two assumptions are highly complex, and a simple account of operant conditioning does not require recourse to either one of them. The presumption underlying the use of biofeedback techniques in clinical practice—that operant training procedures will result in long-term, extralaboratory control of the experimentally altered level of a response system's function—requires that both of these assumptions be made.

The disorders for which biofeedback is being employed as treatment—essential hypertension, migraine and tension headaches, circulatory dysfunction, and the promotion of relaxation and reduced anxiety—all require that the treatment exert a long-term effect beyond the operant control obtained in the laboratory setting. For biofeedback to be useful as a clinical tool, it must produce an alteration that is clinically significant, and such an alteration must be sustained in the absence of the experimental environment. The current widespread use of biofeedback as a treatment procedure assumes that biofeedback therapies have fulfilled these two strict requirements. The examination of the biofeedback literature that follows suggests that such a claim is unwarranted in many cases.

Biofeedback Research

It is not the intention of this paper thoroughly to review and detail the biofeedback literature. Several such thorough reviews are available (Blanchard & Young, 1974; Katkin & Murray, 1968; Shapiro, Mainardi, & Surwit, in press). The overview here is intended only to present chronologically representative studies in each area of biofeedback research on physiological functioning. Special attention is paid to research in which the long-term, extralaboratory effects of biofeedback training have been assessed.

This section is divided into two parts, a review of experimental studies and a review of clinical studies carried out on patients with a target clinical disorder such as hypertension, headache, or anxiety.

Experimental Studies

This overview focuses on studies conducted on three response systems: blood pressure, heart rate, and skin temperature. These three areas have been most heavily investigated. Representative studies reported in the annual publication *Biofeedback and Self-Control* (Kamiya, Barber, DiCara, Miller, Shapiro, & Stoyva, 1971–1976) for each year are cited whenever possible.

In experiments conducted for blood pressure biofeedback (Brener & Kleinman, 1970; Fey & Lindholm, 1975; Shapiro, Schwartz, & Tursky, 1972; Shapiro, Tursky, Gershon, & Stern, 1969) there is an almost completely interchangeable character of methodology and results. Nearly all studies used one, two, or three sessions; provided feedback to half the subjects for increases in blood pressure and feedback to the other half for decreases in blood pressure; and used visual (light) or auditory (tone) feedback signals. Findings show a general trend of greater ability to decrease blood pressure than to increase, with increases (when obtained) of 2–15 mm Hg. Although in terms of instructions to subjects, type of sensory feedback signal (binary or analog), and the presence of material rewards (such as money and *Playboy* magazine slides used in both of the Shapiro et al. studies) these experiments differ slightly, over the five-year period described there are no systematic changes in methodology and no trend toward better training. No follow-up reports to assess long-term effects were conducted for any of these studies.

Studies that provided biofeedback for alterations in heart rate

(Bell & Schwartz, 1975; Bouchard & Corson, 1976; Brener & Hother-sall, 1966; Brener & Jones, 1974; Stephens, Harris, & Brady, 1972; Wells, 1973) reveal the same pattern of results as those for blood pressure, with the potential exception of the Brener and Jones study. Typically, subjects are provided with binary or analog sensory signals (i.e., lights or tones) consequent upon unidirectional changes in heart rate. In these experiments, there appears a general trend toward greater increases than decreases, where obtained increases ranged from 15–34 bpm and decreases ranged from 6–22 bpm (both findings reported in Stephens et al., 1972). The Brener and Jones study is especially interesting because experimental subjects were trained to discriminate vibratory stimuli that reflected only heart rate. Relative to two control groups, one having no discrimination training and one having false discrimination training, the experimental group was the only one to demonstrate significant learning of "successful interoceptive discriminations" (Brener & Jones, 1974). Again, no follow-up data are presented in any of these studies.

The two studies by Bell and Schwartz (1975) and Bouchard and Corson (1976) warrant special attention, as they looked specifically at subjects' performance in the absence of the feedback signal. Bell and Schwartz found that prior to any feedback training for heart rate increases or decreases, subjects could demonstrate some ability to voluntarily increase but not decrease their heart rate upon instruction to do so. With feedback, subjects showed an ability to both raise and lower heart rate relative to resting levels. In a postfeedback phase, in the absence of the feedback signal, subjects maintained an ability to raise and lower their heart rates significantly, suggesting "complete transfer of bidirectional control" (Bell & Schwartz, 1975). Reported increases for this study were approximately 7 bpm at pre-feedback, 10 bpm during feedback, and 8 bpm at postfeedback. Reported decreases were approximately 1 bpm at prefeedback, 4 bpm during feedback, and 4 bpm at postfeedback. A test for what was termed "voluntary control" involved the reversal of the color of the cue lights (discriminative stimuli) for the increase and decrease heart rate conditions. The fact that this procedure produced no significant deficit in learning suggested to the authors that the discriminative cues did not exert a stimulus control effect that could argue against the notion of voluntary control.

The study by Bouchard and Corson (1976) looked at the differential effects of "success" and "failure" contingencies of feedback in heart rate control. These authors also obtained a "no difference" finding between feedback and no feedback phases of their experiment. Reported increases in this study were 3.43 and −.01 bpm during the first feedback trials, 3.23 and −.87 bpm during no feedback, and 4.53 and −.02 bpm during the second feedback for the "success" (positive) and "failure" (negative) feedback groups respectively. Average decreases obtained were 1.68 and 3.41 bpm during the first feedback phase, 1.43 and 5.21 bpm during the no feedback phase, and 3.55 and 7.44 bpm during the second feedback trials for the "success" and "failure" feedback groups respectively. An additional feature of this study that makes it especially interesting for the arguments advanced here is that the authors relate the differential effectiveness of "success" and "failure" feedback to the literature on the Selective Association Principle discussed below. Results showed that heart rate increases are best facilitated by "success" feedback. Bouchard and Corson (1976, p. 73) suggest that "the success and failure signals have different biological impact (activating effects) and, therefore, differentially influence heart rate changes in the increase and decrease directions."

In studies investigating skin temperature or vasomotor control biofeedback (Snyder & Noble, 1968; Steptoe, Matheus, & Johnston, 1974), similar, small, but consistent effects were obtained. Snyder and Noble provided subjects with binary feedback for discrete finger vasoconstrictions and found significantly more of these in their experimental subjects than in controls. Steptoe, Matheus, and Johnston found subjects could learn to produce differential temperatures in their earlobes, but the effects obtained were nonsignificant. No follow-up reports were conducted in either study.

One may conclude that the experimental literature in biofeedback has consistently demonstrated operant conditioning in the autonomic response systems discussed above. However, the learning effects are nearly always very small in terms of magnitude of response alteration, and in the eight-year span described here, very few or no changes in the experimental methodology have been implemented, even in the face of small and still potentially transient results.

Clinical Studies

The importance of reviewing the clinical literature is critical here because these studies more often include some follow-up data, and the biofeedback procedures are applied directly to a particular target disorder so that success may be defined along some other dimension besides statistically significant changes in responding. Success in these studies requires a significant alleviation of the target clinical symptomatology. The areas of research reviewed in this section (following Blanchard & Young, 1974) are electromyographic (EMG) biofeedback for muscle retraining, EMG biofeedback for relaxation training, EMG for tension headaches, and biofeedback for alteration of heartrate, blood pressure, and peripheral vasodilation.

In the area of EMG biofeedback for the retraining of lost muscle group function (Andrews, 1964; Booker, Rubow, & Coleman, 1969; Johnson & Garton, 1973; Marinacci & Horande, 1960; Peper, 1973), some significant measure of success was obtained in all cases. The procedure was basically the same in each study: Subjects were provided with amplified EMG sounds (clicks) from the affected musculature as feedback and trained to increase this activity. Success, however, is not simply the production of higher levels of EMG activity, but constitutes a recovery of function in the affected muscle group. Hemiplegia, often the loss of movement in an arm or a leg on one side of the body resulting from stroke, is the most common disorder treated here. From the finding of return of function in most of these investigations plus the report of follow-ups or long final baselines, it appears that biofeedback has functioned in this capacity to retrain voluntary muscle movement.

For studies employing EMG biofeedback for relaxation training (Garret & Silver, 1972; Jacobs & Felton, 1969; Peper, 1973; Raskin, Johnson, & Rondestvedt, 1973; Wickramasekera, 1972), the results are less encouraging. Subjects in these studies were given EMG feedback contingent upon the EMG activity in the frontalis muscle, which transverses the forehead. It has been claimed (Budzynski & Stoyva, 1969) that reducing EMG activity in the frontalis muscle parallels an overall relaxation in the musculature of the upper body. In these studies, EMG biofeedback was utilized to treat chronic anxiety (Garret & Silver, 1972; Wickramasekera, 1972), insomnia (Peper, 1973), and neck muscle spasms in the trapezius muscle (Jacobs &

Felton, 1969). While subjects in each study showed a significant re-duction in EMG activity, not one clearly demonstrated a therapeutic effect with respect to the symptom for which it was employed (Blanchard & Young, 1974). From this finding one may conclude that EMG biofeedback techniques have not demonstrated the clinical effectiveness of the more involved techniques of clinical relaxation therapy to which it was originally thought EMG biofeedback was a "shortcut" (Brown, 1974).

Investigations employing EMG feedback in the treatment of tension headaches (Budzynski, Stoyva, & Adler, 1970; Budzynski, Stoyva, Adler, & Mullaney, 1973; Epstein, Hersen, & Hemphill, in press; Wickramasekera, 1972) have all demonstrated considerable therapeutic promise. All of these studies report a significant decrease in headache activity. However, for each study—with the exception of the Wickramasekera (1972) study, for which no individual data or statistical analysis are provided—there is one important difference in procedure compared to the other applications of EMG biofeedback: A treatment procedure that combines both frontalis EMG biofeed-back and a technique of relaxation that patients practice at home on themselves is employed. In fact, the most recent of these studies, conducted by Epstein et al. (in press), suggests that the "home relaxa-tion practice" procedure is necessary to maintain the therapeutic effect. The studies previously conducted have not controlled for the possible confounding of the two treatments. While these are some of the most rigorously controlled studies in the area of clinical applica-tions, we are left to conclude that biofeedback alone may not be sufficient to produce the needed effect.

The use of biofeedback to produce heart rate changes is the most thoroughly researched clinical application. Biofeedback of heart rate is used in the treatment of patients with cardiac arrhythmias (Engel & Bleecker, 1974; Scott, Blanchard, Edmunson, & Young, 1973; Weiss & Engel, 1971). Studies reported by Weiss and Engel and by Engel and Bleecker on the treatment of premature ventricular con-tractions (PVCs) report success after follow-ups in over half the cases. The ingenious procedure here involves teaching subjects first to speed and then to slow their heart rate and then to maintain heart rate just outside the range in which PVCs occur. Blanchard and Young (1974) note several methodological problems in these studies as well as in an additional study reported by Engel and Bleecker

(1974) using heart rate decreasing training to treat supraventricular tachycardia and paroxysmal atrial tachycardia (PAT) in a single subject. Engel and Bleecker also report on a patient treated for sinus tachycardia, but no baseline data are provided and no report of the clinical response (i.e., reduction of sinus tachycardia incidences) is given. The fourth study reported by Engel and Bleecker (1974) was performed on a patient who suffered from PAT and episodic tachycardia. Again, while successful reduction in PAT and incidence of sinus tachycardia is reported, insufficient data are provided for an effective evaluation of the treatment procedure (Blanchard & Young, 1974). In the treatment of two cases with sinus tachycardia, Scott et al. (1973) obtained successful reduction in heart rate in both instances. Although this study represents the best controlled investigation of all reported under this heading, Blanchard and Young (1974, p. 582) note: "the failure to find a complete reversal during the return to baseline precludes drawing any definite conclusions from the data."

The use of biofeedback techniques to control blood pressure is indicated in the treatment of essential hypertension. These studies (Benson, Shapiro, Tursky, & Schwartz, 1971; Elder, Tuiz, Diabler, & Dillenkoffer, 1973; Kristt & Engel, 1975; Miller, 1972; Schwartz & Shapiro, 1973) show varying degrees of success in demonstrating learned decreases in systolic or diastolic blood pressure. Both the Benson et al. (1971) and the Elder et al. (1973) studies actually demonstrated decreases in blood pressure to within the range of therapeutic effectiveness (for some subjects). While Blanchard and Young (1974) conclude from these reports that blood pressure biofeedback may show promise, they note several important considerations. In all these studies either no follow-up data are presented, or follow-up data are either negative (Miller, 1972) or found to be subject to serious criticism (Elder et al., 1973). Both the Elder et al. (1973) and Schwartz and Shapiro (1973) studies employed instructions to subjects concerning relaxation. This is especially critical in that a number of studies (Jacobsen, 1939; Paul, 1969; Tasto & Shoemaker, 1973) report that relaxation training techniques can significantly lower blood pressure.

However, an encouraging development in the use of biofeedback techniques to produce long-term reduction in blood pressure in essential hypertensives is reported in a recently published article by Kristt and Engel (1975). In this study, five well-documented essential hypertensives participated in a three-phase study designed to train them to lower their blood pressure. In Phase I, each patient used a standard sphygmomanometer to record his daily blood pressure at home for seven weeks. In Phase II, the patients were hospitalized for three weeks, and were taught to control and lower their blood pressure by use of a noninvasive technique developed by Tursky, Shapiro, and Schwartz (1972) that permits reinforcement of blood pressure change for each heart cycle. During this period, patients were trained to raise and lower their systolic pressure. Phase III was a three-month follow-up period during which each patient again recorded his blood pressures at home. During this posttraining period, patients utilized a blood pressure cuff to mimic the blood pressure lowering techniques they had learned in the hospital. They practiced this maneuver 4–30 times each day. In this highly successful study, all patients reduced their blood pressure to normotensive levels and maintained this reduction during the three-month follow-up period. The implications of this successful treatment will be discussed later in this paper.

In the area of clinical application of biofeedback for learning of peripheral vasodilation, Schwartz (1972) reports two case studies of patients suffering from Raynaud's disease. Raynaud's disease is a severe circulatory impairment resulting in extremely reduced blood flow to the hands and feet. The first case was a man with very cold feet who was given feedback and rewards (e.g., slides) for increasing blood flow in his foot. The training was shown effective long after laboratory sessions were terminated. However, Schwartz (1973) reports a special technique that this patient (a psychoanalyst) employed that may force the conclusion that the effect found may not have been a function of his biofeedback training. The second case was a woman who underwent ten training sessions and showed no clinically significant change.

One of the most forceful demonstrations of the effectiveness of biofeedback applications to clinical problems is exemplified in a recent study conducted by Engel, Nikoomanesh, and Schuster (1974) entitled "Operant Conditioning of Rectosphincteric Responses in the Treatment of Fecal Incontinence." Incontinence is an inability to regulate evacuation voluntarily. With the aid of a combination of biofeedback and feedback of actual rectal muscle distentions (via an inflatable balloon inserted into the rectum), all six subjects showed therapeutically significant improvement in reducing incontinence over follow-up periods ranging from six months to five years. Four of the six remained continent throughout. This study constitutes a clear-cut demonstration of long-term voluntary control resulting from operant conditioning techniques employed in the laboratory.

This review of the clinical literature seems to indicate that only in the areas of EMG biofeedback for muscle group retraining, feedback for sphincter muscle control, and the one reported successful blood pressure biofeedback study has the biofeedback technique demonstrated the establishment of long-term sustained control over the response. However, there is also some evidence suggesting that in both the areas of EMG feedback for tension headaches and heart rate feedback for cardiac arrhythmias the application of biofeedback techniques may promise therapeutic success.

Conclusions

Two conclusions emerge from this brief look at the literature. The first is that, in nearly every area that has been investigated, the biofeedback technique has shown viability in that a conditioning effect is consistently observed. The presentation of feedback stimuli contingent upon internal responses has been effective in nearly every instance in facilitating operant control over particular internal responses.

The second conclusion stems primarily from the clinical literature. Where long-term, extralaboratory effects are evaluated, we find that current biofeedback practices are successful in producing clinically significant, nontransient changes in only a small number of applications. The biofeedback technique results in sustained, long-term control only in the areas of sphincter control, retraining of muscle group activity with EMG biofeedback (as in hemiplegia), and possibly, in the treatment of tension headaches with EMG biofeedback, cardiac arrhythmias with heart rate feedback, and essential hypertension with biofeedback for blood pressure decreases.

In attempting to account for biofeedback's selective success in producing clinically significant, long-term changes, it is important to identify specific differences in the response systems that have evinced such responsivity to the techniques employed from those which have not. In order to do this, two factors for each response system must be identified. First, the nature of the naturally occurring (afferent) feedback that results from changes in the state of the system should be known. Second, such neural circuitry should be examined to discover how it is possible for the system to associate external, experimentally arranged response consequences with the extant afferent feedback to produce learning.

We believe that one of the shortcomings of the current methodological approach in biofeedback research is its dependence upon a single operant conditioning technique. This has resulted in the use of visual and auditory response consequences (feedback signals) as reinforcers in nearly all experiments. A number of researchers have recently challenged certain aspects of this learning paradigm; their writings are neatly represented in two books entitled *The Biological Boundaries of Learning* (Seligman & Hager, 1972) and *Constraints on Learning* (Hinde & Hinde, 1973). These texts develop and substantiate the notion that certain types of response consequences may be more meaningfully associated with certain classes of responses, and therefore, may produce better learning.

Constraints on Biofeedback
Learning

In the last few years, a great deal of attention has been paid to the notion that the learning paradigm shared by many experimental psychologists neglects some important features of what Skinner (1953) has referred to as "the biological component." This negligence, say certain investigators (Bolles, 1973; Breland & Breland, 1961; Garcia & Koelling, 1966; Seligman & Hager, 1972), lies in the observations that organisms may be biologically disposed ("prepared," in Seligman's term) to associate certain stimuli with certain consequences and not as disposed to associate others.

It is claimed that the traditional experimental operant conditioning paradigm has held implicit the assumption that the proper arrangement in time and space of stimuli and their resultant consequences (with no special regard to what these stimuli and consequences are) is all that the careful experimenter must do to insure that his results will be in accord with previous findings. This idea of "equipotentiality," whether implicit in the paradigm or a misunderstanding of what Skinner meant by "the biological component," has been shown to be false in many instances. For a particular organism, it has clearly been demonstrated that certain stimuli are highly associable with certain consequences and others are not. That is, for man, like other animals, certain classes of response consequences are more meaningfully associated with certain classes of responses.

Schwartz (1974) treats the notion of biological constraints in terms of limitations imposed on the subjects such as the physiological and psychological state of the organism, the instructions provided by the experimenter, the neural integration of specific response systems with functionally related systems, and the range of possible response within a given organ system. In his discussion of what is termed "reward constraints," Schwartz touches upon the theoretical account proposed here.

Garcia and Koelling (1966) discovered the principle of selective associability by placing thirsty rats in a situation in which they drank water flavored with saccharine in the presence of a light and a noise. For half the rats, the response consequence that followed was an electric shock to the foot; the other half were exposed to X-irradiation or lithium chloride (both of which induce illness). When later tested to ascertain which elements of the stimulus (light, noise, or sweet taste) were responsible for the obtained suppression of drinking in the presence of taste, light, and noise, Garcia and Koelling found that those rats which had been shocked after drinking drank freely of sweet tasting water and suppressed drinking in the presence of noise and light. Those rats which had been made ill did just the reverse; they drank in the presence of noise and light but avoided sweet tasting water. Meaningful associations between sweet taste followed by later illness, and bright light and noise followed by electric shock were demonstrated, while the complementary associations were not established, and learning (in this case, response suppression) did not occur. In summarizing this and other studies that also demonstrate such "selective associability" of stimuli and their resultant consequences, Bolles (1973, p. 281) concluded:

> The ability to learn is not a general ability, it is highly selective. It should be assumed from the start that a given animal will be easily able to learn some things and will have difficulty learning others. [It is this] idea which I shall call the Selective Association Principle.

Clearly, the notion of the selective associability of responses and their resultant consequences has not been considered systematically in biofeedback experiments. In nearly all the studies, the response consequences have been some visual display or auditory signal or some combination of visual and auditory stimuli. In the typical experiment, a desired response such as an incremental reduction in systolic blood pressure is produced by the subject and a tone sounds or a light flashes. Initial instructions to the subject are usually "your task is to make the light flash," or "make the tone sound," and so forth. It is an understatement to say that the consequent stimuli have been indifferent to the responses, for what, by way of a natural association, do flashing lights and tones have to do with changes in such internal systems implicated in the regulation of heart rate, blood pressure, skin temperature, and so forth?

It should be clear that the method that has been employed in most biofeedback studies may best be retermed "visual or auditory feedback," for it is not biological, response-related information that is being fed back into the organism, but visual or auditory signals that the subject is expected to associate meaningfully with changes in particular biological processes. Thus far, it has been shown that strict dependence upon visual or auditory feedback has produced variable and limited success in terms of clinical applicability.

A proposal to restructure the prevailing experimental methodology (and reinterpret the results of the few clearly successful biofeedback applications) to take into account the significance of natural afferent pathways follows, and a program for new research methods and experimentation will be put forth. In this effort we will attempt to utilize some basic concepts from neurophysiology. Against this background, evidence drawn from the literature and from the premises of the Selective Association Principle project a unique picture of biofeedback learning.

A Theoretical Account of Biofeedback Learning

The differential and selective success of biofeedback applications and the implications from the Selective Association Principle suggest that biofeedback methodologies may be improved by the selection of response consequences that may produce more meaningful associations with the responses being manipulated. In attempting to discover more meaningful response consequences for biofeedback applications, one must first examine the afferent neural pathways that provide natural feedback information in the regulation of normal autonomic functioning.

In his text, *The Human Nervous System*, Noback (1967) defines three classifications of afferent input:

1. The exteroceptive modalities that respond mainly to external agents through receptors located in the skin. Exteroceptive sensations are pain, warmth, cold, and light touch.
2. The proprioceptive modalities that are primarily associated with body position and movement. They include response to such sensations as limb movement, judging of weight, shape, form, vibration, and pressure.
3. The interoceptive modalities that are primarily associated with the visceral activities of digestion and circulation. The fullness of the stomach or bladder, pain from extensive distention of these organs, and muscle cramps are interoceptive sensations.

It is critical to note that one direct implication of this classification is that the feedback stimuli used in the major proportion of biofeedback studies—visual and auditory signals—do not produce direct input into the afferent systems controlling the behaviors being manipulated.

Bearing this in mind, the next step toward a better theoretical understanding of biofeedback involves attempting to account for the long-term success of the several applications reviewed previously: EMG biofeedback for muscle group retraining; the Engel, Nikoomanesh, and Schuster (1974) rectal sphincter control study; and the Kristt and Engel (1975) blood pressure control study.

Proprioception, the somatic afferent feedback sense, is a highly developed and precise system that provides the information used in what has heretofore been exclusively defined as voluntary behavior. The success of the provision of visual and auditory feedback in the retraining of lost skeletal muscle group function may be characterized in terms of reestablishing perception of this neurologically powerful source of information. The hemiplegic subject must "relearn" to attend to such information. The sensory feedback stimuli provided in this instance need only serve as discriminative stimuli to cue the perception of kinesthetic sensation.

As the major theoretical arguments have centered around opposing conceptions of the autonomic nervous system, the question of why the Engel et al. (1974) rectal sphincter control study and the Kristt and Engel (1975) blood pressure control study were so successful becomes crucial.

The ascending visceral afferent pathways from the autonomic nervous system are shown in Figure 6-1 taken from Ruch and Patton (1965). It may be seen here that afferent feedback from some but not all autonomically controlled response systems is referred to the higher sensory processing areas of the brain and that feedback from the rectal sphincters in particular is transmitted upward in this fashion.

Another unique feature of the Engel et al. study (1974) is the particular type of feedback consequence employed. Instead of relying solely upon simple visual or auditory signals, the additional feed-

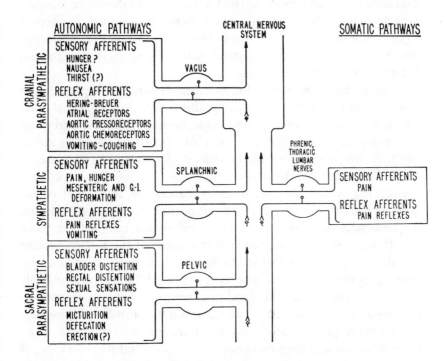

FIGURE 6-1. The ascending visceral afferent pathways. (Reprinted with permission from Ruch, T. C., and Patton, H. D., eds., *Physiology and Biophysics,* Philadelphia: W. B. Saunders, 1965.)

back from the balloon inflation actually served to produce an interoceptive response signaling a change in the sphincter musculature. Thus, this feedback stimulus may be said to have operated directly upon the response system via the natural neural pathways. The employment of response consequences such as the rectal sphincter balloon is very similar to many of the procedures used in Russian "interoceptive conditioning" described by Razran (1961). This procedure should be contrasted with the provision of visual and auditory feedback signals that are transduced by the highly specialized receptors comprising the eyes and ears and referred to their appropriate specialized projection areas of the cortex.

The formulation that is being advanced here may now be summarily stated: In order to insure that the experimentally provided feedback be meaningfully associated with the actual biological change in a given autonomically mediated response system, the response consequences provided by the experiment should be selected with an eye for those that are likely to produce an actual afferent input to the particular response system. The provision of interoceptive input to the sacral parasympathetic system controlling rectal distention is a perfect example.

The highly successful Kristt and Engel study (1975) provides an indication of the viability of the hypothesis that a physiological function (in this instance blood pressure) can be successfully altered when an effective response-consequent signal is chosen. The authors speculate that the patients involved in this study learned to regulate directly their peripheral vascular resistance. The effective feedback (controlling stimuli) in this instance cannot be the visual consequences provided in the laboratory since these were not used during the successful seven-week follow-up period at home. Instead, there is a strong possibility that the continuing use of the blood pressure cuff and the previously learned biofeedback training procedure provided proprioceptive and exteroceptive input more meaningfully associable with changes in blood pressure than did visual signals to the extent that the patient actually learned to control blood pressure level. This is an especially compelling argument in the light of the more dramatic and long-term effects of this procedure than those of previous studies in the same vein that differed in procedure only in the lack of the extremely long "home blood-pressure-reducing practice" procedure.

It now seems plausible to suggest that some response-consequent stimuli may be more effective than others in producing
changes that result in longer-lasting biofeedback learning, and that
there may be systematic reasons for choosing which of the available
stimuli may be best employed with a particular response system. The
suggestion that is being made on the basis of the observed success of
biofeedback applications and the brief look at the afferent feedback
systems is that the external consequent stimuli should be chosen with
an eye for those that are most likely to result in actual afferent input
to the response system being manipulated.

It seems reasonable to suggest that each physiological response
function can be examined and analyzed to enable the researcher or
clinician to choose the most appropriate external response-consequent signal for that function. It can now be argued that the response
consequences that are more in concert with naturally occurring afferent information will be more effective in producing sustained
control of the response system. The rectal balloon, the blood pressure
cuff, the tactile heart rate reinforcer, and the movement of paralyzed
limbs all are examples of such meaningful response consequences
already in use. One can speculate on how the viability and validity
of the hypothesis advanced in this report can be tested. It may be
possible to design well-controlled studies that can directly compare
the effectiveness of traditional sensory (auditory or visual) biofeedback response consequences to feedback reinforcers that can produce a more direct effect on the afferent information that regulates
the physiological systems under study. A reasonable first step might
be the replication of the Engel et al. (1974) and the Kristt and Engel
(1975) studies using a control group that receives only auditory or
visual feedback as a response consequence. It is also possible to initiate a series of studies that can test the use of more selectively associable response consequences to alter specific physiological functions.
For example, the effectiveness of the use of external temperature
control devices that can be readily attached close to the affected
areas of the body could be tested in the treatment of Raynaud's
disease. A controllable heating or cooling device could be utilized to
produce an amplified change in temperature as a response consequence to a natural small fluctuation in skin temperature in the
desired direction. Such a manipulation would alter afferent temperature information that contributes to the natural regulation of skin

temperature. Similarly, a selectively associable response consequence can be produced to reinforce a small natural reduction in
blood pressure in the treatment of hypertension. Pressure cuffs
(Kristt & Engel, 1975) or whole limb pressure devices can be utilized
to produce an amplified controllable alteration in pressure applied to
the arterial walls, thus influencing the afferent pressure information
that contributes to the natural regulation of arterial blood pressure.
A more direct manipulation of blood pressure could be achieved by
directly impinging a positive or negative pressure on the carotid
sinus. Thus, a small reduction in arterial blood pressure could be
directly reinforced by a larger change in pressure as a response
consequence.

These suggestions of more meaningful response consequences
are for the most part speculative, but it is felt here that the application of this theoretical formulation may expand the domain of successful clinical biofeedback practices.

REFERENCES

Andrews, J. M. Neuromuscular reeducation of the hemiplegic with the aid
of the electromyograph. *Archives of Physical and Medical Rehabilitation* 1964, *45:* 530–532.

Bell, I. R., & Schwartz, G. E. Voluntary control and reactivity of human heart
rate. *Psychophysiology* 1975, *12:* 339–348.

Benson, H., Shapiro, D., Tursky, B., & Schwartz, G. E. Decreased systolic
blood pressure through operant conditioning techniques in patients
with essential hypertension. *Science* 1971, *173:* 740–742.

Birk, L., Crider, A., Shapiro, D., & Tursky, B. Operant electrodermal conditioning under partial curarization. *Journal of Comparative and Physiological Psychology* 1966, *62:* 165–166.

Blanchard, E. B., & Young, L. D. Clinical applications of biofeedback training: A review of evidence. *Archives of General Psychiatry* 1974, *30:*
573–589.

Bolles, R. C. The comparative psychology of learning: The selective associa-
tion principle and some problems with "general" laws of learning. In
G. Bermant (ed.), *Perspectives on animal behavior.* Glenview, Ill.:
Scott, Foresman, 1973.

Booker, H. E., Rubow, R. T., & Coleman, P. J. Simplified feedback in neuromuscular retraining: An automated approach using electromyographic signals. *Archives of Physical and Medical Rehabilitation*
1969, *50:* 621–625.

Bouchard, C., & Corson, J. A. Heart rate regulation with success and failure signals. *Psychophysiology* 1976, *13:* 69–74.

Breland, K., & Breland, M. The misbehavior of organisms. *American Psychologist* 1961, *16:* 651–689.

Brener, J., & Hothersall, D. Heart rate control under conditions of augmented sensory feedback. *Psychophysiology* 1966, *3:* 23–28.

Brener, J., & Jones, J. M. Interoceptive discrimination in intact humans: Detection of cardiac activity. *Physiology and Behavior* 1974, *13:* 763–767.

Brener, J., & Kleinman, R. A. Learned control of decreases in systolic blood pressure. *Nature* 1970, *226:* 1063–1064.

Brown, B. B. *New mind: New body.* New York: Harper & Row, 1974.

Budzynski, T. H., & Stoyva, J. M. An instrument for producing deep muscle relaxation by means of analog information feedback. *Journal of Applied Behavioral Analysis* 1969, *2:* 231–237.

Budzynski, T. H., Stoyva, J. M., & Adler, C. S. Feedback-induced muscle relaxation: Application to tension headache. *Journal of Behavior Therapy and Experimental Psychiatry* 1970, *1:* 205–211.

Budzynski, T. H., Stoyva, J. M., Adler, C. S., & Mullaney, D. M. EMG biofeedback and tension headache: A controlled outcome study. *Psychosomatic Medicine* 1973, *35:* 484–496.

Elder, S. T., Tuiz, Z. R., Diabler, H. L., & Dillenkoffer, R. L. Instrumental conditioning of diastolic blood pressure in essential hypertensive patients. *Journal of Applied Behavioral Analysis* 1973, *6:* 377–382.

Engel, B. T., & Bleecker, E. R. Application of operant conditioning techniques to the control of cardiac arrhythmias. In P. Obrist, A. H. Black, J. Brener, & L. V. DiCara (eds.), *Cardiovascular psychophysiology.* Chicago: Aldine, 1974.

Engel, B. T., Nikoomanesh, P., & Schuster, M. M. Operant conditioning of rectosphincteric responses in the treatment of fecal incontinence. *New England Journal of Medicine* 1974, *290:* 646–649.

Epstein, L. H., Hersen, M., & Hemphill, D. P. Contingent music and anti-tension exercises in the treatment of a chronic tension headache patient. *Journal of Behavior Therapy and Experimental Psychiatry,* in press.

Fey, S. G., & Lindholm, E. Systolic blood pressure and heart rate changes during three sessions involving biofeedback or no feedback. *Psychophysiology* 1975, *63:* 563–567.

Fowler, R. L., & Kimmel, H. D. Operant conditioning of the GSR. *Journal of Experimental Psychology* 1962, *63:* 563–567.

Garcia, J., & Koelling, R. A. Relation of cue to consequence in avoidance learning. *Psychonomic Science* 1966, *4:* 123–124.

Garret, B. L., & Silver, M. P. The use of EMG and alpha biofeedback to relieve test anxiety in college students. Paper presented at the American Psychological Association Meeting, Washington, D. C., 1972.

Hinde, R. A., & Hinde, J. S. *Constraints on learning*. New York: Academic Press, 1973.

Jacobs, A., & Felton, G. S. Visual feedback of myoelectric output to facilitate muscle relaxation in normal persons and patients with neck injuries. *Archives of Physical and Medical Rehabilitation* 1969, *50:* 34–39.

Jacobsen, E. Variation of blood pressure with skeletal muscle tension and relaxation. *Annals of Internal Medicine* 1939, *12:* 1194–1212.

Johnson, J. E., & Garton, W. J. Muscle reeducation by use of electromyographic device. *Archives of Physical and Medical Rehabilitation* 1973, *54:* 320–325.

Kamiya, J., Barber, T. X., DiCara, L. V., Miller, N. E., Shapiro, D., & Stoyva, J. (eds.) *Biofeedback and self-control, 1970–1976.* Chicago: Aldine-Atherton, 1971–1976.

Katkin, E. S., & Murray, E. N. Instrumental conditioning of autonomically mediated behavior. *Psychological Bulletin* 1968, *70:* 52–68.

Kimble, G. A. *Hilgard and Marquis' conditioning and learning.* New York: Appleton-Century-Crofts, 1961.

Kimmel, H. D. Instrumental conditioning of autonomically mediated behavior. *Psychological Bulletin* 1967, *67:* 337–345.

Kimmel, E., & Kimmel, H. D. Replication of operant conditioning of the GSR. *Journal of Experimental Psychology* 1963, *65:* 212–213.

Kristt, D. A., & Engel, B. T. Learned control of blood pressure in patients with high blood pressure. *Circulation* 1975, *51:* 370–378.

Mandler, G., Preven, D. W., & Kuhlman, C. K. Effects of operant reinforcement on the GSR. *Journal of the Experimental Analysis of Behavior* 1962, *5:* 317–321.

Marinacci, A. A., & Horande, M. Electromyogram in neuromuscular reeducation. *Bulletin of the Los Angeles Neurological Society* 1960, *25:* 57–71.

McCanne, T. R., & Sandman, C. A. Human operant conditioning: The importance of individual differences. *Psychological Bulletin* 1976, *83:* 587–601.

Miller, N. E. Learning of visceral and glandular responses. *Science* 1969, *163:* 434–445.

Miller, N. E. Postscript. In D. Singh & C. T. Morgan (eds.) *Current status of physiological psychology: Readings.* Monterey, Calif.: Brooks/Cole, 1972.

Miller, N. E., & Banuazizi, A. Instrumental learning by curarized rats of a specific visceral response, intestinal or cardiac. *Journal of Comparative and Physiological Psychology* 1968, *65:* 1–7.

Miller, N. E., & DiCara, L. V. Instrumental learning of heart rate changes in curarized rats: Shaping and specificity to discriminate stimulus. *Journal of Comparative and Physiological Psychology* 1967, *63:* 12–19.

Miller, N. E., & Dworkin, B. R. Visceral learning: Recent difficulties with curarized rats and significant problems for human research. In P. A. Obrist, A. H. Black, J. Brener, & L. V. DiCara (eds.), *Cardiovascular psychophysiology.* Chicago: Aldine, 1974.

Mowrer, O. H. Preparatory set (expectancy). *Psychological Review* 1938, *45:* 45–48.

Noback, C. R. *The human nervous system.* New York: McGraw-Hill, 1967.

Paul, G. L. Physiological effects of relaxation training and hypnotic suggestion. *Journal of Abnormal Psychology* 1969, *74:* 425–437.

Peper, E. Frontiers of clinical biofeedback. In L. Birk (ed.), *Seminars in psychiatry.* New York: Grune & Stratton, 1973.

Raskin, M., Johnson, G., & Rondestvedt, J. W. Chronic anxiety treated by feedback-induced muscle relaxation. *Archives of General Psychiatry* 1973, *28:* 263–267.

Razran, G. The observable unconscious and the inferable conscious in current Soviet psychophysiology: Interoceptive conditioning, semantic conditioning, and the orienting reflex. *Psychological Review* 1961, *68:* 81–147.

Ruch, T. C., & Patton, H. D. (eds.), *Physiology and biophysics.* Philadelphia: W. B. Saunders, 1965.

Schwartz, G. E. Clinical applications of biofeedback: Some theoretical issues. In D. Upper & D. S. Goodenough (eds.), *Behavioral modification with the individual patient: Proceedings of the third annual Brockton Symposium on Behavior Therapy.* Nutley, N.J.: Roche, 1972.

———. Biofeedback as therapy: Some theoretical and practical issues. *American Psychologist* 1973, *33:* 666–673.

———. Toward a theory of voluntary control of response patterns in the cardiovascular system. In P. Obrist, A. H. Black, J. Brener, & L. V. DiCara (eds.), *Cardiovascular psychophysiology.* Chicago: Aldine, 1974.

Schwartz, G. E., & Shapiro, D. Biofeedback and essential hypertension: Current findings and theoretical concerns. In L. Birk (ed.), *Biofeedback: Behavioral medicine.* New York: Grune & Stratton, 1973.

Scott, R. W., Blanchard, E. B., Edmunson, E. D., & Young, L. D. A shaping procedure for heart rate control in chronic tachycardia. *Perceptual and Motor Skills* 1973, *37:* 327–338.

Seligman, M. E. P., & Hager, J. L. *Biological boundaries of learning.* New York: Appleton-Century-Crofts, 1972.

Shapiro, D., Crider, A. B., & Tursky, B. Differentiation of an autonomic response through operant conditioning. *Psychonomic Science* 1964, *1:* 147–148.

Shapiro, D., Mainardi, J. A., & Surwit, R. S. Biofeedback and self-regulation in essential hypertension. In G. E. Schwartz & J. Beatty (eds.), *Biofeedback: Theory and research.* New York: Academic Press, in press.

Shapiro, D., Schwartz, G. E., & Tursky, T. Control of diastolic blood pressure in man by feedback and reinforcement. *Psychophysiology* 1972, *9:* 296–304.

Shapiro, D., Tursky, B., Gershon, E., & Stern, M. Effects of feedback and reinforcement on the control of human systolic blood pressure. *Science* 1969, *163:* 588–589.

Shearn, D. Operant conditioning of heart rate. *Science* 1962, *137:* 530–531.

Skinner, B. F. *The behavior of organisms.* New York: Appleton-Century-Crofts, 1938.

———. *Science and human behavior.* New York: Macmillan, 1953.

Snyder, C., & Noble, M. Operant conditioning of vasoconstriction. *Journal of Experimental Psychology* 1968, *77:* 263–268.

Stephens, J. H., Harris, A. H., & Brady, J. V. Large magnitude heart rate changes in subjects instructed to change their heart rates and given exteroceptive feedback. *Psychophysiology* 1972, *9:* 283–285.

Steptoe, A., Matheus, A., & Johnston, D. The learned control of differential temperatures in the human earlobes: Preliminary study. *Biological Psychology* 1974, *1:* 237–242.

Tasto, D., & Shoemaker, J. E. The effects of muscle relaxation on blood pressure for essential hypertensives and normotensives. Paper presented at the Seventh Annual Meeting of the Association for the Advancement of Behavior Therapy, Miami Beach, Fla., 1973.

Trowill, J. A. Instrumental conditioning of heart rate in the curarized rat. *Journal of Comparative and Physiological Psychology* 1967, *33:* 301–321.

Tursky, B., Shapiro, D., & Schwartz, G. E. Automated constant cuff-pressure system to measure average systolic and diastolic blood pressure in man. *IEEE Transactions on Biomedical Engineering* 1972, *19:* 271–276.

Weiss, T., & Engel, B. T. Operant conditioning of heart rate in patients with premature ventricular contractions. *Psychosomatic Medicine* 1971, *33:* 301–321.

Wells, D. T. Large magnitude voluntary heart rate changes. *Psychophysiology* 1973, *10:* 260–269.

Wickramasekera, I. Instructions and EMG feedback in systematic desensitization: A case report. *Behavior Therapy* 1972, *3:* 460–465.

■7
EEG Biofeedback, Multichannel Synchrony Training, and Attention

LESTER G. FEHMI

It is not possible to present in one chapter a complete review of the field of biofeedback. It is possible, however, to introduce some areas in which research and successful therapy have been done and to provide some references for further study. I will also present evidence that supports the view that EEG activity reflects the scope and flexibility of attentional processes. Finally, I will describe experimental and clinical observations that support the use of EEG biofeedback as a tool in the learning of attentional flexibility and, as a result, in the mitigation of clinical symptoms associated with attentional rigidity.

The basic paradigm for biofeedback training is applicable to all of the various physiological modalities that the field presently encompasses. The modalities that will be discussed here are electroencephalographic (EEG), electromyographic (EMG), temperature, heart rate, blood pressure, and galvanic skin response (GSR). Changes in the physiological process being monitored are reflected by a change in a sensory signal, such as a light or tone. When this feedback signal is appropriately attended to, it is possible for most individuals to learn to control the activity of the monitored physiological process.

Biofeedback training is a unique process by which information of physiological functioning is presented to the trainee. This reestablishes the permissive conditions for learning when existing in vivo feedback systems are temporarily inoperative or not attended to. The experimental comparison of the efficacy of biofeedback training to that of other therapeutic techniques is performed under the false assumption that biofeedback training serves a directive function similar to those of other techniques. In fact, because the function of feedback is to provide information that, in itself, is not directional in nature, biofeedback training may profitably be used in conjunction with other techniques, rather than as a substitute for them. For example, the effectiveness with which a relaxation technique is being learned may be assessed and enhanced by providing EMG biofeedback to both the trainer and the trainee. Since biofeedback training provides the opportunity for change by making information available but does not force change itself nor the direction of change, the results of biofeedback training are greatly affected by often subtle personality variables and biases of the trainees and trainers. Therefore, to evaluate its effects, it appears appropriate to compare other techniques together with biofeedback training to those other techniques alone.

The decision to use biofeedback is the decision to provide an information feedback loop in addition to those that may already exist. By nature, the effects of biofeedback training are individual and depend upon the individual's ability to learn to attend to the spontaneous and volitional changes in the system being monitored or to the associated effects of these changes in the personal, social, and physical environment in which the training takes place. Certain persons, because of past experience, attentional orientation, and physical constitution, have developed and maintained attentional contact with the interoceptive correlates of the changes in physiological function for which biofeedback is provided. These persons may time- and cost-effectively utilize biofeedback as an indicator with which to register and correlate their own experience with spontaneous and volitional changes in the function monitored by the biofeedback signal. When this registration process is complete, the external feedback loop is no longer necessary, and further learning and assessment of self-control may proceed outside the biofeedback setting, with the trainee using direct experience as an index of physiological condition.

Certain other persons, because of past experience, attentional orientation, and physical constitution, have not developed or maintained attentional contact with the monitored function. These persons may effectively utilize biofeedback as an indicator guiding their attention toward intero- and exteroception of processes that vary in accordance with spontaneous or volitional changes in the monitored function. As registration and awareness develop, control improves, and vice versa, until an external biofeedback loop is no longer required for maintenance of self-control of that function.

There exists another group of persons who, because of past experience, attentional orientation, and physical constitution, have neither awareness of nor flexibility of function in the system being monitored. For these persons, biofeedback provides information that the system is invariant in function and does not otherwise directly facilitate the development of awareness or functional control. In this case, techniques supplemental to biofeedback training are necessary in order to stimulate changes in the monitored activity. The flexibility developed by supplemental techniques would promote physiological changes that can be displayed to the trainee for learning purposes.

Since biofeedback information simply creates the permissive conditions for learning but does not, in itself, force change, biofeedback training may be utilized profitably only with an individual showing flexibility along the functional continuum being monitored. Trainees flexible on this continuum can make connections between internal changes and changes in the feedback signal. In addition, they have the flexibility to use the biofeedback information to promote larger incremental changes in the system. Individuals who in the past have developed general attentional flexibility using other techniques, for example, artists, meditators, or dedicated athletes, may benefit more quickly and dramatically from the permissive conditions for learning created by the feedback information.

In contrast, someone with little flexibility of function in the system being monitored learns control very slowly. As an extreme example, one can see that a paralyzed individual, given the opportunity to view his image in a mirror, not only is exposed to less information than is a mobile individual, but he also cannot use the information in order to learn controlled movement because he cannot move. Unfortunately, persons with symptoms that seem well suited to biofeedback training can also be extremely rigid in the physiological system indicated for biofeedback treatment. Thus, they receive a limited amount of biofeedback information, and are limited in their capacity to use such information. However, this response to the information indicates not that biofeedback training is not helpful but, rather, that it should be used in conjunction with other techniques that promote flexibility in the system being monitored. Once system mobility is initiated by other means, the unique opportunities offered by the use of biofeedback techniques may be seized. Small system changes can be practiced until they can be amplified, subtly at first and dramatically later.

Since biofeedback training provides biological information that is not provided by other techniques, it can be used to augment the effectiveness of other processes, such as attention training (Fehmi, 1975), meditation, autogenic training, and relaxation techniques. In our experience, individuals with a moderate amount of experience with other techniques can very rapidly benefit from biofeedback information. They have developed physiological flexibility, but do not have well-developed or subtle internal feedback loops, loops that are usually present in very experienced persons. The potential benefit of biofeedback information was clearly demonstrated to me by a patient with hypertension who responded favorably to biofeedback training within three weeks. Although he had practiced Transcendental Meditation for two years with no evident mitigation of his hypertension, his experience with meditation apparently allowed him very rapidly to utilize EEG biofeedback information together with attention training exercises to reduce his blood pressure. Similarly, I have encountered individuals who had spent most of their meditation asleep and who did not realize they had been sleeping until exposure to biofeedback information. In the biofeedback setting they rapidly learned to develop the mental state associated with presleep. Such individuals could spend a great amount of time sleeping during meditation before developing their own internal feedback loops that would provide the information needed to meditate properly.

Another useful consequence of using biofeedback training together with other techniques is that the equipment provides information to the therapist as well as the trainee. The therapist can use the information to provide a common ground for discussion of subtle physical changes that are difficult to express in words; the opportunity to discuss these changes clearly often facilitates the process of guiding the trainee to his desired goal.

It has not yet been experimentally demonstrated that the specific physiological event that is being reflected by the biofeedback signal needs to be part of an internal experiential feedback loop in order to learn and demonstrate control over the monitored event. An individual may develop control over a physiological event simply by attending to the consequences of physiological changes rather than by attending directly to the changing event. For example, an individual does not have to be specifically aware of muscular tension in order to learn how to relax. An increase in warmth or flexibility may be sufficient effects to signal and reinforce learning relaxation. For another, more complex example, it would be a horrendously difficult task for any human to learn to walk by attending only to EMG biofeedback and an internal experience of muscle tension in discrete muscles. On the other hand, the use of performance criteria themselves as feedback, such as video monitoring of walking, is a simpler and more effective technique that is compatible with the organization of human information processing and neuromuscular systems. Biofeedback would be an appropriate technique in learning to walk if the biofeedback signal were a simple indicator that represented an increasing integration of the complex series of muscle movements associated with walking. The above examples suggest that simple biofeedback techniques do not always represent the most appropriate feedback for learning complex tasks. Although performance can only be as precise as the relevant feedback, the two being tightly knit, the feedback must be appropriate to the learning task.

Introduction to Biofeedback Literature

The references cited below have been selected as examples showing the range of the uses of biofeedback therapy; however, they are not definitive or exhaustive. Those interested in a more complete review may refer to *Biofeedback and Self-Regulation, A Bibliography,* published by the Biofeedback Society of America and edited by Francine Butler and Johann Stoyva. This bibliography contains over 1,100 references to research published through 1972. The Biofeedback Society of America will soon publish a comprehensive bibliography covering more recent research.

Recently, the Biofeedback Society of America has begun publishing a journal, *Biofeedback and Self-Regulation* (Plenum Press); the fourth volume in the series has just appeared. Other journals containing recent research papers in the field are too numerous to mention. Recent research and position papers may also be found in the several volumes of *Biofeedback and Self-Control,* published by Aldine Press and edited by a distinguished board of researchers (Barber, DiCara, Kamiya, Shapiro, & Stoyva, 1976).

Biofeedback training of EMG activity is the most generally accepted modality of biofeedback, and has been used in the treatment of hemiplegia (Johnson & Garton, 1973), tension headache (Budzynski & Stoyva, 1969; Budzynski, Stoyva, & Adler, 1970; Budzynski, Stoyva, Adler, & Mullaney, 1973), anxiety (Raskin, Johnson, & Rondestvedt, 1973), bruxism (Disraeli & Perlis, 1975), torticollis (Russ, 1975), and other types of spasm activity (Marinacci & Horande, 1960). Theoretically, EMG feedback could be used profitably for any problem resulting from or complicated by muscle tension or lack of muscular control in instances where neural connections exist. This form of training has been used successfully to correct foot drop conditions (Basmajian, Kukulka, Naroyan, & Takebe, 1975). In collaboration with Drs. Giuffra and Kreb, I have used EMG feedback with stroke and accident victims at Princeton Medical Center, and have observed rapid learning of control of affected muscular functioning.

Biofeedback training of peripheral vasodilation or temperature has been used successfully in the control of migraine headaches (Peper, 1973; Sargent, Green, & Walters, 1975; Weinstock, 1972), Raynaud's disease (Peper, 1973; Schwartz, 1972), and hypertension (Datey, 1976). Typically, trainees can learn to control peripheral temperature very rapidly, often in one session. As hand or foot temperature increases, the patient feels more relaxed. For these reasons, hand temperature control is often used in our laboratory together with, or as an introduction to, other types of biofeedback training.

Cardiovascular problems have also responded to biofeedback training methods. Systolic and diastolic blood pressure biofeedback have been used in the treatment of hypertension (Benson, Shapiro, Tursky, & Schwartz, 1971; Schwartz & Shapiro, 1973). Heart rate biofeedback has been used in the treatment of patients with atrial tachycardia and premature ventricular contractions (Engel & Bleeker, 1974; Weiss & Engel, 1971).

In our laboratories, attention training and GSR, EMG, thermal, and EEG biofeedback techniques were used in reducing systolic and diastolic blood pressure to below 150/90 from much higher levels. We have encountered only two cases of elevated heart rate (resting rate above 120 bpm), but they also responded to these techniques, bringing heart rate to below 80 bpm.

EEG biofeedback training has been used in the treatment of epilepsy (Sterman, 1973), phobias (Benjamins, 1976), and anxiety (Garrett & Silver, 1972). In addition, EEG biofeedback training has been used with normal subjects in whom it was found that control of various brain waves would increase vigilance (Beatty, Greenberg, Deibler, & O'Hanlon, 1974), improve problem solving (Newton, Bird, & Sheer, 1975), and reduce the needed duration of sleep (Regestein, Buckland, & Pegram, 1973). However, the literature in the area of EEG biofeedback research is controversial, and reflects a confusion that is rooted in what has been the generally accepted method of electrode placement.

The use of traditional clinical and experimental EEG recording techniques, together with standard EEG monitoring equipment using the so-called differential amplifier, has led to some unfortunate problems in the interpretation of EEG biofeedback training results. It has been the custom in both clinical and experimental electroencephalography to take bipolar EEG recordings. A differential amplifier subtracts the electrical activity monitored by one recording electrode relative to ground from the activity monitored by the other so-called reference recording electrode relative to ground. Thus, any equal amplitude and synchronous activity occurring at both electrode sites is canceled. In the case of bipolar recording, both the recording electrode and the reference electrode are placed on cortical sites. Since any cortical site is relatively active and not infrequently synchronous with any other site, it is likely that the EEG record obtained with bipolar electrode placements presents a misleading reflection of the actual EEG activity. A person producing large and equal amplitude alpha activity synchronously at both recording sites would actually show a flat record at the output of the differential amplifier. In that case, the polygraph or oscilloscope record would be flat, and the feedback signal to the subject would indicate that no alpha was present when, in fact, quite large amplitude in phase alpha was present. If activity at the two loci were directly out of phase, the records would indicate a larger response than was actually occurring at either site. My own research, in which I have used monopolar techniques, indicates that high amplitude synchronous brain wave activity occurring simultaneously in the five major lobes of the brain is in fact a desirable condition, a goal for training, and the condition for which the strongest subjective experiences have been reported. For reasons described above, this state would actually be discouraged by EEG biofeedback training programs in which bipolar recording is used. Thus, many of the reports of unsuccessful EEG biofeedback training may be attributed to the use of bipolar techniques, an unfortunate legacy of our past.

Figure 7-1 illustrates EEG monopolar scalp recordings, using interconnected ear lobes as reference, from the occipital lobe at the midline (MO), 2 cm to the right of midline (RO), 2 cm to the left of midline (LO), and a bipolar recording between RO and LO (RO-LO). The above recordings used a ground electrode placed on the neck at the level of the seventh cervical vertebra. Relatively in-phase and out-of-phase brain activity monitored on the right and left hemispheres is denoted by bars under the MO and RO-LO recordings. When RO is relatively in phase with LO, the amplitude of the bipolar differential recordings RO-LO is observed to be dramatically smaller than the amplitude of either RO or LO individually. On the other hand, a monopolar midline recording (MO) reflects in-phase activity by an amplitude somewhat larger than either RO or LO. Conversely, when RO is out of phase with LO, the amplitude of the bipolar differential recording, RO-LO, is observed to be much larger than the amplitude of either RO or LO individually. On the other hand, a monopolar midline recording (MO) reflects out-of-phase activity by an amplitude somewhat smaller than either RO or LO. These actual observations support the argument that bipolar recordings reflect EEG events in such a way as to make likely a misinterpretation of the nature of the underlying activity and a misleading feedback signal in biofeedback experiments. This rationale applies also to the use of bipolar recordings of EMG activity.

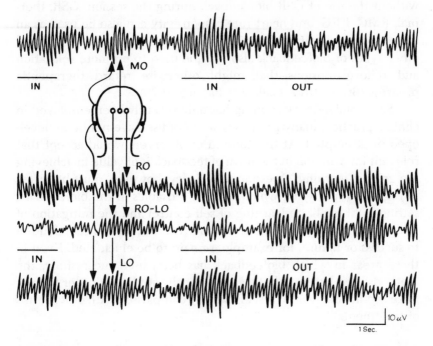

FIGURE 7-1. A comparison of monopolar and bipolar EEG recordings from right and left occipital lobes when brain wave activity is in phase and out of phase. (RO=right occipital; LO=left occipital; MO=midoccipital.)

At this juncture, I would urge anyone utilizing EEG biofeedback to use monopolar electrode placements. Both the ground and the reference electrodes should be placed at some distance from the active recording site, at a relatively inactive location.

Although they are not completely inactive, for many nonexperimental purposes the use of the earlobes for both the reference and ground electrodes is suggested, since they are convenient locations and an improvement over the bipolar scalp configuration. For controlled experiments, other more remote placements may be desirable.

Biofeedback training has been used as an adjunct to other forms of treatment (Benjamins, 1976; Gallon & Padnes, 1976). For example, GSR biofeedback can be used to help locate ideas or stimuli that are associated with anxiety (Bram, 1974). These anxiety-producing stimuli may be subsequently discussed with the therapist, with or without the use of GSR biofeedback during the session. GSR, thermal, EMG, EEG, and heart rate responsivity can also be used as an index of desensitization of anxiety-related stimuli. Similarly, GSR and other types of biofeedback also may be used to promote relaxation and relieve tensions that might otherwise retard therapeutic progress (Bram, 1974; Gallon & Padnes, 1976).

Since biofeedback training has only recently been employed in clinical practice, many promising areas of use have not been developed or attempted. At this time most observers would accept that relevant information in the form of feedback is of value in achieving the goals of learning. Questions of efficacy, however, must be raised in regard to specifying which of these variables in the biofeedback setting most facilitate learning of self-control and the mitigation of symptoms. Personality, belief, and motivational factors contributing to success or failure, for example, remain to be elucidated. Even in those areas in which biofeedback has been used successfully, the methods used have not been systematically studied in order to optimize methodology or to test efficacy by comparison with other forms of treatment.

Multichannel EEG Synchrony Training

In my private practice, I have worked with many patients using EMG, temperature, and GSR biofeedback. In addition, for most patients and nonpatient trainees, for reasons to be discussed, I have emphasized a special form of EEG biofeedback training: multichannel phase synchrony training.

In our laboratories at the State University of New York at Stony Brook and at the Medical Center at Princeton, the subject sits comfortably in a dimly lit, sound-attenuated room. Electrical activity from the brain is monitored by amplifying the potentials through damp, felt pad electrodes placed on the scalp. The subject closes his eyes and begins to perceive a tone or other sensory signal when he is producing an increased amplitude of preselected brain wave frequencies, usually alpha waves. Either by letting his mind wander through different attentional states or by participating in a mental exercise I have developed called Open Focus Training (Fehmi, 1975), he begins to sense the association of processes of attention with presence and absence of the feedback tone. By developing his ability to sustain or prevent the occurrence of the feedback tone, he learns to control the attentional process reflected by the brain wave being monitored.

The major categories of brain waves are classified according to frequency. The slowest waves, delta waves (1 to 4 cycles per second), are associated with deep sleep. Slightly faster waves, theta waves (4 to 8 cycles per second), are associated with emotionally charged or creative imagery, reverie, day dreaming, and presleep stages of arousal. In the theta state, one may feel as if he is actually experiencing or living through his imagery or an old memory, as opposed to having a detached or objective attitude toward his mental imagery. Alpha waves (8 to 13 cycles per second) are associated with a relaxed, alert state of consciousness (Lindsley, 1952). In this state of mind, one perceives and responds effortlessly. When one focuses with effort, cognitively struggles with, or is anxious about a problem or activity, one normally enters a more aroused state of mind, represented by beta brain waves (about 13 cycles per second). Beta is observed to occur when one is relating to his environment or behavior with a critical attitude, tense concentration, or mental effort, all of these conditions being associated with narrow focus of attention.

One major point I would like to communicate in this chapter is that general EEG activity normally reflects either central focus or peripheral focus from any of several sensory systems, rather than simply reflecting unimodal peripheral focus, that is, peripheral focus of a single sensory system. For example, recently it has been hypothesized that alpha blocking reflects a unimodal focus, that is, visual focus (Plotkin, 1976). However, observations made in our laboratory and by other researchers (cited below) have indicated that a reduction in alpha activity is associated with the constriction of peripheral or more central (that is, neural) focus in any or all of the sense modalities upon which attention is focused.

Figure 7-2 exemplifies a general phenomenon related to visual attention. In Figure 7-2, one can see a dramatic increase in the amplitude and abundance of alpha activity at all recording sites

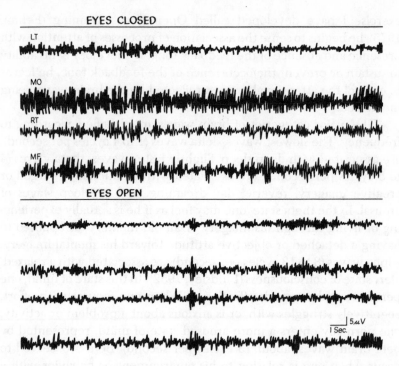

FIGURE 7-2. EEG recording from five brain loci of one subject with eyes closed and eyes open. (LT=left temporal; MO=midoccipital; RT=right temporal; MF=midfrontal.)

when the eyes are closed, as compared to the EEG record from the same individual with his eyes open. The generality of this phenomenon across subjects indicates that under normal conditions in most people either (1) the eyes are habitually focused when open, or (2) that central attention is habitually oriented and concentrated upon visual information when the eyes are open, or (3) that effort, tension, or criticalness is normal to visual functioning, or (4) some combination or all of the above.

Plotkin (1976) recently reported that the single most effective fronto-occipital alpha enhancement condition used in his EEG biofeedback experiment was that of diffusing or blurring visual focus. Since this strategy was tested in the eyes-open condition, his finding is expected and consistent with many earlier findings in the research literature (Lindsley, 1952). The phenomenon demonstrated in Figure 7-2 is compatible with Plotkin's conclusion, in that closing one's eyes would be expected to reduce visual focusing, which mediates an increase in alpha abundance.

Figure 7-3, from unpublished research conducted in 1968, further supports Plotkin's conclusion that the subject's intentional blurring of visual focus tends to increase alpha abundance. When the subject was asked to look for detail, thereby focusing on visual stimulation, alpha activity tended to block on all channels. Note that eyeblinks are indicated on the midfrontal tracing as large excursions. The midfrontal tracings indicate a higher rate of eye blinking and eye movements while the subject was looking for detail, which is generally correlated with a narrowing of focus.

Although it seems clear that visual focus often accompanies a reduction in the presence or amplitude of alpha activity, Plotkin's suggestion that all enhancement of alpha in the feedback situation

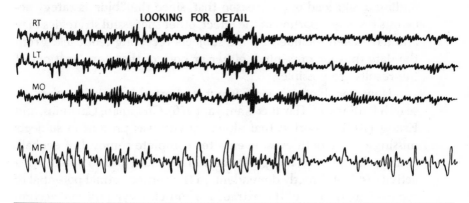

LOOKING FOR DETAIL

RT
LT
MO

MF

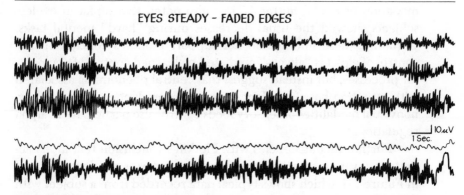

EYES STEADY - FADED EDGES

10 μV
1 Sec.

FIGURE 7-3. EEG recording from five brain loci during the conditions of visual focus.

is mediated by a reduction of visual focusing is inconsistent with my own findings over ten years of clinical observations and experimentation.

I would first like to discuss some apparently contradictory findings within Plotkin's own research. In the report cited above, Plotkin provides evidence that the group that shows the greatest enhancement of alpha is the group that receives both the "diffuse visual focus" strategy and alpha feedback training simultaneously. The groups receiving feedback alone or the strategy alone produce less alpha than the group receiving both. Plotkin suggests that these findings indicate only that greater efficiency of defocusing is learned with alpha feedback. His interpretation of the results is consistent with his view that the abundance of alpha is merely an index of oculomotor activity that mediates visual focus. However, the same finding might lead one to reason that, since the "blur" strategy accounts for only a portion of the effect, other successful strategies may also have been included by the subjects receiving feedback. From the data thus far presented, either or both of these explanations of the results are possible.

However, Plotkin's view is not supported by certain other research findings (cf. Hardt & Kamiya, 1976). Chapman, Cavonius, and Ernest (1971) reported that alpha activity was present in subjects missing one or both eyes, even after complete removal of eyeball, extraocular muscles, and periosteum. They state (p. 1161) that alpha activity is "not directly dependent on the corneo-retinal potential of the eyeball, tremor of the extraocular muscles, eye position, accommodation or eyelid flutter." They also noted that alpha in eyeless subjects showed the usual decreases during "hard" mental tasks. Certainly, these findings do not support Plotkin's conclusion that control of alpha is "always" mediated by learned control of oculomotor processes, but instead suggest that central phenomena associated with attention have an effect upon alpha production or that other, nonvisual modalities of sensory focus control also participate in alpha regulation.

Further inconsistencies with Plotkin's conclusion that alpha activity is always mediated by oculomotor processes are demonstrated in Figure 7-4, which shows typical data recorded from a subject with his eyes open. In the first quadrant is a recording taken while the

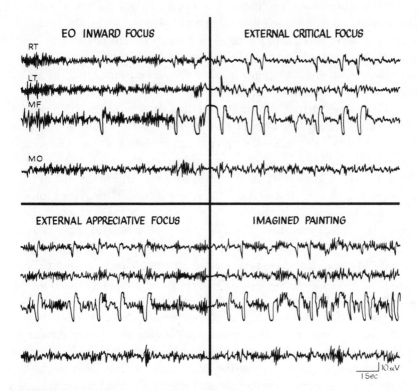

FIGURE 7-4. EEG recording from four brain loci during four conditions of attentional focus. (LT=left temporal; MO=midoccipital; RT=right temporal; MF=midfrontal.)

subject was asked to focus on internal experiences keeping his eyes open. Alpha amplitude and abundance are relatively large for this condition on all tracings but, perhaps, are smallest on the occipital tracing. The second quadrant shows a recording taken while the subject was asked to scrutinize his surroundings in a critical manner. During this task the alpha abundance is low on all tracings. In the third quadrant is a recording taken when the subject was asked to observe his external environment in an appreciative, rather than in a critical, manner. In this quadrant alpha amplitude and abundance is greater than in quadrant 2. The artifacts on the midfrontal lobe tracings during the critical and appreciative conditions indicate that similar amounts of eye blink and gross oculomotor activity occurred in both of these two conditions, yet alpha activity differs considerably. Perhaps because the eyes are open in all conditions, the occipital tracing responds least to changes in condition. However, lobes not directly associated with visual activity, the frontal lobe and the temporal lobes, all show changes in abundance and amplitude of alpha activity as a function of condition.

This observation also suggests that factors other than visual oculomotor control can affect the amount and amplitude of alpha frequencies. In the case of external appreciative focus where the instructions include focusing, one would expect, in accordance with Plotkin's view, that alpha abundance and amplitude should not increase over that in the critical focus condition. However, alpha is observed to increase in the appreciative focus condition when compared to critical focusing. This suggests that a central process associated with the change from critical orientation to appreciative orientation is, in this case, responsible for the changes in alpha abundance. In addition, the changes in alpha activity on the occipital lobe are the smallest changes observed, a finding that does not support the hypothesis that oculomotor processes mediate these changes. Moreover, there is evidence that gross oculomotor activity is similar in both conditions, which suggests that equal levels of visual focus occur in both critical and appreciative conditions. It has been said that Einstein would read complex physics journals and at the same time produce continuous large amplitude alpha activity. As the legend goes, Einstein was observed to produce beta activity only on one occasion, when he discovered an error in reasoning reported in the physics journal that he was reading. Whether or not this anecdote is true, many observations in our laboratory, similar to that presented in Figure 7-4, support the observations that extremes of focused criticalness or judgmentalness are associated with a marked reduction in alpha activity. This suggests that a central phenomenon associated with attention, rather than peripheral sensory focusing itself, is responsible for the modulation of alpha amplitude.

Our observations and interviews with trainees indicate that an individual may produce either alpha or beta waves while engaging in the same activity. Which brain wave state occurs appears to depend upon the way in which the individual generally relates to his experience or behavior: Effortless performance of the task is associated with alpha activity; functioning with mental tension and effort is associated with beta activity. For a given individual over time, there may be a tendency to respond to specific tasks in consistent ways. Thus, one person may play tennis effortlessly, producing alpha all the while, but become tense and produce beta when driving his car. Another person might react oppositely, both cognitively and electrophysiologically. Evidence gathered in our laboratory in collaboration with Schlossman, Saltaformaggio, and Selzer (unpublished) and presented in Table 7-1 supports the view that persons differ in their general attentional approach to tasks, and that a given attentional strategy may be characteristic for certain individuals over a period of time.

The subjects in this experiment were selected by a procedure developed by Day (1967) that was used to categorize them as right movers or left movers. In accordance with this procedure, volunteers were asked a series of questions requiring reflection. The initial direction of eye movement during reflection was recorded. Subjects who consistently moved their eyes in the same direction on at least 17 out of 20 occasions were chosen to participate in the biofeedback experiment. During all periods of the experiment, including baseline periods and rest periods without feedback, the left movers produced more alpha activity than the right movers. Both groups demonstrated ON–OFF control over their alpha activity; that is, they produced more alpha when asked to "turn the tone on" than they produced when asked to "turn the tone off." However, the groups achieved this ON–OFF control in different ways. Only the left movers were able to increase alpha activity above rest levels during the ON periods. The left movers could not turn off alpha activity when asked to do so. On the contrary, right movers produced significantly

TABLE 7-1. Mean Seconds of Alpha Activity per Minute in Right and Left Movers under Four Conditions

Condition	Right Movers	Left Movers
ON	6.76	16.72
Rest I	7.78	14.45
OFF	6.27	13.74
Rest II	7.65	13.70
Mean Rest	7.71	14.07

less alpha during both the ON and OFF test periods as compared to rest period scores.

Bakan (1971) and others have theorized that right and left eye movements during reflection indicate the use of the contralateral hemisphere during memory retrieval or solution of the questions. Functional differences between the two hemispheres suggested by various authors may be summarized by associating the left hemisphere with analytical, objective, and control functions, and the right hemisphere with holistic, intuitive, and passive functions.

In another study by Selzer (1973), using a similar training paradigm as in the study previously cited, it was found that right movers were able to control midfrontal alpha activity using visual feedback but not auditory feedback, while the reverse was true for left movers. In other words, right and left movers appear to utilize different sense modalities more effectively in learning alpha control.

In view of the correlation between EEG activity and states of attention, the findings from these experiments suggest that in some individual adults, at least, the flexibility of scope and direction of attentional focus is restricted. Some persons approach tasks with a predisposition toward effortless into-it-ness or intuition; others tend to strive for greater distance and objectivity. Moreover, these findings suggest that individual predispositional variables may affect the outcome of EEG biofeedback experiments. For example, when one's sampling techniques happen to load a group with either left or right movers, or equal numbers of each, one might expect that, in brief experiments, the results may be partly or wholly negative or not representative of the general population.

A recent pilot experiment in our laboratory suggests even more strongly that no simple statement about any single modality of sensory focus will predict all of the variance in alpha biofeedback experiments. Naïve subjects were instructed alternately to expand and narrow their focus upon two different modalities of experience, visual and somatic. The dependent variable was occipital and parietal alpha integrated energy scores. The results indicate that each modality of focus produced changes in alpha amplitude on all monitored lobes in certain individuals. However, the greatest changes occurred in the lobe that processed the information in which focus was manipulated. Thus, manipulating somatic focus produced greater changes in parietal alpha, above and below rest levels, than in occipital alpha. This experiment also pointed up certain differences between persons. The greatest change in alpha amplitude from narrow focus to expanded focus occurs in the occipital lobe for some persons and in the parietal lobe for other persons.

Many of the phenomena associated with the so-called alpha experience become understandable if the release of these phenomena is viewed as a general reduction of rigidity of focal attention. Furthermore, this view provides a rationale for the use of EEG biofeedback in the treatment of various symptoms through the enhancement of attentional flexibility. Finally, this view, in conjunction with the above evidence, indicates that the power of EEG biofeedback to reflect the general status of attentional flexibility in the various brain systems is a direct function of the number of lobes of the brain reflected in the feedback signal.

Several investigators have undertaken controlled experimental studies of the ability to change various brain wave parameters and the resultant subjective effects (e.g., Brown, 1970; Kamiya, 1968; Mulholland, 1968; Nowlis & Kamiya, 1970). Training often begins with a "play" period during which the subject is encouraged to explore various means of controlling the feedback. In subsequent test periods, he is asked to demonstrate that he can both increase and decrease the particular activity being monitored. "Yoked-control" subjects are matched to these trainees, and are presented a tone that is not contingent upon their brain wave activity since the tone is tape-recorded from other experimental trainees. By comparing the performances of the trainees and the control subjects, confidence is gained that the effects of training are actually a function of the biofeedback rather than of more general conditions. In our laboratories, we have thus been able to demonstrate, under controlled conditions, that persons are able to learn to increase and decrease amplitude and occurrence of various brain wave frequencies from each of the major lobes of the brain: occipital, parietal, frontal, and left and right temporal lobes.

While learned control from each lobe was confirmed, it was also observed that there was only partial generalization of effect to other lobes of the brain. That is, in most people, controlling alpha abundance on any one lobe had only a partial simultaneous effect on all or most other lobes. This result is consistent with the findings of the above-described modality of focus experiment. Less than complete generalization also suggests that learned control of alpha might be facilitated if the feedback signal were to reflect the amplitude of alpha in each of the major lobes of the brain simultaneously so that the effects of focus in each sense modality might be more effectively communicated.

Alpha amplitude reflects the summed membrane potentials of cells beneath the recording electrodes. The greater the number of cells that are becoming simultaneously facilitated and subsequently inhibited in rhythmic succession, the larger are the fluctuations in brain wave amplitude recorded by the EEG. In other words, EEG amplitude is an index of the synchrony of cellular functioning in the cortex of the brain beneath the electrode. Since local synchrony, as reflected by large amplitude EEG alpha activity, is generally observed to be associated with modality-specific diffusion of focus, one might expect that large amplitude alpha which is simultaneously recorded in synchrony from the major lobes of the brain would reflect a more general diffusion of perceptual focus. Thus, brainwave synchrony and relative brain wave amplitude together become the critical parameters or indices of perceptual integration and scope of attention.

The synchrony of EEG activity simultaneously recorded from different brain loci has also been studied in our laboratory. The variables we use in determining phase synchrony may be understood by referring to Figure 7-5. When two waves from different brain loci are rising and falling in synchrony (see waves B and C), they are termed "in phase"; they are described as being "out of phase" if the voltages are changing in opposite directions (see waves A and B). Electronic techniques have been developed in our laboratory that enable us to teach volunteers to control the phase relations of the brain wave activity recorded from each of the major lobes of the brain, or all of them simultaneously. Figure 7-6 shows the results of a phase training experiment undertaken in collaboration with S. Osborne in which subjects received a feedback tone when left and right occipital lobe activity was within ± 15° of "in phase." The subjects were asked to turn the tone ON and OFF alternately. The results demonstrated that the experimental subjects could learn ON–OFF control of the phase relatedness of EEG activity (see open circle traces) while yoked-control subjects could not demonstrate such control over EEG activity (see filled circle traces).

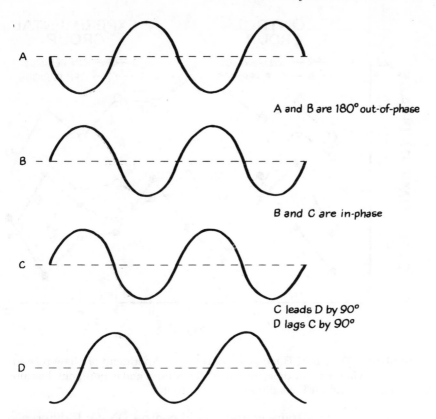

FIGURE 7-5. Examples of sine wave phase relations.

In other experiments in our laboratory, feedback is provided that simultaneously reflects the frequency, amplitude, and phase relations of the activity from the five major lobes of the brain. Five channel EEG biofeedback training is observed to be a more effective procedure than the single channel biofeedback techniques that are presently used in the field. Moreover, phase synchrony among the lobes is observed to enhance the magnitude and frequency of the subjective phenomena associated with alpha and theta.

The most recent double-blind study in our laboratory involved volunteer management executives who undertook a course of multi-channel EEG biofeedback training consisting of twice weekly sessions for ten weeks. The experimental trainees demonstrated that,

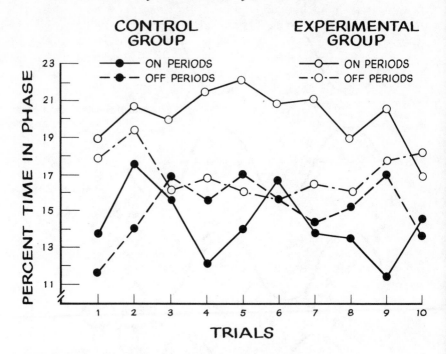

FIGURE 7-6. An EEG biofeedback training experiment of phase related-ness, showing percent time "in phase" for control and experimental groups during ON and OFF conditions over ten trials.

after biofeedback training, they could control ON–OFF difference scores in alpha activity, both with feedback and without feedback (see Table 7-2). These experimental trainees also could increase and decrease their alpha activity above and below baseline without feedback. In addition, after training, the experimental group produced significantly more alpha activity while resting than they produced at the inception of the experiment. The yoked-control subjects showed no evidence of learning control of alpha activity or of change in alpha base rates. After training, the experimental trainees became more flexible in a perceptual sense; that is, they demonstrated less field dependence, using a Gottschaldt test for field dependency. We also asked the trainees to rate themselves on various dimensions of experience and performance. It was found that, after biofeedback training, the experimental executives reported that they were more insightful, more calm, less depressed, more able to concentrate, more self-initiating, more detached from their experience, more observant, more personal (as opposed to formal), more in oneness (as opposed to separateness), and more satisfied with life. None of the above effects were observed by the control subjects. These statistically significant results confirm the changes we have observed to occur in other, less formal experiments as well as in clinical settings.

My primary research interest is in the relationship of EEG activity to attentional processes. Accordingly, I have found that a useful context in which to discuss mental health and disease is in relation to the flexibility of scope and direction of attention. In this view, many symptoms reflect attentional rigidity problems. For obvious examples, the obsessive personality represents an attentional state narrowly focused upon and fixated on certain thoughts or thought patterns; the compulsive personality is narrowly focused and fixed upon certain behavior patterns. Many tension- and anxiety-related psychosomatic problems, such as migraine and tension headaches, are symptoms of the habit of averting narrowly focused attention from fields of concern. Other symptoms may be viewed as manifesting a lack of ability to focus attention.

Many symptoms reflect only the stress associated with habitual narrow focus and directional rigidity. When one is no longer able to attend freely and becomes caught in a compulsively repetitious attentional cycle, a considerable stress and resistance develops against the limiting boundaries. When the trainee learns how to expand his focus again so that the cumulative tension associated with habitual narrow focus and directional rigidity can be reintegrated into a larger field, symptoms disappear as attentional flexibility returns. Symptoms reflecting a lack of ability to focus can also be improved

TABLE 7-2. Double-blind Study of Executives:
p Values of t-Tests Comparing Scores of First Two
Sessions with Scores of Last Two Sessions

Scores in Comparison	Experimental Group	Control Group
ON-OFF Difference Scores— Feedback Periods	$p < .05$	ns
ON-OFF Differences Scores— No Feedback Periods	$p < .05$	ns
Rest Scores	$p < .05$	ns

by training attentional flexibility either in scope or directionality of focus.

· When one greatly diffuses or opens his attentional focus, one can apprehend all of one's experience simultaneously. There is then no necessity to direct or control one's attention in any way, and thus, there is no occasion for control anxiety, the anxiety associated with controlling directionality of narrow focus. This mode of attention, in which one is simultaneously aware of all available experience, is at once an effortless and integrating process. For most trainees, learning how to create the permissive conditions that allow this effortless process to develop is one of the most significant occurrences in the biofeedback setting.

Since most persons have not fully developed their ability to control attentional processes, the state of open focus, which may be developed with the use of EEG biofeedback, is also beneficial to individuals without symptoms requiring therapeutic treatment. As described previously in the discussion of EEG activity in the general population, there is a habitual orientation toward narrow focus of attention, especially in the visual system. This fixation upon visual attention is evidenced, for example, by one's natural tendency to close one's eyes at a concert in order to hear better or when one is trying to clarify body feelings. However, narrow focus of attention may persist even when one's sensory activity is extremely abridged or deprived. In most individuals, for example, rumination of thought often occurs in the absence of distracting external stimuli. Of 30 people who signed up for a biofeedback course recently, 24 complained of insomnia in addition to other anxiety- and tension-related symptoms. Most individuals suffering from even mild insomnia described that, in the course of going to sleep, their focused attention becomes fixated upon their mental activity, thoughts, images, and so forth. They report that they cannot sleep because of the physiological arousal associated with the presence of this stimulating activity. I present this example of attentional rigidity to demonstrate the value of learning to control the scope and direction of one's attention by persons not suffering from symptoms requiring treatment. While there are other ways to learn attentional flexibility, EEG biofeedback training may represent the most cost-effective and time-effective way.

I have found many modalities of biofeedback useful, especially for symptoms associated with pain, tension, and stress. However, my experience has been that the most global and subtle of these biofeedback modalities is that which utilizes multichannel, phase-sensitive EEG biofeedback as an indicator of attention. For any individual, the richness of reality is limited only by his own perceptual or attentional rigidity. In my opinion, multichannel, phase-sensitive EEG biofeedback, properly used, will through the training of attentional flexibility significantly enhance functional capacity and sense of well-being.

REFERENCES

Bakan, P. The eyes have it. *Psychology Today,* April 1971, 64–66.

Barber, T. X., DiCara, L. V., Kamiya, J., Shapiro, D., & Stoyva, J. *Biofeedback and self-control, 1975–1976.* Chicago: Aldine, 1976.

Basmajian, J. V., Kukulka, C. G., Naroyan, M. G., & Takebe, K. Biofeedback treatment of foot-drop after stroke compared with standard rehabilitation techniques: Effects on voluntary control and strength. *Archives of Physical Medicine and Rehabilitation* 1975, *56:* 231–236.

Beatty, J., Greenberg, A., Deibler, W. P., & O'Hanlon, J. F. Operant control of occipital theta rhythm affects performance in a radar monitoring task. *Science* 1974, *183:* 871–873.

Benjamins, J. K. The effectiveness of alpha feedback training and muscle relaxation procedures in systematic desensitization. Paper presented at the Seventh Annual Meeting of the Biofeedback Research Society, Colorado Springs, Colo., Febuary, 1976.

Benson, H., Shapiro, D., Tursky, B., & Schwartz, G. D. Decreased systolic blood pressure through operant conditioning techniques in patients with essential hypertension. *Science* 1971, *173:* 740–742.

Bram, P. Biofeedback techniques in multi-modality treatment. Paper presented at the Fifth Annual Meeting of the Biofeedback Research Society, Colorado Springs, Colo., February, 1974.

Brown, B. Recognition of aspects of consciousness through association with EEG alpha activity represented by a light signal. *Psychophysiology* 1970, *6:* 442–452.

Budzynski, T. H., & Stoyva, J. M. An instrument for producing deep relaxation by means of analog information feedback. *Journal of Applied Behavioral Analysis* 1969, *2:* 231–237.

Budzynski, T. H., Stoyva, J. M., & Adler, C. S. Feedback-induced muscle relaxation: Application to tension headaches. *Journal of Behavior Therapy and Experimental Psychiatry* 1970, *1:* 205–211.

Budzynski, T. H., Stoyva, J. M., Adler, C. S., & Mullaney, D. EMG biofeedback and tension headache: A controlled-outcome study. *Psychosomatic Medicine* 1973, *35:* 484–496.

Chapman, R. M., Cavonius, C. R., & Ernest, J. T. Alpha and kappa electroencephalogram activity in eyeless subjects. *Science* 1971, *171:* 1159–1161.

Datey, K. K. Temperature regulation in the management of hypertension. Paper presented at the Seventh Annual Meeting of the Biofeedback Research Society, Colorado Springs, Colo., February, 1976.

Day, M. E. An eye-movement indicator of individual differences in the physiological organization of attentional processes and anxiety. *Journal of Psychology* 1967, *66:* 51–62.

Disraeli, R. I., & Perlis, D. B. Dental application of biofeedback. Paper presented at the Sixth Annual Meeting of the Biofeedback Research Society, Monterey, Calif., January–February, 1975.

Engel, B. T., & Bleecker, E. R. Application of operant conditioning techniques to the control of the cardiac arrhythmias. In P. Obrist, A. H. Black, J. Brener, & L. V. DiCara (eds.), *Cardiovascular psychophysiology: Current issues in response mechanisms, biofeedback and methodology.* Chicago: Aldine, 1974.

Fehmi, L. G. Open focus training. Manuscript of workshop presented at the Sixth Annual Meeting of the Biofeedback Research Society, Monterey, Calif., January–February, 1975.

Gallon, R. L., & Padnes, S. C. EMG biofeedback and the relaxation response. Paper presented at the Seventh Annual Meeting of the Biofeedback Research Society, Colorado Springs, Colo., February, 1976.

Garrett, B. L., & Silver, M. P. The use of EMG and alpha biofeedback to relieve test anxiety in college students. Paper presented at the Eightieth Annual Meeting of the American Psychological Association, Washington, D.C., September, 1972.

Hardt, J. V., & Kamiya, J. Some comments on Plotkin's self-regulation of electroencephalographic alpha. *Journal of Experimental Psychology* 1976, *105:* 66–99.

Johnson, H. E., & Garton, W. H. Muscle reeducation in hemiplegia by use of electromyographic device. *Archives of Physical Medicine and Rehabilitation* 1973, *54:* 320–325.

Kamiya, J. Conscious control of brain waves. *Psychology Today* 1968, *1:* 57–60.

Lindsley, D. B. Psychological phenomena and the electroencephalogram. *Electroencephalography and Clinical Neurophysiology* 1952, *4:* 443–456.

Marinacci, A. A., & Horande, M. Electromyogram in neuromuscular reeducation. *Bulletin of the Los Angeles Neurological Society* 1960, *25:* 57–71.

Mulholland, T. Feedback electroencephalography. *Activas Nervosa Superior* 1968, *10:* 410–438.

Newton, F. A., Bird, B. L., & Sheer, D. E. Conditioning and suppression of 40 Hz EEG activity in humans: An analysis of voluntary control and subjective states. Paper presented at the Sixth Annual Meeting of the Biofeedback Research Society, Monterey, Calif., January–February, 1975.

Nowlis, D. P., & Kamiya, J. The control of EEG alpha rhythms through auditory feedback and the associated mental activity. *Psychophysiology* 1970, *6:* 476–484.

Peper, E. Frontiers of clinical biofeedback. In L. Birk (ed.), *Seminars in psychiatry* (Vol. 5) New York: Grune & Stratton, 1973.

Plotkin, W. B. On the self-regulation of the occipital alpha rhythm: Control strategies, states of consciousness and the role of physiological feedback. *Journal of Experimental Psychology: General* 1976, *105:* 66–99.

Raskin, M., Johnson, G., & Rondestvedt, J. W. Chronic anxiety treated by feedback induced muscle relaxation. *Archives of General Psychiatry* 1973, *28:* 263–267.

Regestein, Q. R., Buckland, G. H., & Pegram, G. V. Effect of daytime alpha rhythm maintenance on subsequent sleep. *Psychosomatic Medicine* 1973, *35:* 161–175.

Russ, K. L. EMG biofeedback of spasmodic torticollis: A case presentation. Paper presented at the Sixth Annual Meeting of the Biofeedback Research Society, Monterey, Calif., January–February, 1975.

Sargent, J. D., Green, E. E., & Walters, E. D. The use of autogenic feedback training in a pilot study of migraine and tension headaches. *Headache* 1975, *12:* 120–125.

Schwartz, G. E. Clinical applications of biofeedback: Some theoretical issues. In D. Upper & D. S. Goodenough (eds.), *Behavior modification with the individual patient: Proceedings of the Third Annual Brockton Symposium on Behavior Therapy.* Nutley, N. J.: Roche, 1972.

Schwartz, G. E., & Shapiro, D. Biofeedback and essential hypertension: Current findings and theoretical concerns. In L. Birk (ed.), *Biofeedback: Behavioral medicine.* New York: Grune & Stratton, 1973.

Selzer, F. Autoregulation of mid-frontal alpha activity as a function of the direction of conjugate lateral eye movements. Unpublished Ph.D. Dissertation, State University of New York, Stony Brook, 1973.

Sterman, M. B. Neurophysiologic and clinical studies of sensorimotor EEG biofeedback training: Some effects on epilepsy. *Seminars in Psychology* 1973, *5:* 507–524.

Weinstock, S. A. A tentative procedure for the control of pain: Migraine and tension headaches. In D. Shapiro, T. X. Barker, L. V. DiCara, J. Kamiya, N. E. Miller, & J. Stoyva (eds.), *Biofeedback and self-control, 1972.* Chicago: Aldine, 1972.

Weiss, T., & Engel, B. T. Operant conditioning of heart rate in patients with premature ventricular contractions. *Psychosomatic Medicine* 1971, *33:* 301–321.

8
Hypnotism and Altered States of Consciousness
ANDRÉ M. WEITZENHOFFER

Whatever one may say hypnotism is, it should be recognized from the outset that today, as in much earlier days, opinions are very much divided on its exact nature, and even its factuality. The majority of people have believed, and continue to believe, in the reality of hypno-suggestive phenomena. On the other hand, there has always been a small minority of self-dubbed skeptics (Weitzenhoffer, 1963a) dedicated to the proposition of debunking hypnotism. There is Bailly's (1784) famous report on mesmerism, prepared for the King of France, debunking hypnotic phenomena, then known as mesmeric phenomena. Somewhat arbitrarily, I take 1841 as the beginning of hypnotism per se, this date marking the introduction of the term "hypnotism" into the literature. There were Ernest Hart (1896) and his followers in the 1890s who literally cried "humbug" to all hypnotic phenomena, and in this era we have had Sarbin (Sarbin & Coe, 1972) and his followers insisting that all hypnotic and suggested behavior is role playing; while Barber (1969) and his co-workers disclaim the existence of hypnosis as a state and the reality of many induced phenomena, but do seem to admit the existence of suggestion.

It is not my intention to review the arguments of Sarbin or those of Barber, as I have done this in detail elsewhere (Weitzenhoffer, 1971b, 1974a), and it would take us too far afield. The fact that I am writing this chapter is an indication that I do not hold to their views. My position, as expressed in all of my writings and detailed in my first book on the subject (Weitzenhoffer, 1953), is that there is a state of hypnosis, and there is suggestibility. These two are what hypnotism is all about.

Looking at the other half of my topic—namely, "consciousness" —here, too, we find that the majority consider it a fit topic of discussion, while there is a minority going back at least to the beginnings of behaviorism that insists it is not permissible to talk or even think about it. I am a member of the majority, and take the position that it is permissible to talk about it.

Lack of satisfactory definitions and of objective criteria for consciousness is a major feature shared by hypnosis as a state and by consciousness. Both are quite intangible; whatever we can say about either depends largely upon reports of personal experiences, and is, thus, founded upon highly private, subjective data.

It would seem then that any attempts to relate hypno-suggestive (hypnotic) phenomena to consciousness are doomed to failure from the start. How can one relate two unknowns to one another? Is it scientifically tenable to attempt this or even to write about either?

I will briefly address myself to this latter issue in the remainder of this introduction. Since this is not the primary topic of the chapter, I will only touch upon some of the major issues involved and offer here the gist of some of the arguments I see as bearing on the matter. I will do so by addressing myself to three issues I perceive as constituting main stumbling blocks in the minds of many critics.

MUST ALL PROPER OBJECTS OF SCIENTIFIC DISCOURSE BE DIRECTLY OBSERVABLE OR MEASURABLE? Since the physical and biological sciences have stood the test of time and have proven themselves to be good examples of what science is about, we might turn to these for the answer to this question. For instance, the existence of the planet Pluto was mathematically established well before it could be pointed at and measured. The existence of viruses was established long before they could be seen, measured, and their nature identified. Furthermore, in this instance, the subscience of virology developed successfully. Finally, even though no one has seen or directly measured the semiconductor holes that are the basis of transistors, their effective control by engineers has revolutionized technology. Many other examples are available. These will suffice to answer the first question in the negative.

MUST ALL PROPER OBJECTS OF SCIENTIFIC DISCOURSE BE DEFINA-BLE? It is a well-established fact that any universe of discourse must contain, indeed begin with, a certain minimal set of undefined terms and axioms or their equivalent. The remainder of the discourse, then, evolves out of this basic set through construction according to certain rules. The contents of these sets are flexible, but that there must be such sets is a fact. Furthermore, while there are minimal sets, and it is desirable to work with them, it is permissible to work with more complex sets, and in practice this is often the case. Such sets are, of course, reducible to minimal ones without loss. For instance, in geometry, points and circles may be taken as undefined elements, even though it is possible and usual to define a circle as the locus of all points equidistant from a given point and to take points only as undefined. On the other hand, we could take circles but not points as undefined elements and define points in terms of the contact and intersection of circles.

Furthermore, to state that some element is an undefined element does not preclude descriptively talking about it. Axioms and theorems frequently serve this function. The axiom that there is a straight line that contains any two given points does not define either point or line but does tell us something about the properties of points and lines and their relation to each other.

In keeping with these remarks and those of the previous section, I take the position that it is just as valid to consider such concepts as "consciousness," "altered state of consciousness," "thought," "volition," and "hypnosis" as undefined terms of our universe of discourse as it is to take other terms and try, quite unsuccessfully, to define the former in terms of the latter. And, just as I can validly say many things about such undefined elements of geometry as points and lines, so I can validly say many things about consciousness, volition, hypnosis, and other undefined terms that are part of our everyday language.

DO SUBJECTIVE PHENOMENA LIE OUTSIDE THE DOMAIN OF THE SCIENTIFIC STUDY OF BEHAVIOR? In its effort to place psychology on a solid scientific foundation, behaviorism originally set forth the tenet that only observable behavior is a fit topic for scientific study. As pointed out, this view has not been supported by the history of science. If, then, the study of subjective phenomena (hence, of the private, experimental world of man) is to be excluded from scientific investigations of behavior, this must be done on some other basis. Like consciousness and hypnosis, *behavior* lacks a satisfactory definition. Anyone who doubts this needs only to consult English and English's *Dictionary* (1958). Loosely speaking, as the authors point out, behavior is anything an animal (hence, also, a human) does. For present purposes this will do, particularly since, as English and English also encouragingly remark in their summation, nearly everyone who uses the term *behavior* seems to be referring to the same thing, regardless of how they define it. When we talk about the human animal, we can further observe that his behavior falls roughly into two main categories: communicative (informational) behavior and noncommunicative behavior. Also, we can observe that what we call subjective experiential phenomena become data and part of our universe of discourse through and only through our interpretation of communicative behaviors. It seems to me that the difficulties that arise in the study of subjective data lie much more in this matter of interpretation by the experimenter or observer than in the data per se. To the extent that verbal utterances are as much a motor act as any other motor act and are as directly publicly observable and recordable, I have always had some difficulty in understanding how behaviorism could exclude verbal reports about subjective events from scientific study—particularly since, in many instances, verbal responses clearly are responses to an observable stimulus, namely, another verbal utterance in the form of questions or instructions from the experimenter. The above difficulty has been compounded by the fact that it is impossible to work with communications about subjective events *qua* responses without placing any linguistic interpretations on them. They can be treated as one treats eye blinks or salivation conditioned to the sound of a bell. I do not recommend this approach as either productive or enjoyable, but if one wishes to be a strict behaviorist and deal with subjective phenomena, it can be done. On the other hand, I do not believe this is necessary in order to study subjective events scientifically. The canons of the scientific method definitely do not call for it. As a matter of fact, physics, which is usually considered to be science par excellence, recognizes that, in the final analysis, the basic data of science are completely subjective. Is it not, then, somewhat inconsistent to deny scientific validity to subjective reports?

A basic weakness of the behavioristic treatment of subjective data can be seen in connection with the following: There is a phenomenon called "animal hypnosis." One of its presumed characteristics is "insensibility" to pain as demonstrated by the "hypnotized" animal not reacting to painful stimuli by, say, not withdrawing its paw when pinched with forceps. But tonic rigidity is also a feature of this state, and as Steiniger (1936) years ago thoughtfully pointed out, the reason the animal does not respond to the stimulation could be that, although it does experience pain, it is paralyzed! Unfortunately, animals cannot talk, and we cannot readily know which alternative is correct. However, there also are now a number of reports, such as that of Stephen (1968), indicating that supposedly surgically anesthetized human patients have had to undergo rather painful experiences while being unable to communicate this fact at the time and while not showing any reflex signs of pain either. If the patients had communicated pain while still showing no pain reflexes, the anesthesiologist and surgeon would surely not have discounted the reports because the reflexes were missing. Yet, this is exactly what has happened in reverse when investigators who label themselves skeptics (Weitzenhoffer, 1963a) have observed physiological changes characteristically associated with pain also occurring in hypnotized subjects who had received suggestions of analgesia and who reported no pain. These skeptics have denied the reality of the suggested analgesia. Curiously and paradoxically, these same investigators have obviously been quite willing to accept reports of experienced pain at face value, for how else would they have known that physiological "objective" signs were valid indicators?

I would like to propose in this connection that (1) leaving out all questions of meaning, verbal utterances that are consistently and repeatedly elicited from a subject under controlled conditions have the same validity as, say, bar-pressing to a flash of light or salivating to the sound of a bell in conditioning experiments; (2) if there is a consensus by observers regarding the meaning to be ascribed to these verbal utterances, this meaning is a valid datum, too.

Consciousness and Altered
States of Consciousness

With this statement of my position regarding the scientific status of consciousness and related matters, I shall now present some thoughts about them to serve as background for a later discussion relating hypnotism and consciousness. These thoughts have largely been a product of my frustration and despair of finding in the extant literature any satisfactory answers to three basic questions: What is consciousness? What is an altered state of consciousness? And, more specifically, how do we determine the existence of either one? I must emphasize that these thoughts are not meant to be a theory. Also, in the space of one chapter, I shall not be able to do more than give the gist of these thoughts, with a minimum of documentation.

Consciousness is a highly personal, private experience, but one about which we can communicate meaningfully. Yet, in the final analysis, it is clear that I can know directly only of my own consciousness, and only indirectly of yours and others'. I know of others' consciousness primarily through two sources: (1) my conclusion that since you and I and others are built alike and function alike, we most likely share the experience of consciousness, too; and (2) communications from others that support this conclusion, in particular, their own assertion that they are conscious. It seems to me there is something remarkable about this ability we have to communicate consciousness. At times it is as though there were some sort of associated direct apprehension of the presence of this condition in others through channels other than our usual senses. If I were to seek for evidence of extrasensory perception, I would be inclined to look for it in this area.

Since it is my consciousness that I know best, it is to it that I first turn for data. I ask myself, "How do I know that I am conscious?" The answer, Descartes' famous dictum, *Cogito ergo sum*, comes to mind. Although he may have said this more in an effort to assure himself of his existence, it seems to me it was also an assertion regarding his consciousness. In any event, with a slight modification it can serve this purpose. I would, therefore, rephrase the above to "I am aware of thinking; therefore, I am conscious; therefore, I exist."

Going a step further in this self-examination, I note my experience of consciousness is instantaneous and immediate, and really does not depend upon my having thoughts about it or any thoughts in particular. I experience, and that is the essence of my consciousness, just as I experience my existence of the moment directly, without having to deduce it. There is no deductive or inductive process evident. I know, I apprehend, my consciousness in a most direct manner.

I experience many things. These many experiences form the content of my consciousness, and one of the distinctive aspects of consciousness is the fact that the experience of consciousness itself is part of this content. Although the pure, primitive, raw experience of "self" might be identified with this aspect, I am of the opinion that what we usually refer to as the experience of self or self-consciousness is something more elaborate. The content of consciousness varies continuously. Normally, its basis includes the ongoing impulses from exteroceptors and interoceptors, the activity of those neural elements that are responsible for mnemonic material, and the activity of those elements responsible for thoughts.

Also, as I conceive it, the very overall, ongoing activity of the nervous apparatus itself provides a content of sort. This activity creates a background "noise," something akin to the retinal self-light, and is the basis for an elementary, unstructured, experience of consciousness. When, and only when, even this content is lacking, then there is lack of consciousness, that is, unconsciousness. This experience should be distinguished from amnesic experiences.

Consciousness with variable content and lapses of consciousness seem to me to be the two most basic and only clear-cut experiences we have with regard to consciousness.

To speak of "altered states of consciousness" has become quite the vogue. The idea seems to be that some individuals, possibly all individuals, can at times be "conscious," yet not conscious as they "normally" are (Tart, 1975). To me it seems preferable to take altered states of consciousness also as an undefined term of the universe of discourse. But perhaps something more definite can be said if one takes a closer look at some of these presupposed altered states.

To start, one might note that although the literature does contain allusions to consciousness other than our normal consciousness, the more usual view is that of alterations of, presumably, one and only one consciousness. This last view probably comes closest to the true state of affairs—at least from the subject's standpoint. When one begins to inquire of oneself and others what it is that serves as the basis for saying consciousness has been altered or that one is in some other state of consciousness, besides just a raw feeling of change, one finds evidence that it is the content of consciousness that is experienced as change and little else.

For instance, consider sleep and, more particularly, the dream state, which presumably is a universal experience and which is viewed today as being an altered state of consciousness. How is this condition different from normal, waking consciousness, insofar as the dreamer is concerned? Quite clearly, when we dream we are conscious and can even be quite sharply so. The main change we experience seems to be in the content of our consciousness. It is true that there are other changes. For instance, the source of the content is primarily internal. The thought processes, especially those involved with judgment, reality testing, and decision making, also show changes. These, however, are features that we, as observers, may be able to point out, but that are not experienced as such by the dreamer. With, possibly, the exception of those rare instances when a dreamer recognizes in his dream that he is dreaming, the dreamer in general has no particular awareness of being in a different state of consciousness. He is not even particularly conscious of the content of his consciousness having been altered, even less so of functioning differently than usual. In brief, he does not experience himself as being differently conscious. Any statement he may make regarding an alteration of consciousness is always post facto and very much influenced by factors extraneous to the dream situation.

Of course, we should not disregard evidence of changes in the thought processes, in the degree of reality testing, and so on, as other possible independent different bases for speaking of an alteration in consciousness. It could be that content is only one of many dimensions characterizing consciousness. On the other hand, one also should not overlook the possibility that such other changes as we, the observers, conclude to have taken place may have a different interpretation. They may simply reflect the change in content just referred to. It is easy to conclude, for instance, that a dreamer's thought processes are alogical and even illogical, when actually they have been quite logical, considering the kind of information available to the dreamer's consciousness. For example, when I was about 13, I dreamed of being killed by someone putting a gun to my head and shooting me. There was no pain, no physical experience of any kind, or any change in my feeling of being. I remember thinking in my dream, more in a reflective manner than with surprise, "So, this is what it is like to die—nothing changes." I cannot say with any certainty what my expectations in the waking state would have been at that time with regard to what I would have experienced if thus shot. I seriously doubt that they would have concurred with the dream experience, my perception of waking reality being at variance with that of the dream reality even then. Yet, in retrospect, I find the events of the dream were basically logical. Never having been shot nor having died before, what else could I have experienced? Nothingness? In what shape? For how long? I feel I experienced nothing different simply because there was no basis for me to experience anything else, and that was, indeed, the most logical outcome under the circumstances. In other words, the basic stuff dreams are made of can only be the accumulated waking experiences of an individual. Nothing new can be created, only new organizations or structures. However, it would not have been any less logical had I gone on to experience myself in Heaven, Hell, or Purgatory, on some other planet, or in some other dimension, according to what might have become available for content and what particular other determinants of my dream content and structure had been active. As a sort of postscript, let me add that a case was reported to me some years ago of a man who had attempted suicide by shooting himself in the head. Although the bullet had penetrated his skull, he suffered minimal injury, apparently not even losing consciousness, and apparently experiencing so little of a physical nature that he thought he had missed his head until he became aware of the blood coming from his wound! Indeed, was my dream alogical or illogical? Clearly, whether or not a dream is logical depends on the premises with which we start and what kinds of data we have.

Grounds for speaking of altered states of consciousness have also included such data as reports by drugged and hypnotized individuals that their vision is blurred, that objects seem to be in a fog, that the light in the room has dimmed, that objects seem unreal, and so forth. There are also reports of body-image distortions. Regarding these, we should first note that, once again, we are talking about a change in the content of consciousness from which, at best, a change in consciousness itself might be inferred, unless we arbitrarily identify consciousness with its content. Second, at least in the case of hypnosis, the blurring appears to be a transitory condition that can be understood from the fact that the external visual apparatus is affected by the procedures used to induce hypnosis (Weitzenhoffer, 1971a) in ways that might well be expected to lead to visual distortions. One may get similar results for near and not-so-near objects by looking at infinity (out in space) and thereby appear in a trance, or putting on a friend's glasses. Since I doubt that in the latter cases one would seriously advocate speaking of an alteration in consciousness having occurred, I question the validity of doing so in the other instances just discussed, without a closer look at what actually lies behind the experiences. The case of hypnosis supports this position.

The reported unreal quality of objects is difficult to analyze because subjects are usually unable to specify much more than this. Possibly, it denotes a true change in consciousness, but maybe not. We do know that certain drugs, such as barbiturates, have a descending depressive action on the central nervous system. Something of this sort seems to occur during natural sleep, too, although not usually in an orderly, continuous, sequential fashion. We can speculate with some legitimacy that vision might become less distinct, that light stimulation might become less effective as neural transmission, neural excitability, and other aspects of the processing of visual stimuli are depressed by barbiturates. Thus, if half of the synapses— or half of the neurons normally excited by a given light intensity— become decommissioned, we would expect that a lesser intensity— hence, a dimming—of light might be experienced, even though the light had not changed. In the area of audition, we would expect pitch to be affected, that is, if the volley theory is valid. This is not to say that such changes as the above might not be associated with other alterations that are the basis for a concurrent change in consciousness, but the visual fogging would still have to be viewed as just that and not as a fogging of consciousness. If vision is fogged at the level of the lens by a cataract, we certainly do not think in terms of alterations of consciousness. I question that we are more entitled at this stage of our knowledge in doing so just because the source of the fogging is the brain.

If it is reasonable to posit that the cerebral processing of retinal impulses can be altered by drugs, blows on the head, sleep, and possibly, by suggestion, it is also reasonable to posit the strong possibility that other effects on the central nervous system can cause alterations of processes basic to the cognitive functions and to consciously determined behavior in general. Whether or not we should say these effects also directly affect consciousness per se is another matter.

These remarks lead me to say a few words regarding the evidence from recent so-called state-dependent learning studies. On first examination, the reported data would seem to offer strong evidence for the existence of more than one state of consciousness—until one examines more closely what is involved in learning, recall, and related phenomena. Whether or not consciousness is altered, retrieval may be appreciably affected if the psychophysiological conditions existing at the time of acquisition were appreciably different from those existing at the time of retrieval. A mechanism for this, discussed in terms of a Hullian model, will be found in an article of mine (1954, 1955) written about the effects of hypnosis upon learning and recall.

Assuredly, we could identify consciousness with its content, and any change in its content would carry with it the alteration of consciousness. Or we could identify consciousness with reality testing, and any alterations in reality testing would thereby constitute an alteration in consciousness. But, can we rightfully assert that the very young child, whose reality testing we can all agree is quite different from that of an adult or from that which he will exhibit later on, is any less conscious than an adult? Certainly the child experiences the world differently. His imaginary playmates may be extremely real. His world may be peopled with very real goblins. For him, wishing and doing may be undifferentiated. But to say on any of these accounts that his consciousness is different must be questioned.

We could go on in this vein. I feel the point has been made. I will however, report that I have gone on to examine other facets of altered consciousness, with essentially the same kinds of results. Change in content consistently comes up as a dominant feature, and other recorded changes are consistently found not to be pathognomonic of altered consciousness except by fiat.

With new tools and techniques becoming available and our knowledge in other areas expanding, this picture may change in the future. To me, these observations suggest that, possibly, consciousness is an all-or-none phenomenon. Either we are conscious or we are not. Qualitative and quantitative aspects are not intrinsic to it, but instead, are superimposed. Consciousness has variable content, but content is not consciousness. It merely dresses it up, shapes it. I am also inclined to view consciousness as an emergent phenomenon, a concept going back to Broad (1951) that has since had both adherents and detractors, Turner (1965), Sperry (1969), and Eccles (1976) being among the most recent writers to make use of it. Speaking for myself, I understand by "emergent property" a property that grows out of or is an expression of the existence of a certain configuration of interactions between certain elements. It depends for its existence upon there being specific elements and upon these interacting in specific ways. It is, therefore, a product of structure and composition, and might be said to be a superordinate property or manifestation. In this context, consciousness is then to be seen as a manifestation of certain constellations of active neurons interacting in certain ways. One can find many counterparts of this in the physical world. The properties of stereoisomers seem a case, as are those forces in the nuclei of atoms known as exchange forces. Although this model is open to the possibility that a unique subassembly of neurons (center) must be part of the overall system before consciousness can be present, this may or may not be the case. I use the term "system" in its mathematical sense: a set of elements possessing a structure.

As for the role of special centers, it has been postulated by Eccles (1973, 1976) that language is an essential element of consciousness. This being the case, the neural subsystem that makes language possible would have to be one of the elements of the overall system out of which consciousness emerges. There can be no question that communication is essential for our knowledge of the consciousness of others. I do not see, however, that it must follow that only those organisms or only those parts of an organism which can communicate with us have consciousness. I suspect that behind this notion to the contrary lies a confounding of the process of thinking with language. As adult human beings we are wont to think in words. However, thinking can be partly or completely wordless and entirely in terms of sensory imagery. At the start of this section, I referred to Descartes' *Cogito ergo sum*. Without language, he certainly would not have been able to make this statement. It is difficult to see how he could even have reflected on this issue. On the other hand, he could still have pictured himself going for a walk, reexperienced previous olfactory, visual, and other sensory experiences associated with this act, and, thereby, "thought" about taking a walk, without benefit of words. Thus, as I see it, language provides consciousness with a richer content, one that includes many possible levels of abstraction. It certainly adds a unique dimension to consciousness, but I question that its lack prohibits consciousness. I am not even convinced that communication about consciousness is absolutely essential to our apprehension or inference of consciousness in other organisms, although I admit that for purposes of scientific inquiry it seems an essential tool. We can only speculate about the consciousness or lack of consciousness of the left hemisphere in split brain cases, or about its presence or absence in animals and plants.

The Domain of Hypnotism

Hypnotism is an outgrowth of mesmerism and, more particularly, of the discovery by de Puységure in 1785 that some individuals, when mesmerized, appeared to pass into a state of sleep not unlike that exhibited by individuals in a state of natural somnambulism—thence, its designation as artificial or magnetic somnambulism. We owe the term *hypnotism* to James Braid, who, in 1841, also demonstrated that upward, visual fixation on a small, relatively near, bright object seemed sufficient to bring about mesmeric sleep. A further contribution of his was his gathering of data pointing the way to the attribution of most hypnotic (hence, mesmeric) phenomena to the effects of suggestion. I say "further" because there are more than just hints of this in an earlier report on mesmerism by Bailly (1784). Other writers of this era may also have alluded to suggestion effects but it would seem that credit for openly propounding that suggestion was the basis of all hypnotic phenomena must go, first, to Liébeault (1889) and especially his collaborator Bernheim, who succinctly stated his thesis in the dictum, "There is no hypnotism, there is only suggestion" (1917). Most often, this statement has been misunderstood to mean Bernheim did not believe in a hypnotic state. But as I have shown elsewhere (Weitzenhoffer, in press) there can be little question that although Bernheim believed suggestion brought hypnosis about, he also believed hypnosis was an authentic, induced physiological condition, quite like natural sleep.

Since 1886, when Bernheim wrote his first and most influential work, a gradual and subtle, but radical, change in the definition of hypnotic somnambulism and suggestion has occurred that, in my opinion, has led many members of the scientific community to view hypnotism quite differently, without ever realizing this has happened. In brief, hypnotism in our time is not what it was in Bernheim's time (in 1886), nor has it been for many years. This is a serious matter because many investigators of hypnotism have been led to examine something quite other than what Bernheim, his contemporaries, and his predecessors studied and wrote about. For this reason, I have felt obliged since 1970 to distinguish between *classical hypnotism* and *modern hypnotism*. I believe a great deal of the controversy, the ambiguities, and especially the lack of real progress characterizing twentieth-century hypnotism research can be ascribed to the above situation. The pertinence of these observations to the topic of this chapter is obvious. What we can say about hypnotism in its relation to consciousness may well depend upon what we hold hypnotic phenomena to be. As we are beginning to see here, we may have to look at two apparently different sets of data. The situation is, in fact, appreciably more complex.

The Meaning and Nature of Suggestion

The term *suggestion* has a colloquial and a related technical meaning. We are concerned with the technical meaning. The first clear and detailed exposition of its use in the context of hypnotic phenomena is found in Bernheim's 1886 work. There one finds that, for Bernheim and his comtemporaries, suggestion was the label for certain communications—mainly, but not exclusively, verbal—that had the following two defining characteristics:

1. They elicited *automatisms,* that is, *nonvoluntary* behavior.
2. The elicited behavior was always a *transformation* of the dominant idea or ideas contained in the communication into a more or less exact behavioral counterpart or representation.

This view of suggestion is what I have called *classical suggestion* (Weitzenhoffer, article submitted for publication). The combined features of nonvoluntariness and of a transformation with the elicited behavior constitute the *classical suggestion effect,* or suggestion-effect, for short. Both defining features are frequently masked by the wording of suggestions, which may appear as command-like, instruction-like, or even request-like communications. This, possibly, has been a factor causing modern hypnotists to stray from the above conception of suggestion. It should be emphasized that Bernheim (1947) and his contemporaries viewed the effects of suggestion as very real and as being both psychological and physiological. In particular, just as Bernheim viewed suggestions of, say, muscular rigidity as bringing about actual, visible muscular contractions, so he posited that suggestions of sleep also brought about the same actual, nonvisible, neural changes as those responsible for natural sleep. This suggested sleep was, of course, classical hypnosis.

The classical view of suggestion, which I espouse as the only reasonable one, has one certain important corollary that, I must admit, had escaped me until fairly recently, and that seems also to have escaped the attention of other researchers, including Bernheim. This is simply that one can never know a priori that a communication is or will be a suggestion, but only that it was one. One can intend a communication to be, that is, to function as, a suggestion by eliciting a suggestion-effect. But until this effect has actually taken place and the presence of its two crucial characteristics has been verified, there is no basis for speaking of a suggestion rather than of some other type of communication. I repeat, a suggestion can only be known to have been so post facto. This leads to the natural linguistic distinction between *intended suggestion* and *effective suggestion* or, simply, plain *suggestion.* It can be agreed, for the sake of brevity, that one will thus speak of communications that would function as effective suggestions.

The shift to the contemporary view of suggestion was gradual, subtle, and insidious, and grew out of efforts to apply the scientific method to hypnotism. No one individual or work can probably be held solely responsible for this shift, but it is my feeling that Hull's classical work (1933), and my own (Weitzenhoffer, 1953) did much toward firming up this view. The development shortly thereafter of the Stanford Scales by Weitzenhoffer and Hilgard (1959, 1962) and their wide acceptance led to the final wide and unfortunate acceptance in scientific circles of a conception of suggestion that essentially eliminated completely the nonvoluntary features of the classical definition as a criterion. Such forerunners as the scales developed by Davis and Husband (1931), by Friedlander and Sarbin (1938), and other earlier attempts at measuring suggestibility during the 1930s do, of course, share in this dubious honor.

I do not believe the majority of us who paved the way toward this event did so because we disagreed with Bernheim and consciously wanted to depart from the classical definition. It was more the case that, in our ardor to be scientific, we chose to rely more and more on an operational definition of suggestion, suggestibility being "measured" by specifically designated instruments, such as the Stanford Scales. Hypnotism research from about 1930 on has become increasingly perfused with measurements of suggestibility that exclude or at least ignore the defining nonvoluntary feature of classical suggestion. One consequence of this is that the data regarding suggestibility collected during this period generally confound individuals who respond nonvoluntarily to intended test-suggestions with those who respond voluntarily.

To return to the principle topic of this chapter, the relationship of hypnotic phenomena to consciousness, it can now be seen more clearly why it has been necessary to go into such details. For one thing, since volition is intimately connected with consciousness, it may make a difference for our discussion whether or not we view suggestion as eliciting nonvolitional acts. It may also make a difference whether or not we look at relevant data from hypnotism research solely guided by the results of measures ignoring the nonvoluntary factor.

Before going to the next topic, hypnosis, let us go back to the statement made earlier that the classical concept is the only reasonable one. My reason for saying this is much easier to state now than it was then. It evolves out of the fact that when one carefully examines the kinds of communications going on during the production of hypnotic behavior, one discovers there is nothing objectively distinguishable about many of the communications a hypnotist will refer to as "suggestions." I say "many" recognizing that there is at least one form of expression more likely than others, under certain conditions, to elicit a suggestion-effect. This is one that informs the subject that certain events that will take place, or are taking place, will originate, or are originating, from within him, without being of his conscious making. But there are many other forms of communications for which my statement does hold. When asked what made them suggestions, the hypnotist often will explain that he "intended" them to be so. While we can conceive and have evidence that the hypnotist's intent can and does get communicated and, hence, could play a part here, further analysis is found to lead to a dead end, and to the eventual conclusion that the definition of suggestion ultimately lies in its effects.

However, the strongest arguments for my accepting the classical definition are the results of research I undertook starting in 1970 (Weitzenhoffer, to be published). Its aim was to determine whether or not there was any basis for speaking of "ideo-motor action," a mechanism postulated by Bernheim and other earlier investigators, to account for suggested motor responses. In brief, 100 subjects were given an opportunity to respond to two modified forms of the Hands Together test-item of the Stanford Scale of Hypnotic Susceptibility, Form A (Weitzenhoffer & Hilgard, 1959, 1962). In one modification, the subjects were essentially told that their extended hands would move toward each other at a signal. In the other modification, the subjects were requested (instructed) to move their hands together. The amount of movement occurring in a fixed time interval was recorded, as well as other aspects of the response. The subjects were then asked to compare the experience of the movement of their hands in the two situations. Subsequently, the verbal responses of the subjects were submitted to a content analysis. The results of this study showed unquestionably that nonhypnotized subjects, responding to an intended suggestion, fall into two groups: (1) those who experience the classical suggestion-effect, and (2) those who do not. The difference in experience is characteristically summed up by one subject's comment: "The first time [referring to the suggestion], I did not do it . . . my hands just moved. The second time, I did it!" For those readers who may have some concern about order effects here, let me reassure them by adding that a counterbalanced design was used in this connection.

Presumably, there are neurophysiological concomitants of the suggestion-effect. Bernheim, and many others, have thought so. Jasper and Penfield (1949) and Penfield (1954) have presented evidence that voluntary motor activity is associated with a blocking of beta activity in the prefrontal areas. This suggests a potential way of checking further the existence of the suggestion-effect, the prediction being the absence or a decrease of beta blocking when it occurs. Both Jasper and Penfield gathered their data with electrodes implanted in the exposed cortex of brain surgery patients. My efforts to obtain the necessary cooperation to replicate and adapt their experiment to the present issue having met with strong opposition, I have tried to devise means of doing the same by means of scalp electrodes. After two years of effort in this direction, I have become convinced that any application of the Jasper and Penfield findings will have to be done on the open brain in some milieu more amenable to this type of work than the one I am in.

There is another promising avenue of approach here, suggested by the work of Deeke, Scheid, and Kornhuber (1969) and of Kornhuber (1973) with the "readiness potential." Here, the prediction would be that the suggestion-effect would be associated with a lessened readiness potential and even with an absence of or with some distortion of it. Since scalp electrodes can be used, the ethical-administration problems associated with research on the exposed brain are circumvented. There is, however, an instrumentation problem, as this kind of investigation requires expensive, sophisticated equipment that I do not have.

The "Power" of Suggestion

In Bernheim's view, suggestion effects come about through the elicitation of ideo-dynamic action. Briefly, the theory here is that there exists a mechanism in everybody whereby (left unimpeded by the higher cortical processes frequently subsumed under the heading of the executive or ego functions) ideas lead to direct, immediate, reflex-like corresponding behavior. According to whether the evoked response is motoric or sensory, Bernheim also wrote of ideo-motor and ideo-sensory action. Feeling that the affective system can also be thus activated, I add to this list ideo-affective action. Bernheim was not the only one to use those terms. William James (1950) did so at length and, before Bernheim, William B. Carpenter (1852, 1880) did, too, being probably the first one to specifically use the expression "ideo-motor action" in this context. It was also in about this same period that Chevreul was calling Ampere's attention to this very same phenomenon. All of these investigators were of the firm opinion that suggestion-effects reflected a basic property of the human nervous system in the same way as, say, Pavlovian conditioning does. Whatever theory one may hold here, the phenomenology of suggestion leads to the postulate that the human organism has a substrate for many simple to highly complex automatisms, that is, behaviors that need not be voluntarily initiated or even come to conscious awareness, or that, when initiated voluntarily, can go on independent of further volitional control. These automatisms may be as simple as the experience of an unstructed flash of light, or a jerk of a finger, or consist of the most complex behavior imaginable. Theoretically, and as uncritically reported in the literature, the possibilities are awesome as well as extraordinary, because whatever the idea communicated by the suggestion is, it would seem to be capable of setting into motion a corresponding automatism.

Tested in the laboratory, the power of suggestion has indeed been shown to be both remarkable and not so remarkable. I reviewed the data in 1953 and again in 1959. As I view the state of the art today, I do not see the overall picture I presented then as appreciably changed. There is evidence for and against the notion that suggestion has remarkable powers. Probably, the truth lies somewhere in between. On the whole, the trend in contemporary hypnotism research has been to report results going against the reality of the many extraordinary, if not marvelous, effects that earlier writings described and that are still popular beliefs. In light of the confusion existing as to what is meant by a suggestion and by hypnosis, modern laboratory findings should be taken with a grain of salt. By the same token, one should not take all earlier research at face value. There is such a thing as healthy skepticism. Furthermore, the effort to test the so-called reality or authenticity of suggested phenomena has frequently led investigators to perform experiments that could not possibly shed light on the issue and to introduce procedures bound to lead to negative results. For instance, in view of the known neurophysiology of the pupillary reflex action to light and, also, of nystagmus induced by rotation, it is highly improbable that a suggested blindness or a suggested hallucination of being whirled in a Dunlap chair could have any effect on these phenomena. Yet, it has been the recorded presence of the pupillary reflex and the absence of rotatory nystagmus that has been used by modern writers as clear-cut evidence that induced blindness and hallucinated rotation are not real!

For details I will refer the reader to two previous works of mine in which this analysis has been carried further (Weitzenhoffer, 1971b, 1974a). What few people realize is that the behavior of a highly suggestible subject is rarely, if ever, fully determined only by the suggestions, instructions, and requests made to him. There is usually considerable place for his own elaborate contributions to his response. Characteristically, the subject faced with the effects of a suggestion, but not told how he is to react to it, will then follow his own inclinations. The latter will depend on a great many factors, including some other rather subtle suggestion-effects and his previous experiences with suggestions. Behavior following a suggestion is frequently a mixture of a suggested effect and the natural reaction of the subject to the suggested effect. Thus, a subject may indeed see and hear a suggested roaring lion charging him as a suggested effect. Whether he runs, cowers in abject terror, stands there watching with a smile, or finally does nothing may all be determined by personal and other factors having nothing to do with the suggestion, being in some cases consciously and voluntarily determined behavior and in some cases a natural reflex act. Inexperienced investigators of hypnotic-suggestive phenomena are prone to be unaware of this, with unfortunate consequences for their research and, especially, their conclusions. In this connection, I will mention one other feature. I call it the "principle of best approximation" (Weitzenhoffer, 1953). This is not a true and tested scientific principle but more a rule of thumb based on informal observations on my part. If a highly suggestible individual is unable to produce the exact behavior called for, he will usually produce that which is his best approximation. But, because it is an approximation, it may frequently lack authenticity in the eyes of the observer, who will then judge the suggestion-effect pretended. Thus, told there is a vase on the table in front of him, a subject may see it quite vividly but, when told to pick it up and examine it, may not have the corresponding tactile sensations, and his manipulation of the vase will appear a pretense.

I am of the opinion today, as I was in 1953, that suggestions can bring about remarkable effects in highly suggestible individuals, including physiological changes. I believe the failure of modern scientific methods to substantiate this more fully lies, in large part, in the approach behavioral scientists have taken. At worst, modern behavioral laboratories have not unambiguously shown that the many remarkable phenomena ascribed to suggestion by the early literature cannot be produced. It is worth noting in this connection that the disparity that exists regarding the kinds of suggested manifestations clinicians seem to obtain when using suggestion techniques and those manifestations occurring in laboratories can readily be understood in terms of the fact that clinicians are not encumbered by the limitations the scientific method imposes on what they can produce.

Hypnosis

One of the most important controversies in the field of hypnotism regards "hypnosis." Is there a state of hypnosis or not? And, if there is one, just what is it? We saw earlier that hypnosis is merely a label initially substituted for such expressions as "artificial somnambulism," "induced somnambulism," "lucid sleep," and other terms. Essentially, these expressions aim to indicate that the presumed condition in question shows the characteristics of both sleep and waking. Alas, when in due time the acid test of physiological measurements was applied, it became evident that sleep was one thing hypnosis was not. Indeed, it was found indistinguishable from normal wakefulness. This initially shocking finding is really not surprising when one recognizes the fact that, with respect to overall intellectual functioning and in many other ways, the hypnotized person is essentially unchanged. Given the right instructions and permissions, he is capable of carrying out the same activities as when not hypnotized. This suggests that a relatively intact nervous system is present and that what happens physiologically, assuming hypnosis is a real state, is such that the use of scalp electrodes, even supplemented by signal averagers and spectrum analyzers, is too crude a method to detect any underlying changes. I am convinced, after a great deal of work of this nature, that only by using cortically and subcortically implanted electrodes are we likely to elucidate this further. My own efforts to secure the necessary cooperation to do this unfortunately have had the same fate as my efforts to study the suggestion-effect in brain surgery cases.

Lacking this sort of information, what are the arguments for talking about hypnosis, and what can we say regarding its nature and its relationship to consciousness? It can safely be said that, from at least Bernheim on, hypersuggestibility—or, more precisely, an associated increase in suggestibility—has been used as a major criterion of hypnosis. This feature had actually been recognized much earlier by de Puységure in connection with his discovery of artificial somnambulism, and was singled out by such researchers and practitioners as Bertrand (1826) and Despine (1880). It remained for Hull and his co-workers to formally demonstrate, in the 1930s, the occurrence of this enhancement in a limited situation. What Hull's laboratory did was to show this enhancement in the case of suggestibility for one specific intended suggestion (1933). The laboratory demonstration that this was a much more general effect was done by Weitzenhoffer and Sjoberg (1958). Our findings were replicated by Barber and Glass (1962), still later by Andersen and Sarbin (1964), and finally by Hilgard and Tart (1966). Although the Barber and Sarbin groups placed somewhat different interpretations upon the reasons for enhancement, the fact was well demonstrated, even though still on an appreciably smaller scale than that existing in practice outside the laboratory. As some readers will guess, their interpretation was that, while the procedures had led to an enhancement, it could and should be ascribed to other factors than hypnosis.

In addition to hypersuggestibility, a number of other characteristic features were originally associated with artificial somnambulism, and later with hypnosis. Some of these, as originally listed by Bertrand (1823) have been discussed elsewhere (Weitzenhoffer, 1963b). I will mention only two more. First there is a reported increase in vicarious (through the hypnotist) volitional control by the subject of functions ordinarily not accessible to voluntary control by either hypnotist or subject. For instance, changes in heart rate by direct effort of will are not normally observed, but there are reliable reports that suggestions of rate changes can be effective in the hypnotic state. Second, there are reports by presumably hypnotized subjects of experiencing an inner change. This has usually been interpreted as indicating the occurrence of an altered state of consciousness.

There also exists a more comprehensive set of so-called objective clinical signs of hypnosis that many hypnotists use. This list (Weitzenhoffer, 1953, 1974a) includes such features as fixity of gaze (trance stare), tonic immobility, psychomotor retardation, and others. Some of these "symptoms" have been verified in the laboratory, for instance by study of spontaneous eye movements and rate of blinking (Weitzenhoffer, 1969, 1971a). Others remain to be thus examined. In the meantime, it should be clearly kept in mind that these are transitory features that usually give way to other manifestations brought about by the very actions the subject is called upon to exhibit. For example, while it is indubitable that the inactive hypnotized subject whose eyes are open will tend to exhibit considerable reduction of saccadic eye movements, particularly when first hypnotized, any subsequent instruction or suggestion that calls for utilization of his visual apparatus will obliterate this feature. Certain signs, furthermore, must be seen as resulting from the kinds of suggestions, and even instructions, given to the subjects in the course of inducing hypnosis. They are, thus, basically, induced artifacts. For instance, one is more likely to observe increased alpha production as a consequence of the subject's being instructed to relax, and especially of his closing his eyes, whether or not he enters a hypnotic state. The entire traditional sleep of hypnotized subjects seems a by-product of the suggestions, as is the actual sleep in which the induction may culminate (Weitzenhoffer, 1953). This is not to say that procedures causing these features are not useful, but it is a caution not to read more into their occurrence than there is. Failure to do so can only lead to ambiguity and controversy, as it clearly already has. Hypnosis has a protean quality of which one must beware.

In the light of these observations, it is understandable that researchers, and hypnotists, have turned to "hypersuggestibility" as the criterion of hypnosis par excellence. Unfortunately, in their zeal to utilize it, the majority have overlooked an important issue: Hypersuggestibility has meaning only if a comparison is made between two conditions of suggestibility. Therefore, as I have repeatedly pointed out (Weitzenhoffer, 1963, 1974b; Weitzenhoffer & Sjoberg, 1958), it has come to pass (and this goes back at least to Hull) insofar as scientific hypnotism is concerned, that, invariably, subjects are "hypnotized," their suggestibility then and only then measured, and this measure is then used as an index of how "deeply" hypnotized they are. It never seems to occur to the hypnotist that possibly there has not been any increase in suggestibility, and that from this standpoint alone, there is no reason to believe the subject is at all hypnotized! That even appreciably suggestible subjects exposed to an induction may not show an increase was well demonstrated by myself and Sjoberg (1958) with replications by others (Andersen & Sarbin, 1964; Barber & Glass, 1962; Hilgard & Tart, 1966). But this is really old stuff. Bernheim emphatically pointed out as far back as 1886 not only that many individuals show appreciable suggestibility without benefit of any induction of hypnosis, but that this suggestibility may be as great as that seen in some of the best hypnotized subjects; and that while many subjects (even those who are otherwise appreciably suggestible) show an enhancement following an induction of hypnosis, there are also those who do not. From the standpoint of research on hypnotic phenomena, other than the state of hypnosis itself, this last is probably of no great import because, quite clearly, and going back at least to Braid, it is suggestibility and not hypnosis per se that has been the topic of interest. Indeed, had it not been for suggestibility, interest in hypnotism would probably long ago have become merely academic, for suggestions are used to produce hypnosis, and suggestions are used to produce all of the other phenomena of hypnotism. Why, then, bother to hypnotize? Well, simply because an induction-of-hypnosis procedure does appear to lead to greatly enhanced suggestibility. Obviously, if one's aim is to utilize a person's suggestibility, it makes sense to maximize it first.

If the laboratory has not told us much about what hypnosis is, it has given us one important bit of information. In my 1970 study (Weitzenhoffer, to be published), all subjects who had participated were also invited to go through the same procedure after being hypnotized. (For the research-oriented reader, let me add that half of the subjects went through the hypnotic phase first and the non-hypnotic one next; for the other half, this order was reversed.) The results were most revealing. They not only showed again the existence of a suggestibility enhancement, often appreciable, but the investigation showed this enhancement to affect the subject specifically at the level of volitional control, that is, at the level of his automatisms. What was enhanced was his capacity to respond non-voluntarily, not just his willingness or proneness to respond in general. Furthermore, and much to my surprise and that of my assistants, conclusive evidence accrued serendipitously that, with hypnotized subjects, intended instructions and requests frequently function as suggestions, also eliciting nonvoluntary behavior (Weitzenhoffer, 1974b). Thus, as observed earlier, the determination of which communications are to be called suggestions can only be done properly post facto.

Whether or not the transformational aspect of the suggestion-effect is also directly affected, presumably positively, is not clear. This may be more of an indirect effect from the increased automatism.

In any event, these findings on the effects of the induction of hypnosis on the suggestion-effect are in keeping with Bernheim's writings, which I feel are representative of the consensus of his era. They constitute the essence of that which I have called the classical hypnosis effect (hypnosis-effect, for short), namely, the enhancement of classical suggestibility through action at the level of an increased lessening of volitional participation or, perhaps better, a spreading of automatism. There may be other effects, but this seems to be the crucial one.

We saw earlier how failure to take automatism into account in determining the effectiveness of intended suggestions may have led to serious confoundings in hypnotism research. How serious it may be can now be seen when one realizes that the presence of suggestibility has been extensively used to decide whether a person was or was not hypnotized. Furthermore, the degree of suggestibility, as measured by the number and types of intended suggestions receiving responses, and the amount and quality of the responses have also been used extensively to determine the so-called depth of hypnosis. I need not elaborate this point further. If this is not enough, there is more. Remember that researchers, including myself, have quite universally failed to take into account that the earmark of classical hypnosis was also an increase, a change, a difference, in suggestibility—not just the presence of suggestibility, no matter how high. There is a saving grace here in that very high suggestibility more often than not is associated with hypnosis, if one may speak of hypnosis. Hence, the assumption that highly suggestible subjects who have undergone an induction of hypnosis are hypnotized in the classical sense is often justified. Not so with those subjects who show lesser degrees of suggestibility.

With the strong likelihood that a double confounding has been introduced into the scientific study of hypnotism since Bernheim, and particularly in the past twenty-five to thirty years, it is no small wonder that 204 years after it all started (if we take Mesmer as the starting point), we still do not know who will be hypnotizable and who will not be, or even who will or will not be suggestible, without putting a person to the actual test; nor are we any nearer to understanding why they are or are not. Small wonder that we remain as uncertain today about the reality of the many phenomena described in the literature as we were twenty-five years ago, when I summarized the existing facts in my *Hypnotism: An Objective Study in Suggestibility* (1953).

Let us go one step further in this effort to elucidate what it is we are talking about under the label *hypnosis*. Hypnotism proper began with the discovery of artificial somnambulism. Modern hypnotists still speak of somnambulism in connection with hypnotism, but do so rather questionably. They perceive hypnosis as lying on a continuum measured in terms of suggestibility, the suggestibility of a hypnotized subject also being his depth of hypnosis. Arbitrarily, they have agreed that any individual who falls in the higher ranges of these so-called scales of hypnotic depth or susceptibility will be said to have reached a somnambulist stage or state, or to be in a hypnotic somnambulism. This is reasonable enough, for only those subjects who possess the highest suggestibility can come anywhere near producing the kinds of phenomena that have been associated with classical artifical somnambulism (classical hypnosis). But it is my opinion that relatively few individuals classified as somnambules on the basis of modern scientific criteria are so in the classical sense. The true classical type of somnambule is not particularly abundant, at least has not been in the last thirty or so years. Were they more abundant in earlier days? Perhaps not. But I do not want to go into an issue here that is not really relevant to our discussion. What is relevant is that for one more reason we must seriously question that scientific hypnotism, as viewed, used, and studied in at least the last thirty years in the United States, is at all that which we read about in the older literature. This is not to say that classical somnambulism is not encountered in the practice and study of modern hypnotism. Of course, it still occurs, but it is confounded with all sorts of other manifestations, which might be better summed up under the heading of states of heightened suggestibility, or better still, suggestion states, as Bernheim himself advocated.

Although classical somnambulism is characteristically associated with greatly enhanced suggestibility, it appears to involve something more that I cannot precisely specify. In any case, whatever it is, classical somnambulism seems to occur much more as a quantum jump than as a step or range of steps on a continuum of suggestibility. There are strong indications in many of the classical works on hypnotism of Bernheim's era, including his own, that we may be looking here at two or more kinds of conditions associated, in part, with heightened suggestibility. There are also indications that perhaps one should really think plurally in terms of various suggestibilities, but in another sense than the one in which this has been done in modern times and as described in a number of available texts (Barber, 1969; Hilgard, 1965; Weitzenhoffer, 1953).

There are two other aspects of hypnosis as a state to which we need to return before we can go on to our final topic. There are many reports suggesting that with classical somnambules (and also with nonsomnambules who, nevertheless, have a high degree of hypnotic suggestibility), it is possible to bring about physiological and psychological changes in a controlled fashion otherwise not available to control. This has usually been taken as evidence and as a measure of their greater suggestibility. There is, however, an alternative way of looking at this, also suggested by existing data, that instead of reflecting greater suggestibility, it is a reflection that certain channels of control have become available, suggestibility having little to do with it directly. For instance, one might understand the reported control of heart rate by hypnotized subjects instructed to do so as being a result of the lifting of a neural blocking normally present and preventing direct cortical control. Similarly, with so-called suggested hypermnesia. The latter could result from other types of blocks being lifted, or dissolved, or from neural changes associated with the induction of hypnosis temporarily making new pathways available. In brief, I am speaking of hypnosis as a state facilitating certain processes independently of any suggestion-effects, these processes then becoming available and adding their effects to any suggestion-effect. This is a dimension of hypnosis that has unfortunately not been touched upon to any degree.

The other feature I want to go back to is the experience of hypnosis. There are strikingly consistent reports by presumably hypnotized individuals that they experience a definite change when they are hypnotized. It is a change that many experience at the instant of passing into the state. It is described sometimes as similar to the flipping of a switch. Unless given some help by the experimenter, these subjects usually have difficulty in finding appropriate words to describe the experience. It is truly indescribable. Few subjects initially ascribe depth or degree to it, although they may describe its quality as varying. They may speak in terms of degree about other experiences they have concurrently with that of hypnosis, but this is clearly something else. It is true that in the course of time most subjects, perhaps all, come to ascribe depth to their experience of hypnosis. I suspect this is largely an artifact introduced by the hypnotist's usual insistence on depth being present, although it could be that hypnosis does have depth, and that it takes a while for most subjects to acquire the ability to estimate it. Here, again, one must be wary of the insidious effects unwitting suggestions, instructions, and communicated information have upon what hypnotized subjects experience and come to believe. The procedure of simply asking a subject how deeply hypnotized he is, or to compare his present hypnosis for depth with a previous one, may seem quite straightforward and innocuous. However, it is full of pitfalls, as I have discussed elsewhere (Weitzenhoffer, 1960a, b), and can readily create an artifactual depth in what would otherwise be an all-or-none situation.

There are two further experiences reported by hypnotized subjects, especially those classifiable as somnambules, that are worth noting. Many subjects have great difficulty in describing how hypnosis is different from their nonhypnotic state. The more articulate express the fact that when hypnotized their mind is extraordinarily free of all material extraneous to the situation, including sensations and random thoughts. It seems to be a state of effortless concentrated attention. It is interesting that in 1841 James Braid described hypnosis as a condition of "monoideism." That and only that which is pertinent is experienced. If the situation calls for no special activity, the condition is one of concentrated attention on nothing. Thus, we see that it is content which appears to differentiate consciousness with hypnosis from consciousness without it. Recent investigative work on my part stimulated by some of the questions raised in writing this chapter is beginning to provide evidence that subjects essentially left to their own devices regarding the experience of hypnosis, indeed, do not perceive it as an altered state of consciousness as much as they perceive it as involving a change in content.

The final aspect of hypnosis I want to touch upon in this section is one that has consistently come up since the time of de Puységure. There is evidence that for highly suggestible subjects, especially those who are also hypnotized, suggestions are extremely compelling and frequently associated with a seeming desire or need to satisfy the hypnotist's demands without question. I realize this has been one of the most controversial issues in this area. The compelling feature is usually not one the subject normally experiences and, therefore, can report upon. In order for it to appear, it is necessary for the response to the suggestion to be impeded from within or from outside the subject. Only then can the subject experience this compelling quality. Thus, the subject must first oppose the suggested effect in order to experience its force. Similarly, the experimenter is not likely to observe evidence of this aspect unless impediments to the carrying out of the suggestion are introduced.

Suggestion, hypnosis, and hypnotic phenomena per se have been the main topic of this section. In the next section, we will turn our attention more specifically to questions of consciousness as they bear upon hypnotism, and the converse.

Automatisms, Hypnotism, and Consciousness

I believe it can be safely stated that most individuals today, including even modern researchers, who speak of hypnotism still do so with the phenomenology of classical hypnotism in mind, although, admittedly, with a great deal of confusion regarding what is actually involved. Additionally, it seems to me that if hypnotism has any relevance to problems of consciousness, it is mainly when understood in the classical form. Thus, my particular emphasis upon the latter.

As thus far discussed, it is anything but clear that hypnosis constitutes an altered state of consciousness. But what of the phenomena that can be induced through intrahypnotic and extrahypnotic suggestions; that is, with suggestions given in the presence or in the absence of hypnosis? A listing of the variety of effects (Hilgard, 1965; Weitzenhoffer, 1953) one can presumably produce shows a majority of phenomena that can readily be eliminated as having no appreciable bearing upon matters of consciousness. A great many others touch on it only in the fact that they alter its content, sometimes quite appreciably, but still, consciousness per se seems to remain unaltered. However, there remain certain aspects of hypnotic behavior that do seem to have a bearing on consciousness and that go beyond the issue of mere content, at least as we have discussed it thus far.

As we saw earlier, automatisms are the essense of hypnotic phenomena. Automatisms are any segment or the whole of covert and overt behavior not experienced by the behaving individual as having been, or being, voluntarily determined by him. Since intention is intimately connected with consciousness, it would appear that here we have an area where hypnotism and consciousness may meet in a possibly fundamental way.

The study of automatisms is not simple because automatisms are usually seen enmeshed in a web of intentional behaviors. Typically, a behavior can be initiated voluntarily, but then proceeds automatically, either being self-terminating or being terminated by events outside the individual's control. On the other hand, a behavior can start at an automatic level, go on thus, but be voluntarily terminated. Many behaviors have a voluntary initiation and termination, but are otherwise automatic. These two last types of behavior are usually perceived by individuals as being voluntary, although, at best, they are only partially so.

As Bernheim emphasized, automatisms are a normal aspect of our everyday life and pervade it. Possibly, as much as ninety-nine percent of normal waking behavior takes place at an automatic level, and one might well say that automatism is the rule rather than the exception. Much of what passes in our mind as intentional behavior is only partially so, and sometimes minimally so. Examine any typical, routine activity of yours, and you will readily see that all you do volitionally is initiate it. After that, it goes on quite automatically. Frequently, it is self-terminating or terminated by external agencies, so that voluntary termination may never be involved. However, just because a behavior is an automatism does not mean it must lie outside the content of consciousness. It is, again, an important fact that once voluntarily initiated, automatisms tend to drop out of consciousness, but can usually be intentionally brought back into it, without the behavior becoming any less automatic. The individual merely observes the automatism progress, without interfering with it at the voluntary level. For many automatisms, intentional control has precedence, and one sees many activities that are a mixture of alternating segments of intentional and automatic behavior.

Automatisms can apparently be extremely complex, showing intelligence and intention-like features. They can be quite lasting. Just how complex is not clear, but there are reasons to believe that most intentional behaviors have an automatism counterpart. Stated another way, just about everything that can be done intentionally can occur as an automatism. Additionally, there are automatisms that normally cannot come under intentional control, so that the domain of automatisms is potentially wider than that of intentional behavior.

Two or more compatible automatisms can occur simultaneously and proceed independently of each other or in a coordinated manner. Similarly, voluntary and automatic behavior can coexist independent of each other. The reader will readily find examples of this in his own life. Some automatisms are innate but, for the most part, they appear to be acquired. There are several forms of acquisition generally discussed in psychology under the heading of "learning." The conversion of originally solely intentional acts into automatisms is one of the more important forms of acquisition . Acquired automatisms, especially those arising from conversion, are usually more amenable to voluntary control. Separate automatisms can become combined and integrated in a variety of ways, through such processes as chaining and branching. The more complex combinations constitute topological nets. Any eliciting and combining of existing automatisms into a new automatism may be thought of as induced automatism. Other automatisms are simply elicited, or evoked, when called forth.

Although we tend to operate automatically much of the time, conscious control can normally supersede at any time. This is particularly true in the case of interactions between two individuals where the behavior of one is the object of communications.

Suggestion in the framework of classical hypnotism is the elicitation and induction of automatisms, starting with the full regalia of potential automatisms an individual possesses. Whether it is all in the nature of ideo-dynamic action, as Bernheim (and, later, William James) viewed it, or whether there is more is not entirely clear. For the time being, we shall simply speak in terms of existing automatisms. The basic effect is that in the absence of conscious interference —and this latter is essentially the essence of intentional control— ideas elicit automatisms. Keep clearly in mind that the extent of this interference need not be great. It can consist of a brief holding back of the responses, allowing the so-called executive functions of the individual to appraise the situation and decide whether or not the automatism should be allowed to go on. I make no pretense of fully understanding what the executive apparatus involves. I will admit that, like consciousness, it is a concept that retains considerable vagueness. It is a mental apparatus, and it is a conscious one. Its functions are many, and have been sufficiently described by others (Bellak, Hurvich & Grediman, 1973; Rappaport, 1967); therefore, I do not feel I need repeat this effort. It suffices that the balance between automatism and the executive apparatus control is what seems to be most directly involved in hypnotism. The usual way of eliciting an automatism in the suggestion situation is by establishing an atmosphere conducive to the subject's allowing the suggestion-effect to occur. Some individuals are apparently able to voluntarily inhibit their executive functions and allow the automatism to occur, particularly if the automatisms are strong. Others have to be led gradually into doing this or shown how to do it. It is also possible, on occasion, to bypass the executive apparatus. This seems to have been the essence of Janet's "suggestion by distraction" (1889) and Bernheim's explanation of why suggested sleep and natural sleep, as he understood them, facilitate the suggestion-effect. In this instance, the neural mechanisms underlying the executive functions are seen as decommissioned in part or wholly by the sleep state. This notion receives support from the observed facilitating effects of subanesthetic doses of barbiturates and anesthetic agents in general and our knowledge of their pharmacological action.

What distinguishes hypnotic suggestibility in the case of classical hypnotism (hence, somnambulism) is the tremendous degree of generalization that takes place. It is not just a generalization of suggestibility, as I once put it (Weitzenhoffer, 1953), meaning by this an increase in the number of automatisms one can evoke; it is more in the nature of a shift, a changeover on the part of the subject from partial automatism to complete or near complete automatism. That is, he responds in toto or nearly so with a massive automatism. His entire behavior is now an automatism. Furthermore, I am of the opinion this is not something that necessarily gradually builds up. One gets the impression of a gradual buildup from induction techniques and the kinds of manipulations used to produce a so-called deepening of hypnosis, as well as from techniques used for training subjects to be good hypnotic subjects. What seems to happen in many cases is something best compared to the sudden mass crystalization of a supersaturated salt solution. One adds one crystal, another, and so on, with nothing happening until, all at once, as one adds the critical crystal, the whole liquid solution turns solid, or a least a large crystal conglomerate appears. Here, however, the analogy ends, because in most instances, once the mass automatization has occurred, it becomes easy to reinstate it without going back through the preliminary buildup.

With most subjects, one has to go through some sort of training session or repeated inductions. But there are some rare individuals who do not need this. This is understandable if we can conceive of some individuals perceiving from the start what is required of them and thereby making the conscious, intentional act of turning off, so to speak, their executive control, even to the extent of making its reinstatement an operation contingent upon instructions from the hypnotist. This is what I referred to in earlier writings as a voluntary abdication of the use of volition (Weitzenhoffer, 1963b, c). Of course, I am now speaking of hypnosis in its pristine form. In practice, we hardly ever see it thus because of the many ways in which we, the hypnotists, clinicians, experimenters, and subjects shape it. Hypnosis is basically extremely malleable, chameleonic; hence, the difficulties in identifying it.

Having traveled this far we now come to one of the more intriguing aspects of hypnotism. Although the discovery of the existence of the class of phenomena to be discussed goes back well before this time, physicians using hypnosis in the middle 1950s became enamored of a technique frequently called the "finger questioning technique." Although I believe its origins lie in some of the teachings of Milton H. Erickson, probably the foremost medical hypnotist of this century, its wide dissemination and use seem more attributable to two highly influential teachers of hypnotism, former students of Erickson: David B. Cheek, a physician, and Leslie M. LeCron, a psychologist. Briefly, the technique is one whereby the hypnotized subject is told to let his "unconscious" answer questions by moving various fingers to indicate "yes," "no," and "I do not know." From there to instructing the unconscious to use its supposedly marvelous "powers" to bring about cures is but a step. In short time, hypnotism sessions came to take on all of the aura of the spirit séances of the nineteenth century. The new twist was that now the hypnotist not only interacted with the subject but behaved, too, as if some other, independent, intelligent, conscious entity were present. Details of the techniques used, with a critical analysis of them and their results, will be found in two articles I wrote at the time (Weitzenhoffer, 1960a, b). One consequence was that Cheek (and, later, others) began to make fewer references to talking to the unconscious, and increasingly spoke of "ideo-motor questioning," inasmuch as I had made a pretty good case for the argument that elicited ideo-motor responses were really involved here. Otherwise, the picture remained much the same. The technique and its variations continue to be in use in medical circles. The idea of tapping the hypnotized patient's unconscious by various means was nothing new, one of the oldest and most widely used methods for this being that of induced automatic writing. What distinguished the Cheek-LeCron method from older techniques was that the hypnotist frequently behaved as though the source of information, that is, the unconscious, was an entity distinct from the conscious subject. In brief, the situation was being treated as one might treat one involving two classical co-conscious personalities.

It was probably inevitable that someone would make use of this technique for investigative purposes. It is surprising this did not take place sooner. Recently, Ernest R. Hilgard (Hilgard and Hilgard, 1976) has adapted it, with some modifications, to investigate the nature of hypnoanalgesia, speaking of "the Hidden Observer" as the informant.

Hilgard believes that by using this technique, he has evidence that hypnotized subjects function at two levels of awareness. At one level, they feel no pain when told to be anesthetic, but at another level, which can be tapped, they are very much aware of the pain. From there, Hilgard has gone on to formulate his "neo-dissociation" theory of hypnosis. Divested of modern terminology, and references to split-brain data and computer-like diagrams, this theory does not appear to be essentially different from Janet's (1925) earlier dissociation theory of hypnotic behavior, and the prefixing of neo- appears to be unjustified.

Hilgard's data, like the less-well-controlled results obtained by Cheek and LeCron, while intriguingly suggesting and exciting for the study of consciousness, may have a basic flaw. That is, the techniques used probably create the Hidden Observer as an artifact. Basically, what Hilgard does in one group of experiments is (1) to instruct the hypnotized subject he will feel no pain, and (2) to tell him there is a part of himself, of which he is unaware, that can continue to experience the pain and will report on it by means of finger signals; namely, pressing one of a number of buttons identifying the degree of pain experienced. Hilgard has used other modifications, such as automatic writing and even vocal apparatus of the subject. Although it cannot be conclusively demonstrated from Hilgard's reports that this is so, there are sufficient details available to support the tentative conclusion that, most likely, the technique induces a motor automatism that directly connects appropriate hand movements with sensory data. Simultaneously, the latter is kept from being part of the content of the subject's consciousness by another elicited sensory automatism. Agreeing with Eccles (1976) that the nature of the brain is such that the most sophisticated computer cannot approximate it, the above situation is somewhat analogous to an airplane pilot told to turn on the autopilot and who, having done so, then goes to sleep or to attend to matters other than the flight of the plane. Sophisticated autopilots not only fly planes, but can independently record just about anything and report it. I see no more of a need to introduce a Hidden Observer in connection with Hilgard's experiment than to do so in the case of the autopilot.

Although Hilgard's discussion of the Hidden Observer in terms of independently functioning multiple "cognitive structures" strongly suggests he may be thinking along lines of a co-conciousness, as yet he has not explicitly presented it as such. In any case, Hilgard's use of the Hidden Observer and the Cheek-LeCron finger technique are strongly reminiscent of earlier work done on the experimental production of multiple personalities by means of suggestions (Weitzenhoffer, 1960b). These experiments and the Creek-LeCron-Hilgard material are of obvious interest to us, inasmuch as they may be situations in which one or more consciousnesses other than the subject's have been brought into being. I say "may" because experimental production of multiple personalities are open to the same kinds of questions as I have just raised, and the exact nature of the final product remains a moot issue.

It is not that I question the existence of multiple consciousnesses in a single body. My own experiences with a few natural occurrences of multiple personalities, especially one case I have followed for over seven years, leaves no question in my mind as to their reality. The problem I have referred to lies in their experimental production and the usual naïveté of the experimenters in respect to both the intricacies of induced automatisms as well as those associated with multiple personalities per se. The creation of pseudo-multiple personalities is relatively easy, and can even be done quite unwittingly. Whether or not one can produce additional true consciousnesses on demand in any hypnotized individual is something else. The possibility is there, and equally important, there probably are individuals with such a personality structure that true multiple consciousness can be induced in them when they are hypnotized. Such individuals, I am of the opinion, might be thought of as having latent multiple personalities, and are likely to manifest them to varying degrees with very little help from the hypnotist other than his hypnotizing them.

One feature that gives particular reality to some instances of naturally occurring multiple consciousness is their very real sense of identity, of distinct self, which they communicate. The concept of self, of personal identity, takes on an altogether different dimension when viewed in this context. I believe most of us have a tendency to relate our sense of identity to the distinctness of our body from that of other individuals. Multiple consciousnesses cannot do this. Along this line, one of the most thought-provoking statements one consciousness, in a natural case of multiple personalities, has made to me has been the assertion, "I am a personality, not a person. That other one is the person." When I inquired into the distinction, it was explained to me, with some condescension, that persons have a physical body, and that this particular consciousness did not happen to have one!

Tempted as I am to speculate on the origins and nature of the self and of the sense of identity and how it relates to consciousness within the rough model I have sketched, I must forego this pleasure. It would anyway remain just that, speculation. Instead, I will go back to an earlier question: What constitutes an altered state of consciousness? More specifically, what is the basis for saying an alteration has occurred? I have stated that content appears to be the main, and possibly only, feature of consciousness that changes in so-called cases of altered consciousness. Identity is a part of that content, but it also appears of a rather different nature than other contents. Whatever the case, I would propose that if we are to speak of changes in consciousness, perhaps we ought to reserve this for instances in which the identity associated with consciousness is changed.

If we go back to the earlier issue of whether or not hypnosis is an altered state of consciousness, it is just possible we might now be able to come up with a different answer than our original one. Actually, I do not know that we can, because I lack the necessary data at this time. But consider: Traditionally, going back at least to Braid, hypnosis was associated with a subsequent spontaneous posthypnotic amnesia. Braid held it to be the sine qua non of hypnosis. Later, Bernheim emphatically made it a criterion of induced somnambulism, believing it to have a physiological basis (this in spite of the dominant role he ascribed to suggestion in the production of many other signs of hypnosis). Later researchers increasingly took the position that the amnesia was a suggested artifact and increasingly incorporated an intrahypnotic suggestion of posthypnotic amnesia in their routine as a further test of depth of hypnosis. Admittedly, it is a difficult issue to test today. For my part, I am not satisfied with the artifact theory. An amnesia may indicate, among other things, an inability to bring back into the content of consciousness something that was previously part of this content. It may also indicate that something was never available as a content to consciousness. If, as I have proposed, suggested somnambulism is a shift to a massive, overall automatism, particularly one associated with the same dropping out of normal conscious cognitive activities as are seen in dreamless sleep, is it also possible that this is accompanied by a loss of identity, of self, even of consciousness? For the most part, those reports we have of subjects' experiences in hypnosis are from individuals who do not appear to have been in a somnambulistic state. This would be the case for those who remember without help. As for those who remember because amnesia-lifting suggestions are given, not only is there ambiguity about the condition they were in, but we must also be concerned regarding unintended effects such suggestions may have had on the reports. In brief, I do not know of the existence of any satisfactory reports from somnambules regarding their actual state of mind. But here and there one gets glimpses suggesting things may be quite other than we have come to believe, and that there is an area worth further careful, sophisticated, and methodical investigation. It could turn out that hypnosis (suggested somnambulism), after all, is an altered state of consciousness by virtue of lacking the subject's normal identity, or by virtue of not being associated with any consciousness at all. Some of Janet's (1889) writings contain material suggestive of the first alternative. My own speculative inclinations are to view the general automatism constituting hypnosis as being of sufficient complexity as to be associated with an emergent consciousness, but one that is initially without identity, identity being acquired subsequently as the new consciousness is given an opportunity to function within the hypnotic state. Even then, such identity as is acquired must remain subject to the fact that the executive functions of the hypnotized individual are, at best, merged with those of the hypnotist or, at worst, have no independent existence from his.

As I pointed out earlier, the extreme malleability of the hypnotic state makes it an extremely difficult object of study. Not only is it shaped by what goes on before the induction and by the induction procedures, but it continues to be shaped by what follows. Furthermore, the subject brings into the situation many highly personal factors affecting the outcome. I have been speaking in terms of ideal conditions leading to an unadulterated form of induced somnambulism. The fact that more often than not we do not encounter this is what probably led such early investigators as Charcot, his students, and his colleagues to eventually recognize the existence of induced conditions, which they referred to as *états frustes* and *états imcomplets*. Data regarding these conditions are really insufficiently detailed to warrant any attempt to discuss them further in these pages. However, further efforts to examine hypnosis within the context of problems of consciousness ought to take them into account. I feel this is particularly important since a great many of the individuals we see hypnotized today, particularly outside of the laboratory situation, probably are individuals who develop those not-quite-somnambulistic conditions. These are individuals in whom complex automatisms can be detached from the control of their executive apparatus and externally controlled. With these individuals, the issue of identity becomes an intriguing matter because, frequently, although they retain a sense of identity, this identity does not include the elicited automatisms. Their occurrences may be part of the content of their consciousness, but only as something external to their selves. Characteristically, such a subject will comment, "I know it must be me doing it . . . but it just doesn't seem it's me!"

In brief, we have a situation here where the content of consciousness may remain intact or not, but in any case, the sense of identity is, let us say, restricted. Is this a basis for speaking also of an alteration of consciousness?

Personally, I am disinclined to do so. Some readers may feel differently, and I admit the question needs further examination.

If by now the reader feels confused about what hypnosis is, let me reassure him he is not alone. The problem seems to be largely a semantic one. If it had been recognized from the start that hypnosis was simply another term for artificial somnambulism, and if one had stuck to this by then defining hypnotism as the use of suggestions with individuals in and only in an induced state of classical somnambulism, and then gone on to perhaps follow Bernheim's idea of generally speaking of states of suggestion, probably none of the confusion would exist. I offer the reader the above consideration as one solution to his confusion.

A Final Note

It would seem most reasonable to assume that consciousness and hypnosis are mutually relevant. However, if this is the case, what appears to be the situation for the time being is that neither can illuminate the other. The overall picture suggests that by using suggestion methods one should be able to devise experiments that could throw light upon consciousness. Conversely, it seems that if we understood consciousness better we might be more in a position to elucidate the nature of suggestion phenomena. The problem is that both consciousness and suggestion states essentially remain enigmas. To say we need to study them further seems trite. Hypnotism has been a topic of intensive scientific study for over 135 years. Consciousness has been a topic of study for even longer. Perhaps the complexity of these topics is such that nothing better could have been accomplished in that period of time. Considering the advances made in other disciplines in that period, I doubt it. Speaking only of hypnotism research done during the last forty-five years, I find that much of it and the associated writings have been of low scientific caliber. There has been far more pseudoscience than science in it. Except for a small minority, investigators in this area have been on the whole a pretentious and opinionated lot, basically ignorant in spite of their academic training, and frequently poorly grounded even in their very chosen field of inquiry. They have been prone to shallow thinking, the overuse of technical jargon, the abuse of statistics, and various forms of unintentional and intentional intellectual dishonesty. They have been far more concerned with convincing others, frequently with evangelistic fervor, of their beliefs and convictions and with winning academic and professional laurels than with ascertaining the truth. In this process, they have preferred the easier and more expeditious path of selective rediscovery, replication, disconfirmation, and demonstrations of the obvious, the already-known, and the inconsequential to the more arduous path of judicious building upon past findings. I am also led to reflect that what an investigator does is very much influenced by the necessity of satisfying the stated and unstated demands of academia or of the organization he works for, those of his professional peers, of the scientific community at large, of society, of grant-giving agencies and their representatives—not to mention those of the editors of scholarly journals and their referees. And, while the existence of these forces does not excuse such features as poor workmanship, ignorance, and dishonesty, in all fairness they must also be held to account for their deleterious effects upon scientific progress. This is, of course, an old story and perhaps not too much can be done in this area. However, other aspects of the situation I have just described can be improved. Until then, however, needed answers may be long in coming.

REFERENCES

Andersen, M., & Sarbin, J. R. Base rate expectancies and motoric alterations in hypnosis. *International Journal of Clinical and Experimental Hypnosis* 1964, *12:* 147–156.

Bailly, J. S. *Rapport des commissaires de la faculté et de l'Académie chargés par le Roi de l'examen du magnétisme animal,* 1784. (The text of this report can be found in a great number of works, in particular in Bertrand [1826], where the text of several other reports made by members of the King's commission are also given.)

Barber, T. X. *Hypnosis: A scientific approach.* New York: Van Nostrand Reinhold, 1969.

Barber, T. X., & Glass, L. B. Significant factors in hypnotic behavior. *Journal of Abnormal and Social Psychology* 1962, *64:* 222–228.

Bellak, L., Hurvich, M., & Grediman, H. K. *Ego functions in schizophrenics, neurotics and normals.* New York: John Wiley & Sons, 1973.

Bernheim, H. *Automatisme et suggestion.* Paris: Félix Alcan, 1917.

———. *Suggestive therapeutics* (2nd ed., 1886). New York: London Book Co., 1947.

Bertrand, A. *Traité de somnambulisme.* Paris: J. G. Dentu, 1823.

―――. *Du magnétisme animal en France.* Paris: J. B. Baillière, 1826.

Broad, C. D. *The mind and its place in nature.* New York: Humanities Press, 1951.

Carpenter, W. B. On the influence of suggestion in modifying and directing muscular movement, independently of volition. *Proceedings of Royal Institution of Great Britain* 1852, *1:* 147–153.

―――. *Principles of mental physiology.* New York: Appleton-Century, 1880.

Davis, L. W., & Husband, R. W. A study of hypnotic susceptibility in relation to personality traits. *Journal of Abnormal and Social Psychology* 1931, *26:* 175–182.

Deeke, L., Scheid, P., & Kornhuber, H. H. Distribution of readiness potential, pre-motion positivity, and motor potential of the human cerebral cortex preceding voluntary finger movements. *Experimental Brain Research* 1969, *7:* 158–168.

Despine, P. *Étude scientifique sur le somnambulisme.* Paris: F. Savy, 1880.

Eccles, J. C. Brain, speech and consciousness. *Die Naturwissenschaften* 1973, *60:* 167–176. (Also in Eccles, J. C. *The understanding of the brain.* New York: McGraw-Hill, 1973.)

―――. Brain and free will. In G. G. Globus & M. Grover (eds.), *Consciousness and the brain—A scientific and philosophical inquiry.* New York: Plenum, 1976.

English, H. B., & English, A. C. *A comprehensive dictionary of psychological and psychoanalytical terms.* New York: Longmans, 1958.

Friedlander, J. W., & Sarbin, R. T. The depth of hypnosis. *Journal of Abnormal and Social Psychology* 1938, *33:* 281–294.

Hart, E. *Hypnotism, mesmerism and the new witchcraft.* New York: D. Appleton, 1896.

Hilgard, E. R. *Hypnotic susceptibility.* New York: Harcourt, Brace & World, 1965.

Hilgard, E. R., & Hilgard, J. *Hypnosis in the relief of pain.* Los Altos, Calif.: William Kaufmann, 1976.

Hilgard, E. R., & Tart, C. T. Responsiveness to suggestions following waking and imagination instructions and following induction of hypnosis. *Journal of Abnormal Psychology* 1966, *71:* 196–208.

Hull, C. L. *Hypnosis and suggestibility.* New York: Appleton-Century, 1933.

James, W. *The principles of psychology* (1890).New York: Dover, 1950.

Janet, P. *L'automatisme psychologique.* Paris: Alean, 1889.

―――. *Psychological healing. A historical and clinical study* (Vol. 1). London: George Allen & Unwin, 1925.

Jasper, H., & Penfield, W. Electrocorticogram in man: Effect of voluntary movement upon the electrical activity of the precentral gyrus. *Archiv für Psychiatrie und Nervenkrankheiten* 1949, *183*: 163–174.

Kornhuber, H. H. Cerebral cortex, cerebellum and basal ganglia: An introduction to their motor functions. In F. O. Schmitt & F. G. Worden (eds.), *The neurosciences: Third study program.* Cambridge: MIT Press, 1973.

Liébeault, A. A. *Le sommeil provoqué et les états analogues.* Paris: Octave Doin, 1889.

Penfield, W. Mechanisms of voluntary movement. *Brain* 1954, *77*: 1–17.

Rappaport, D. States of consciousness. A psychopathological and psychodynamic view. In M. Gill (ed.), *The collected papers of David Rappaport.* New York: Basic Books, 1967.

Sarbin, T. R., & Coe, W. C. Hypnosis. *A social psychological analysis of influence communication.* New York: Holt, Rinehart, Winston, 1972.

Sperry, R. W. A modified concept of consciousness. *Psychological Review* 1969, *76*: 532–536.

Steininger, F. *Die Biologie der sogennante "tierischen Hypnose." Ergebnisse der Biologie* 1936, *13*: 348–451.

Stephen, C. R. Awareness during anesthesia. In M. T. Jenkins (ed.), *Common and uncommon problems in anesthesiology.* Philadelphia: F. A. Davis, 1968.

Tart, C. T. *States of consciousness.* New York: Dutton, 1975.

Turner, M. B. *Philosophy and the science of behavior.* New York: Appleton-Century-Crofts, 1965.

Weitzenhoffer, A. M. *Hypnotism: An objective study in suggestibility.* New York: John Wiley & Sons, 1953.

————. The influence of hypnosis on the learning processes. Some theoretical considerations. *Journal of Clinical and Experimental Hypnosis*, Part 1, 1954, *2*: 191–200; Part 2, 1955, *3*: 148–165.

————. *General techniques of hypnotism.* New York: Grune & Stratton, 1957.

————. *Research in hypnotism: 1953–1958.* Office of Naval Research report. *ONR*: 452: LP: gbs. Group Psychology Branch. Psychological Sciences Division, Washington, D.C., 1958.

————. Reflections upon certain specific and current uses of the "unconscious" in clinical hypnosis. *International Journal of Clinical and Experimental Hypnosis* 1960, *8*: 165–177. (a)

————. Unconscious or co-conscious? *American Journal of Clinical Hypnosis* 1960, *2*: 177–196. (b)

————. "Credulity" and "skepticism" in hypnotic research: A critical examination of Sutcliffe's thesis and evidence. Part 1. *American Journal of Clinical Hypnosis* 1963, *6*: 137–162. (a)

————. The nature of hypnosis. I. *American Journal of Clinical Hypnosis* 1963, *5:* 295–321. (b)

————. The nature of hypnosis. II. *American Journal of Clinical Hypnosis* 1963, *6:* 40–72. (c)

————. Eye-blink rate and hypnosis. Preliminary findings. *Perceptual and Motor Skills* 1969, *28:* 671–676.

————. Ocular changes associated with passive hypnotic behavior. *American Journal of Clinical Hypnosis* 1971, *14:* 102–121. (a)

————. Hypnose: Schein oder Wirklichkeit? [Hypnosis: Fact or Fiction?] in A. Katzenstein (ed.), *Hypnose. Aktuelle Probleme in Theorie, Experiment, und Klinik.* Berlin: Fischer Verlag, 1971. (b)

————. *Hypnosis and hypnotherapy.* Tape 4. Behavioral Sciences Tape Library. Fort Lee, N.J.: Sigma Information, 1974. (a) (Typescript copies available from the author.)

————. When is an "instruction" an "instruction"? *International Journal of Clinical Experimental Hypnosis* 1974, *22:* 258–269. (b)

————. "What did he (Bernheim) say?" *Proceedings of the Seventh International Congress of Hypnosis and Psychomatic Medicine* (in press.)

————. The suggestion-effect. (Article submitted for publication).

Weitzenhoffer, A. M., & Hilgard, E. R. *Stanford Scales of Hypnotic Susceptibility, Forms A, B, and C.* Palo Alto, Calif.: Consulting Psychologist Press, 1959, 1962.

Weitzenhoffer, A. M., & Sjoberg, B. M., Jr. Suggestibility with and without an induction of hypnosis. *American Journal of Clinical Hypnosis* 1958, *1:* 15–24.

■9
Altering States of Consciousness through Sensory Deprivation

PETER E. SUEDFELD and RODERICK A. BORRIE

If one accepts Tart's definition of an altered state of consciousness (ASC) as "one in which [the individual] clearly feels a *qualitative* shift in his pattern of mental functioning" (Tart, 1969, p. 2), the production of ASCs has been a widely publicized hallmark of sensory deprivation beginning with the initial studies using that technique with human subjects. For example, in the very first book published about this type of experimental situation (Solomon, Kubzansky, Leiderman, Mendelson, Trumbull, & Wexler, 1961), there were chapters reporting data such as the following: Of 29 subjects, 25 reported some form of hallucinatory activity with the hallucinations being mostly in the visual modality and progressing from simple percepts, such as dots of light or lines, to complex ones including full-blown animated scenes; objects in the visual field—the walls of the room and stimuli consisting of geometric figures—were seen to move and change shapes immediately after the subject was released; the subject felt that his body was altering in size, pattern, location, or texture; subjects found it difficult to distinguish between states of waking and sleeping; and thoughts and emotions became less rational and more primitive.

Similar data, and particularly further reports of visual and auditory hallucinations and changes in body image, were found in many other early studies. No wonder, then, that in his exhaustive review, Ludwig (1966) listed "reduction of exteroceptive stimulation and/or motor activity" as the first in his summary of techniques that produce ASCs. Of course, such conditions include a wide variety of environments besides the experimental sensory deprivation chamber. ASC-like phenomena have been reported in the literature dealing with every one of these environments, with the similarities among them appearing to be much more striking than the differences. Hallucinations, fantasies, withdrawal states, and major shifts of effect and cognition all abound in the reports (Lilly, 1956; Suedfeld, 1974). Among these are the situations encountered by solitary flyers, sailors, prisoners, and explorers; reduction of sensory acuity or of mobility because of illness or the treatment of illness; religious and mystical trance states. These last, as well as what is commonly called brainwashing, are quite frequently based upon excessive, rather than insufficient, stimulation. Thus, distinctions should be made between ASCs accompanying meditation and those occurring as a result of dancing and drumming rituals.

If we take the results of experimental research as the epitome of reduced environmental stimulation effects, the changes that can be categorized as ASCs merge gradually into changes in which the subject feels a quantitative shift in perceptions, intellectual activities, emotional responses, and so on, but without the drastic qualitative alteration that defines the ASC. In many cases, it is quite difficult to draw a clear demarcation line. As a matter of fact, it has been argued that many of the phenomena originally reported as hallucinations and other qualitative shifts in experience were actually the effects of dreaming or dream-like states, either misreported by the subjects or mislabeled by the experimenters, or both. Many subjects in sensory deprivation experiments report that they find it difficult to distinguish clearly between the waking and sleeping states; a considerable segment of confinement time is apparently spent in hypnogogic or hypnopompic transition periods; and other forms of stimulation, such as spontaneous neural firing in the retina, residual stimuli in the experimental chamber, or inputs arising from the subject's body itself, may be perceived and elaborated until they are reacted to as though they were rather complex fantasized inputs.

In the following section a summary will be presented of the major types of ASC reports and interpretations in the sensory deprivation literature, together with alternative explanations of the phenomenon where these have been offered. An attempt will also be made to distinguish among the effects of the major methods used to induce what is generally called sensory deprivation. These are: reductions of patterned input by the use of translucent goggles and white noise, reduced variability of input by immobilizing the subject's head or entire body in a frame of some sort; and reduction of absolute levels of sensory input either by confinement in a dark and silent chamber or by immersion in water. The effects of these widely different techniques are surprisingly similar, and some recurrent patterns have also been found; these shall be indicated where they are relevant to the question of ASCs.

1. HALLUCINATIONS. As was mentioned before, the high level of hallucinations reported in the original perceptual deprivation studies at McGill University was one of the most dramatic and frequently cited effects. As a result of the vividness and dramatic nature of these reports, the matter of hallucinations received considerable further attention from investigators. Some problems quickly arose because of the difficulty of identifying exactly what reported sensations can legitimately be described as hallucinations. Since in most situations at least some stimuli remained in the environment, some of the descriptions given by the subjects were seen as possibly due to such stimulation, whereas in other experiments there was a difficulty in distinguishing between hallucinations (sensations without an objectively identifiable stimulus) and illusions (where actual physical stimuli are misinterpreted or distorted). Even more important from the point of view of the implications of the technique, the term *hallucination* was frequently interpreted as pointing up a parallel between sensory deprivation and a miniature psychosis; but unlike the hallucinations of psychotics, those of deprived subjects tended to be mostly visual rather than auditory, and in the few studies where clinical criteria were applied, they very seldom met the standards of being uncontrollable, "out there," scannable, and apparently real (Suedfeld & Vernon, 1964). Eventually, as a way of defusing if not

resolving the controversy, the custom arose of labeling such reports as RVS (Reported Visual Sensation) or RAS (Reported Auditory Sensation), with further elaboration of the specific nature of the percept being done on an individual basis rather than attempting to produce replicable categories (Murphy, Myers, & Smith, 1963). A further classificatory scheme has defined the types of reported sensations on the basis of their complexity and meaningfulness. Type A includes flashes of light, changes in diffuse ambient light, abstract or geometric forms, and various kinds of noises; Type B is made up of meaningful objects or living beings—either seen or heard—and music (Zuckerman, 1969a).

A review covering almost all of the research (Zuckerman, 1969a) came to the following conclusions. There are no major differences in the production of reported sensations as a function of type of sensory deprivation technique used, as a result of intermittent stimulation during the experiment, as a result of mechanically reduced mobility, or as a result of increasing time in the chamber. Most reports are of visual sensations, and typically progress within a particular subject from the simple Type A experiences to the more complex Type B.

It appears that complex visual phenomena tend to be experienced more than the simple ones when the subject's eyes are open (Kempe, 1973). These are also more likely to be controllable by the subject himself, not scannable, reported to be multicolored, reported as occurring in the eye or inside the head rather than in the external environment, three-dimensional rather than two-dimensional, more realistic for the subject, and reacted to as being more pleasurable, than simple phenomena.

Experience of Type A phenomena appears to be facilitated if the orientation given to the subjects implies that visual sensations are to be expected, although the more complex types of experience do not seem to be affected by this variable. In retrospective reports, subjects who were sensitized to the possibility of sensations by being told ahead of time to report those that they had are more likely to mention Type B phenomena, although they do not report a higher number of these during the experiment itself. Sensations are more likely to be reported during states of medium or high arousal, although this does not necessarily mean that the actual experience necessarily occurs in such states. There is no evidence that any particular personality type is more likely to produce reported sensations than any other; the few reports of such relationships have typically been preliminary and unreplicated. One thing that is fairly clear is that "most [RVSs] seem to be transient impersonal phenomena of no dynamic or pathological significance" (Zuckerman, 1969a, p. 125).

Zuckerman's interpretation of reported sensations in sensory deprivation is that the subject reacts to stimulus reduction either by falling into sleep, focusing attention on his own thoughts and feelings, or continuing to scan the interoceptive and exteroceptive environments for inputs. Under these conditions, he may react to bodily produced stimuli or the distortion of residual stimuli in the environment, eventually perhaps becoming more sensitized to organized images stemming from higher central nervous system loci. High arousal or reduction of competing stimuli may intensify these images, and the lack of contextual cues as to location and nature may help to result in the image being "perceived" as an external one. It is possible that the search for stimuli, involving mental and perceptual effort, may fatigue the subject to the point where imagery is experienced, sometimes in elaborate forms (Horowitz, 1970). All of this is a far cry from the bizarre interpretations of sensory deprivation as a "model psychosis," or as a way of inducing altered states of consciousness mechanically and almost universally, particularly since the frequency of such phenomena is not all that great when—as few experimenters have done—the data are compared with those of a normal-environment baseline (Myers, Murphy, Smith, & Goffard, 1966).

Some experimenters have also reported that their subjects had experienced nonveridical perceptions in the other sensory modalities. These have included the smell of tobacco smoke going into the chamber during a therapeutic study on smoking cessation, striking alterations in the taste of food, tingling or other sensations in the fingertips, and feelings of motion either of the room itself or of the individual within the room. Unfortunately, systematic investigations of these reports have been few. One reason for this is the relative scarcity of the reports themselves. But more important is the difficulty of identifying hallucinatory phenomena in these senses as opposed to illusions or dreams/daydreams, as well as the fleeting nature of the experiences and the relatively poor vocabulary available to analyze them. In fact, reported sensations in the minor senses, just like other processes in these modalities (e.g., vividness of memory, ability to discriminate stimuli), have not been studied nearly as thoroughly as the equivalent phenomena in vision and audition, a major gap in the sensory deprivation literature.

2. ILLUSIONS. Illusions, in the sense of altered perceptions, have been found routinely as a result of sensory deprivation. Unlike hallucinations, there is relatively little problem in definition here. Upon being released from the chamber, subjects have experienced some degree of disturbance in the perceptual field, with such problems as difficulty in focusing, the merging of objects into backgrounds, a loss of three-dimensional perception, and increased acuity of color vision and hearing (Bexton, Heron, & Scott, 1954). Later studies have confirmed these findings, and added such effects as apparent spontaneous motion in the visual field, changes in the stability, position, size, and shape of objects, and so on (Doane, Mahatoo, Heron, & Scott, 1959). It should be pointed out, however, that there is some inconsistency in the reports, with several laboratories having been unable to replicate these or at least a major portion of these findings.

In his review of the literature, Zubek concluded that:

> The weight of the experimental evidence indicates that conditions of reduced sensory input do not produce a variety of dramatic and unusual distortions of the perceptual environment as reported initially from the McGill laboratory, at least as derived from qualitative observations. . . . Among the tests which are impaired are electrical flicker, Gottschaldt Embedded Figures, Bender-Gestalt, spiral aftereffect, figural aftereffects, reversible figures, Müller-Lyer illusion, phi-phenomenon, "perceptual lag," visual reaction time, and visual vigilance. Color perception is also impaired but only after durations longer than a day. On the other hand, such visual measures as depth perception, the constancies, brightness discrimination, c.f.f. [critical flicker frequency], and visual acuity do not appear to be affected by either short-term or long-term periods. An increase in visual functioning, as measured by a tachistoscopic recognition technique, can also occur but only after short-term deprivation. [1969, p. 252]

In other modalities, researchers have found improvement in auditory vigilance, faster reaction time to auditory stimuli, and improvements in sensitivity to tactual, pain, and gustatory stimulation. Delayed auditory feedback and kinesthetic acuity are not affected;

tactual form discrimination and tests of spatial orientation show decrements.

Interestingly, when subjects are deprived of single modalities at a time, as opposed to more general sensory deprivation, the transferability of effects is quite clearly demonstrated. For example, increases in tactual, pain, olfactory, and gustatory sensitivity as well as in auditory discrimination are produced by visual deprivation, and immobilization without other forms of restriction can also produce the effects more usually obtained by general sensory deprivation. Effects are apparently mediated at a central neural point, since there is transferability both across sensory modalities and across brain hemispheres: Elimination of input to one side of the body produces increased sensitivity in the same modality from the contralateral receptor.

In this context, there are interactions with methodological details such as duration of time, type of condition, time of test administration, and the reaction of the subjects to sensory deprivation itself. It appears, for example, that the lag between the termination of the deprivation condition and the initiation of the testing procedure may greatly affect the results, with immediate poststimulation tests usually showing the most consistent changes. However, some phenomena have been found to persist for up to a day after release. Also, it appears that deprivation of approximately two days seems to produce greater changes than durations either shorter or longer than that. This is in contrast to the findings on cognitive changes, which seem to peak at around twenty-four hours (Suedfeld, 1969a).

It should not be inferred that the relationship between duration and illusions is a simple curvilinear one. For example, Zubek and Bross in a number of papers have found what they call the "Depression-Enhancement Phenomenon": Changes in critical flicker fusion of the nonoccluded eye after monocular deprivation (1) decrease after six hours of deprivation, (2) return to baseline by the end of nine hours, and (3) continue to increase for up to two weeks. This appears to be a fairly consistent pattern (Zubek, Bross, & Harper, 1976), although the direct cause of the effect has yet to be established (Harper & Zubek, 1976).

Another aspect of illusions is changes in body image, including such experiences as feelings of floating or movement and similar distortions of orientational perception (Cappon & Banks, 1961). As with pseudohallucinations (Myers et al., 1966), such experiences are more frequent in everyday life than is commonly realized. In fact, Cappon and Banks found them to be reported more often as occurring in normal situations than in experimental treatments including perceptual deprivation, sleep deprivation, caloric stimulation of the labyrinth, inhalation of N_2O and CO_2, and an anxiety situation. Other sensory deprivation experimenters have found high frequency rates of changes in body image, sometimes quite dramatic ones. Once again, the early studies from McGill University report the highest proportion of these, with much less striking experiences appearing in later research. Normal-environment baselines were not collected in these studies. One might thus conclude, in view of the work of Cappon and Banks, that distortions of orientational perception in sensory deprivation are in fact quantitative (and perhaps merely minor quantitative) changes, and therefore do not really qualify as evidence of an ASC.

Time perception also tends to change in sensory deprivation. The majority of subjects appear to underestimate the time spent in the condition. This is rather surprising since a more logical prediction would be that the long stretch of unfilled time would be experienced as even longer than it really is. While some personality factors appear to be related to time estimation (Cohen, Silverman, Bressler, & Shmavonian, 1961; Vernon, 1963), the general direction is quite consistent across studies and techniques.

3. DREAMS, DAYDREAMS, AND FANTASY. This is the general area where one might expect the most interesting effects of sensory deprivation to occur in the context of ASC. Not surprisingly, perhaps, it is also the area where the least amount of systematic research has been done. To a great extent, this is a function of changes in scientific fashion. Most of the sensory deprivation research cited in this chapter was performed between 1950 and 1970. Since that period, the volume of experimental research on the effects of restricted stimulation with human beings has declined, and much of the current literature deals with the relevance of the technique to therapeutic and other applied or semiapplied situations. Thus, during the very same time that the investigation of dreams and related phenomena—fantasy, imagery, and the like—was becoming acceptable and being put on a scientific basis, workers in sensory deprivation turned their interest to other areas. What is available is a few scattered, uneval-

uated reports of the subjective comments of the individuals participating in sensory deprivation experiments.

One exception to this is the work of a group at Allan Memorial
Hospital in Montreal (e.g., Azima, Vispo, & Azima, 1961), who used
sensory deprivation in a procedure they call "anaclitic therapy."
Anaclitic therapy is based on the desirability of fostering dependency
needs systematically, and to encourage deep regression and disorganization of the body schemes in order to establish a nurturing
relationship between the patient and the therapist. This relationship
could then be used to reduce feelings of anxiety and guilt in the
former. Azima et al. did find a great deal of regressive fantasizing and
affect in mentally disturbed patients during sensory deprivation,
with the patients concentrating on problems arising from fixations in
the pregenital phases of their lives. Figure drawings, alterations of
body image, and the appearance of primitive fantasies and behavior
all demonstrated a high degree of regression. The investigators
hypothesized that the deprivation condition produced a state of dependency similar to that of infancy, coupled with a need for gratification provided by the therapist.

In less-controlled investigations of this phenomenon, one of the
things that has become fairly obvious is that sensory deprivation
subjects spend considerable time sleeping (Vernon, 1963) and that
they find it difficult to discriminate states of wakefulness, drowsiness,
and actual sleep. In fact, this continuum becomes much more continuous in sensory deprivation than it appears to be in normal conditions. It has been proposed that many supposed hallucinations
experienced by sensory deprivation subjects are in fact dreams or
daydreams (Suedfeld, 1975). This hypothesis is supported by the
dominance of the visual modality in both dreams and deprivation-
related reported sensations, in contrast to psychotic hallucinations
(Kubie, 1950). At any rate, reports of dreams and daydreams are
extremely numerous in the sensory deprivation literature (Schultz,
1965), with the content of the dream frequently being related to the
sensory deprivation situation itself (Vernon, 1963). Some investigators have reported a relatively high number of unpleasant dreams,
but this does not appear to be universal, and may be more closely
related to the degree of stress and anxiety induced by the experimental orientation procedure than by sensory deprivation itself.

The ability to enjoy one's fantasizing and daydreaming has been identified as one of the few personality variables that appear to be systematically related to sensory deprivation tolerance. One set of findings indicates that effectiveness of control over primary processes is related positively to tolerance of sensory deprivation (Goldberger, 1961; Leiderman, 1962; Wright & Abby, 1965). On the other hand, a similar relationship is found when one looks at the ability to relax and enjoy primary process experiences. Some subjects do consider such phenomena as visual sensations to be pleasant, whereas others interpret them as symptoms of dysfunction (Goldberger, 1961; Myers et al., 1966). Several authors have emphasized the importance of the subject's emotional/cognitive set (for a review, see Suedfeld, 1969b). A recent example is the finding that in a water immersion study when subjects were in general open to nonnormative experiences of many sorts, reactions were frequently euphoric ("so much enjoying my time there . . . like a super, super, super sauna . . . socializing with myself, confronting, exchanging myself, transition, adequate, real . . .") even though the objective categories included what are usually called aversive effects: changes in body image, distortion of time perception, mood shifts, and RVSs (Hoffman, 1977).

Suedfeld (1975) has hypothesized that the attempts of the organism to maintain a reasonably normal level of stimulation under deprived conditions leads to the generation of unusual levels of fantasy and imagery; individuals who, because of personal characteristics or cultural background, accept these as interesting or at least neutral adapt better to the situation than those who react to them as indicators of pathology, thereby arousing anxiety. The increased sensitivity of receptors to even low-intensity stimuli, which are then elaborated into the basis for nonveridical experiences, may be at the physical basis of this process (Fiske, 1961).

Related to this question is the matter of creativity in sensory deprivation. While it has been found that performance on unstructured tasks is impaired by deprivation (for a review, see Suedfeld, 1969a), this does not provide an adequate test. There have been reports (Smith, 1975) of the use of sensory deprivation to foster productivity by highly creative individuals. While this may be an illusion, in the sense that subjective estimations of performance may be high without a concomitant actual change (somewhat similarly to various kinds of drug effects), it certainly deserves objective study.

An experiment currently being planned is to isolate volunteers from groups of highly creative individuals (e.g., artists, writers, inventors, scientists), and to obtain ratings of performance produced during and/or after the experiment to see whether any verifiable alterations have occurred. From a psychoanalytic point of view, the relationship between original creative behavior and primary process would imply that such individuals should be highly tolerant of and positively responsive to the sensory deprivation situation.

The relationship between so-called sensory deprivation effects and responses to nondeprivation procedural factors has been demonstrated by the work of Orne and Scheibe (1964). It appears that the paraphernalia and forms used in early sensory deprivation experiments could produce some of the effects in themselves, even without any deprivation. The finding seems to indicate that some sensory deprivation research, in the early years at least, did not sufficiently differentiate between the anxiety and stress effects deriving from nondeprivation factors and the effects of sensory deprivation itself. In the realm of ASCs, it has been said that "with the element of fear removed, the imagery of sensory deprivation becomes like the imagery of daydreams, quite familiar and usually not anxiety-producing" (Leiderman, 1964).

In his later work, Lilly elaborated findings from his early statements about the prevalence of imagery, particularly unpleasant imagery. One interesting remark in Lilly's early publications (1956; Lilly & Shurley, 1961) is that prolonged water immersion produces psychotic-like behaviors, including savior types of delusions and conversations with inanimate objects. Recently, Lilly (1973) emphasized the mystical nature of these experiences: the possibility, after hours of meditation and contemplation in the tank, of tuning in on networks of communication and of civilizations other than our own. Still later, in experiments combining immersion with LSD, he discovered the ability to leave his body and return to it at will. From then on, he discusses out-of-the-body, inside-the-body, and other ASC phenomena as having been real ones in contrast to his previous identification of them as delusional. This same change occurs in his attitude toward his two "guides," disembodied points of consciousness who first appeared to him during an almost lethal accident and who repeatedly reappeared in later sensory deprivation experiences. These experiences included a wide variety of trips into the universe, inside his own body, and into other realms of consciousness.

Among other, although perhaps less dramatic, nonphysical trips was the experience of one of our own subjects who, finding the air in the chamber to be getting stuffy, attempted unsuccessfully to contact the monitor via the intercommunications system. Since he had been previously informed that the monitor would always be available through this method, he became quite annoyed and decided to leave the experiment. He departed from the chamber, walked up to the main floor of the psychology building, and met and conversed with an acquaintance who lives in a distant city. They had a fairly long conversation, which was only terminated when the monitor's voice over the intercom broke in to awaken our subject who was, of course, still lying on the bed inside the sensory deprivation chamber. Had the termination of the dream not been through such an explicit and abrupt intrusion from the monitor, the subject probably would have continued to believe that the experience was a fantasy or an out-of-body voyage. It is impossible to estimate to what extent similar reports are due to dreams being indistinguishable from waking or hypnogogic phenomena in the sensory deprivation setting or to other contaminants such as the interaction of sensory deprivation and drugs.

Examples and Theoretical Approaches

As we have mentioned, subjective experiences during sensory deprivation are by no means homogeneous either between people or within one person over time. While there are certain common denominators, the individual experience is a personal one built to a large extent around internally generated stimuli. We can cite some examples from one of our latest studies, in which 20 women stayed in sensory deprivation for 24 hours each as part of a therapeutic procedure (Borrie, in preparation). Upon release, they reported their subjective experiences informally to the question, "What was it like?" and their observations were recorded.

The following reactions were reported by these subjects (numbers in parentheses are the number of subjects reporting that particular phenomenon): pleasant (6), relaxing (6), hot and stuffy (5), uncomfortable (5), specific reports of dreams (7), confused (3), tense (2), boring (2), enjoyable (2), frightening (2), thinking about problems (5), time passed slowly (2), restless (1), unpleasant thoughts (4), unusual experience (1), visual hallucination of lights (1). In addition, three other subjects terminated before 24 hours because the experience was too unpleasant. One of these reported becoming extremely upset about not being with her family and suddenly feeling an urgent need to be with her children. A second left merely because she was bored and upset; she expressed no specific unusual thoughts other than a need to get out of deprivation. Both of these subjects left after 5 hours. The third dropout began crying after one half hour, but expressed a desire to continue with the session. She remained upset for another 15 minutes when she agreed that it would be best to leave. It seems that sensory deprivation had brought back strong childhood memories of having been locked in a root cellar, a small underground room. In our chamber, she felt as if a great weight were pushing down on her chest, and she was trying to push it off as if she were trying to open the cellar door from the inside. She was extremely distraught and remained quite agitated for several hours after this experience.

One aspect of these reports, as well as of other studies, is the tendency to emphasize the unusual, out-of-the-ordinary event. This tendency exists not only in published accounts of the research but also in the self-editing of the subjects when they record their experiences. For instance, while only two of our subjects volunteered that they were very bored, when questioned several others admitted to being quite bored. Boredom, although it is a common experience in sensory deprivation, is not a particularly bizarre experience and is perceived as hardly worth reporting. Some other ordinary phenomena were that the chamber was very pleasant, relaxing, uncomfortable, or stuffy. Specific dreams and specific thoughts were described by many subjects. Only one participant had an RVS, which was of Type A.

Sensory deprivation imposes no restrictions on the continuum of possible inner experiences that would inhibit a particular type of subjective state. The range of inner experience in sensory deprivation is therefore identical to that found in the normal environment. Conditions of reduced external stimulation may, however, increase the probability of some types of reactions above that of their occurrence under normal levels of stimulation. Fischer (1975) has presented "a cartography of inner space" that links the varieties of subjective states to arousal levels. With successive increases in arousal, one proceeds through the conscious states: sensitivity, creativity, anxiety, acute schizophrenic states, catatonia, and mystical rapture. In the direction of decreased arousal, Fischer borrows the names of various meditative states since Eastern cultures have made much more detailed analyses of these states.

In that some subjective experiences are bound to specific states of arousal, sensory deprivation may increase the probability of different subjective states by affecting arousal level. Unfortunately, the relationship between sensory deprivation and arousal is neither simple nor clear. It is probable that arousal is not a single unidimensional continuum but a set of related dimensions that are connected to different systems of the body. Since we have discussed elsewhere the problems of working with arousal as a single dimension (Borrie & Suedfeld, 1976), suffice it to say here that sensory deprivation does not have a clear unitary effect on arousal.

Aside from the complexities involved in determining precisely what is meant by the term "arousal," there are considerable individual differences in how deprivation affects arousal levels and arousal differences within the same individual over time. To illustrate this, consider the following alternative reactions in a hypothetical example. Upon entering the chamber and settling on the bed, the individual is slightly anxious because of the novelty of the situation. This initial increase in arousal, combined with the absence of external stimulation, produces the previously mentioned increase in sensitivity to the situation. On the other hand, an individual who is not fearful may engage in reverie and problem-solving processes related to his own recent activities. For him, a raise in arousal level may lead to increased creativity and problem-solving ability.

Another complication stems from the fact that most subjects fall asleep within a matter of a few hours (Vernon, 1963). Waking up from sleep in a sensory deprivation chamber can be a confusing experience if one has momentarily forgotten where one is. The surprise of this misorientation can cause an immediate increase in arousal and considerable anxiety. If, on the other hand, this confusion does not occur, arousal will remain low, and the individual may stay in a half awake, half asleep state conducive to hypnopompic imagery. Later in the session, boredom and its associated arousal increase may occur (Berlyne, 1960; London, Shubert, & Washburn, 1972).

These alternative possibilities demonstrate that ASCs and other deprivation phenomena are strongly influenced by the cognitions of the particular individual. The low level of stimulation certainly affects those cognitions, and may also have a more direct—though as yet unclear (Zubek, 1969)—effect on arousal. The specific content and the interpretation of deprivation-linked ASC experiences are determined by individual factors. Subjects who practice meditation, for example, report that deprivation enhances their meditation state and allows achievement of deeper levels of consciousness. One subject who was a practicing Buddhist was reluctant to leave the chamber because she was having "extremely informative dreams." These subjects' experiences were viewed as quite positive because of their prior experience with similar states. To an individual who is unfamiliar with such conditions, deep relaxation can be interpreted as loss of control in the same way as dreams can be interpreted as hallucinations.

Although we now know that actual hallucinations are quite infrequent in sensory deprivation, some of the explanations developed to account for RVSs are useful in analyzing subjective reactions in general. The most promising formulations are really theories of consciousness and attempt to explain normal thought processes as well as unusual ones. One of these is the continuity hypothesis (Savage, 1975), which views different subjective experiences as a continuum of states that are not sharply distinguishable from one another, and argues that these experiences evolve from one to the other. In this theory, sensations, perceptions, thoughts, fantasies, dreams, memories, illusions, and hallucinations are all similar in kind. Traditionally, there are three dimensions on which each subjective experience can vary and is therefore distinguished from other experiences. These are vividness, coherence, and voluntariness. Savage (1975) has shown these three dimensions to be unreliable criteria in distinguishing among subjective experiences; however, it is probable that each type of subjective experience can vary along each of the dimensions. Unfortunately, this type of theory of consciousness tends to be descriptive rather than explanatory.

Recently, Horowitz (1975) outlined an information-processing approach to hallucinations that appears quite comprehensive as an explanatory model. In this model, four properties are necessary for the occurrence of the "ideal" hallucination. An understanding of these properties will aid us in explaining other subjective experiences as well. First, Horowitz posited that we function subjectively in three separate yet interrelated systems: an enactive system, an image system, and a lexical system. The enactive system is the subjective memory and experience of motor actions. In the image system "sets of information derived from perception, memory, thinking, and fantasy are combined, compared, and recombined. There are separable subsystems of image representation based on the separate sensory systems of organization" (Horowitz, 1972, cited in 1975, p. 168). The lexical system, which deals with language, is the most complex. It is the last to develop in the individual, and is difficult to separate from the other two systems. In its pure state, "lexical representation is conceptualized as actionless (no subvocal speech) and imageless (no auditory, visual, or kinesthetic accompaniments)" (Horowitz, 1975, p. 169).

According to Horowitz, when the image system is more highly activated than the other two, the person becomes more likely to hallucinate. The time-bound dominance of one representational system over the others may give each subjective experience its own unique quality. For example, Horowitz suggests that the experiences of sequence and time are most closely linked with the lexical system. Therefore, when a subjective experience is represented chiefly in the image system and only poorly in the lexical system, the image will have a timeless, "standing alone" quality. A similar sort of link has been proposed by others (Paivio, 1971).

The second property that leads to the experience of a hallucination is the increase of internal input to the image system. Here, Horowitz uses a dual-input model of image formation (West, 1962), suggesting that a central image system receives input from both internal and external sources. Internal sources of information could be increased under the following circumstances:

a. Relative reduction of external input with no relative lowering of activity (receptivity) of the representational system.
b. Increase in capacity of the representational system without increase in availability of external signals.
c. Augmentation of internal input due to arousal of ideas and feelings secondary to drive states.
d. Reduction of usual or "homeostatic" levels of inhibition over the internal inputs.

e. Alternation of the transition between "matrices" [regulatory processes for matching perception images with cognitive schemata], permitting internal inputs to gain more representation on matrices oriented to, and more often associated with, perception. [Horowitz, 1975, p. 177]

When external signals are ambiguous, internal mechanisms would again be allowed more freedom for organization and elaboration. Sometimes an ambiguous input cannot be validated externally because its source is within the optical system itself, "either from the anatomic characteristics of the eye or arising in the bioelectrical circuits for pattern receptivity in the retinal ganglionic network or at higher cell arrays in the optical-cortical pathway" (Horowitz, 1975, p. 180). The idea of perception as a constructive process (Neisser, 1967) mediated by the needs of the individual is important here. When an ambiguous input, such as an entoptic phenomenon from within the eye, is mixed with the expectancies, memories, or fantasies of the receiver, the resultant representation may be appraised as hallucinatory.

The third property of the information-processing cycle that leads to bizarre experiences is the impairment of the way information is processed. As an image is matched to the individual's cognitive schemata, it may become mislabeled, mistranslated, or misinterpreted in many different ways so that an erroneous appraisal occurs. An image may appear too briefly to be correctly interpreted. An overabundance of images with less emphasis on the lexical system could make it difficult to provide appropriate labels. An intense need, e.g., for stimulation, might cause a normally unacceptable image to be appraised as real.

The fourth property is the impairment of control over cognition. When this happens, unplanned and intrusive images occur and do not fit well into the meaning of the experience. Horowitz (1975) suggests that unbidden images can occur after stressful events "as eruptive representation of usually warded-off ideas and feelings," and as an unconscious attempt to transform an emotional state.

While these properties are usually present in the hallucination experience, many other factors vary individually. For instance, the person's characteristic mode of thought can make a difference in the appraisal of an image. Some individuals use imagery more in their normal thought processes, while others rely more heavily on verbal processes (Paivio, 1971). Horowitz (1975) suggests that a particularly vivid image occurrence is more likely to be labeled as hallucinatory by the person who is a verbal processor than by one who normally thinks in images. The more novel the experience, the more probable is its evaluation as nonveridical. Individual differences in interpretation also result from differences in expectations, wishes, and fears. For instance, the perception of a random shape caused by seeing some entoptic elements might be judged to be a snake if the appropriate fears and expectations were present. Such expectations, an active memory, or fantasy images can all serve to intensify internally generated images.

Consideration of these properties and individual differences is also useful in understanding information processing as it occurs in both normal and atypical circumstances such as sensory deprivation. The four information processing properties are influenced in specific ways by deprivation conditions, and these effects interact with individual characteristics to produce a unique subjective experience. First, deprivation can initiate a shift to image representation by eliminating cues that would encourage use of the enactive or lexical systems. When the individual is immobilized or confined, the propensity for enactive representation, while not eliminated, will be greatly reduced. In the same manner, the removal of verbal communication to the individual eliminates an input that would tend to keep representation in the lexical system. Of course this does not stop verbal processes, but it may lessen the likelihood of verbal thinking.

In addition to experiencing an absence of verbal communication, the subject in sensory deprivation is also removed from visual stimulation so that the same argument may be raised regarding image representation. It is possible that the absence of time or sequence cues also affects the predominant mode of representation. That is, the link between verbal processes and perception of sequence and time (Paivio, 1971) may work in both directions. Horowitz (1975) hypothesized that a shift away from the lexical system would give an image a timeless quality, but a situation with a timeless quality may inhibit the use of the verbal representational system, thus promoting an increased use of image representation.

An extreme example of timelessness of the sensory deprivation experience is the case of one of our subjects, who seemed very surprised at being told that it was time to leave. This particular subject was only scheduled for 12 hours in the chamber. Upon release, he refused to believe that he had been in the chamber for more than a few minutes. Since the clocks confirmed his belief, and there were no windows in the laboratory, it was necessary to take the subject to a window so that he would see that 12 hours had actually elapsed. The obvious explanation of this subject's experience is that he went immediately to sleep and slept for the entire 12-hour period. Nevertheless, it is unusual that he could sleep that long and be entirely unaware of having been asleep. Since most of our research utilizes a 24-hour confinement period, subjects do not usually become this disoriented. However, as was mentioned previously, misjudgment of elapsed time is extremely common in deprived subjects.

The effect of sensory deprivation in increasing the level of internal stimulation is more clear-cut. Horowitz's first circumstance under which internal input goes up was the reduction of external input without a decrease in activity or receptivity. This as well as several other factors cited by Horowitz are present in sensory deprivation. There has been much support for the hypothesis that deprivation raises the individual's need for information (Jones, 1969) and that individuals strive for an optimal level of stimulation (Schultz, 1965; Zuckerman, 1969b). When external stimulation is no longer available in adequate amounts, the individual will increase his production of internal information and/or increase his receptivity to internal and residual stimuli already present. Higher information need will promote the reduction of inhibitions against internal input in order to achieve a more optimal stimulation level. This allows the individual's other needs to contribute a greater portion of the internal input, especially since the normal concerns with the usual responsibilities of ordinary days have been temporarily suspended. Another result of increased information need is that heightened receptivity to external stimuli makes the subject more likely to notice events occurring in the optical system itself.

Internal factors can augment or reduce the expectancy of a perceptual representation. The individual's current wishes, fears, or knowledge of the situation can provide enough framework in such an ambiguous setting (a walk-in inkblot, as Vernon [1963] has called it) to allow interpretation of some rather uncertain stimuli. Two examples of olfactory hallucinations illustrate this phenomenon. While olfactory hallucinations are quite rare in sensory deprivation, the two instances reported by subjects in our laboratory are notable in their clarity and in the certainty of the subjects that they were reporting real phenomena. The first case was that of a subject undergoing treatment to stop smoking. During the 24-hour period of deprivation she heard tape-recorded messages concerning the hazards of smoking cigarettes. While listening to these messages, the subject smelled cigarette smoke and was convinced that smoke was being pumped into the chamber as part of the treatment procedure. No smoke was actually present. A second case was a male, in deprivation as part of a treatment for overweight. His judgment of time happened to be quite good, and in the morning he smelled the distinct aroma of fresh coffee. He claimed the coffee smelled so good he could taste it. So convinced was he of this perception that he told the monitor over the intercom that the coffee she was making certainly smelled good. Of course, no coffee was actually being made.

Sensory deprivation also has an effect on the individual's ability to process information correctly. On one level it hampers reality testing. At its most basic this is illustrated by the fact that the complete absence of light makes it difficult to differentiate between having one's eyes open or closed. The unavailability of this basic reality test contributes to the more complex problems of distinguishing the various stages of sleep and wakefulness. Subjective phenomena related to different levels of these stages become hard to discriminate. For example, the occurrence of a hypnopompic image can be quite confusing. As the individual awakes from a very vivid dream there are few cues available with which he or she may appraise the experience. Confusion occurs as to whether the image was a hallucination, a dream, or merely a vivid thought.

Another possible impairment in processing has been hypothesized by Suedfeld (1972), who proposed that sensory deprivation causes cognitive disorganization, making it difficult to judge and organize available information. While this construct was originally posited to account for the decreased ability of sensorially deprived subjects to process external input, it is likely that it also affects the processing of internally generated input. Deprivation-induced cognitive disorganization could prevent accurate appraisal of thoughts and images, and may allow some aspects of a fantasy or memory to become disproportionately important. This could promote misinterpretation of internal representations and contribute to a "strangeness" of the subjective experience. For example, one subject began after five hours to think of her family at home. This thought led to thoughts of her children and their need for her. This idea became more and more salient until it was all she could think about. She began to think that she could hear her children calling her. At this point she terminated the session and rushed home feeling quite upset and anxious. While it is impossible to identify the part that cognitive disorganization played in this experience, it is likely that it did impair this subject's ability to appraise accurately the thoughts she was having.

Another factor that affects one's judgment of a situation is an intense need. Such a condition can selectively alter the perception of an image so that it fits more closely with the individual's need at the time. In sensory deprivation, the predominant need is the one for more input, particularly external input. Stimulus need may contribute to the acceptance of internal image experiences as real perceptions of external phenomena. However, the realization that such perceptions are impossible under the subject's present circumstances could lead to the alternative labeling of the experiences as ASC, hallucination, fantasy, or dream.

Many of the dreams reported in sensory deprivation have the common quality of seeming to fill the subject's increased stimulus need. A recurrent theme is the dream about being in the chamber, lying on the bed, and having some sort of interruption. This interruption can be as simple as someone walking in and sitting on the bed to talk with the subject. Sometimes it is more dramatic, such as one subject's dream that a group of people broke a hole through the wall and came in to have a party. Knowing that this was not supposed to happen, the subject attempted to shoo the celebrants back out through the hole. Another respite from sensory deprivation seems to come from dreaming about escaping or being let out of the chamber. In one case, this type of dream seemed to be fulfilling a second need as well. A subject in sensory deprivation as part of an overweight treatment dreamed that a group of people came to get her out of the chamber and took her to a banquet where she was the guest of honor. She sat at the head of the table because she was doing so well on her diet. After having only a glass of juice at the banquet, she returned to the chamber to finish her session.

The reduced mobility of the subject may also affect the interpretation of an experience. The absence of kinesthetic cues can not only suppress the enactive system of representation, but can contribute to an out-of-the-body experience. Fischer (1975) has said that voluntary motor performance will break down the "realism" of, and essentially end, an out-of-the-body experience. While in most sensory deprivation experiments the subjects are not physically immobilized, they are usually instructed to lie as still as possible. This allows the internal inputs an even broader degree of interpretation since there is little connection between perception and external inputs. Immobility therefore removes one further anchor in reality. An example of this type of experience can be seen in the following self-report from our own research:

> Somewhere near the beginning of the session I decided to meditate and found it easy to get very relaxed in a short time. One goal of meditation is to get away from the surface yammering of your conscious mind. That's the running monologue that seems to accompany everything. Anyway, this meditation was particularly successful. Somewhere along the line I became aware of myself standing next to the bed. It wasn't really next to the bed but slightly above the bed on the side where the wall was. I could see myself very clearly as one sees another person. Strangely, however, I was also aware of myself and my body lying on the bed. This was the self that felt like me. I was inside the one on the bed. At the realization that there were two of me, I became quite excited about the possibility of talking with this other me. When I was going to talk to this self next to the bed, I became very aware of my body. It now seemed to be not on the bed but floating weightlessly slightly above it. The feeling of weightlessness then became a tingle all over. This tingle quickly turned into a tremor which grew to the point that my whole body was quaking. Every part of me was shaking so violently that I was aware of nothing else. Finally I was afraid the quaking of my body was going to disturb the people in the next room. At that thought, all was still again. My body was as relaxed as if nothing had happened. My other self was gone. It was like waking from a dream, which it may well have been. It's funny though that at no point, not even when I was shaking, was I frightened or upset. It was very exciting.

The fourth property of impaired control over cognition seems to be common in sensory deprivation. Horowitz (1975) has postulated that stress, drugs, or the lowering of the usual defensive overcontrol can allow the intrusion of unbidden images that have a startling effect because of their salient and unintentional quality. Deprived subjects often report that in the later portion of their stay they become unable to concentrate on any one thing; their "mind wanders," and thoughts come in an uncontrolled stream of consciousness. This loss of control or inability to maintain a single line of thought seems to increase with time in deprivation. It is possible that this phenomenon is part of the increase in cognitive disorganization that occurs as a function of stimulus reduction. Gradual loss of cognitive control is frequently reported in the literature, again with wide individual differences. For example, Haggard, Ås, and Borgen (1970) found that persons from rural environments with low stimulus levels suffered very little loss of cognitive control during experimental sensory deprivation, in contrast to urban dwellers adapted to high stimulation, whose thinking became incoherent.

Control or the perception of control over subjective experiences is an important variable in the reaction to those experiences. Actually, one frequently reported negative effect of sensory deprivation is the inability to maintain a line of thought. Subjects who report having been able to concentrate on and solve some of the problems that had been bothering them early in the sensory deprivation session become disturbed when they are no longer able to do this. Subjects who are able to relax and enjoy the flow are the ones who suffer least from this loss of control, in accordance with the theories cited previously (Goldberger, 1961; Kammerman, 1977; Lilly, 1956; Myers et al., 1966; Suedfeld, 1975).

Conclusion

If one takes a retrospective look at the literature in human experimental sensory deprivation, one finds that its role in the induction of ASC is considerably more restricted than is commonly thought. Reports of hallucinations and delusions tend to be unverified or at best dubious. Changes in perceptual and affective reactions are typically not qualitatively different from those experienced in normal environments, although there may be some quantitative shift.

It is probable that this kind of low-intensity ASC (if it can be called an ASC at all) is characteristic of the experiences of most deprived subjects. However, there seem to be others who undergo much more intense alteration for some reason. One possible explanation of this difference is the ability of the majority of subjects to maintain control over their cognitive and perceptual processes to a greater extent than the minority, whose states of consciousness alter as a result of a reduction of secondary process dominance. Among this minority, some find the experience distressing and react with a general disorganization and negative affect that frequently result in their leaving the chamber. Others, however, can either relax and enjoy the flow of fantasy or can turn it to creative functions, what Goldberger (1961) called primary process functioning in the service of secondary process. Such experiences may decrease the subject's fear of unusual conscious states, possibly with a decrease in the use of unnecessary or inappropriate defense mechanisms and a concomitant improvement of personality integration (Kammerman, 1977; Lilly, 1956). The results may in some cases be not only conducive to self-actualization, but may be specifically therapeutic for various problems.

One thing is fairly certain: The interesting aspect of sensory deprivation in relation to ASCs is not in the production of so-called hallucinations or the fleeting changes in time perception or body orientation, some of which are artifactual and none of which appears to be terribly important. Rather, the interesting and promising aspects of the experience are those related to dreams and fantasies. These are also the aspects that are the least thoroughly investigated and the least understood, even though the hypothetical explanations of sensory deprivation effects revolve around them. Given the changing emphasis and volume of research activity in this field, it may well be that the mysteries will remain mysterious.

REFERENCES

Azima, H., Vispo, R., & Azima, F. J. Observations on anaclitic therapy during sensory deprivation. In P. Solomon, P. E. Kubzansky, P. H. Leiderman, J. H. Mendelson, R. Trumbull, & D. Wexler (eds.), *Sensory deprivation.* Cambridge: Harvard University Press, 1961.

Berlyne, D. E. *Conflict arousal and curiosity.* New York: McGraw Hill, 1960.

Bexton, W. H., Heron, W., & Scott, T. H. Effects of decreased variation in the sensory environment. *Canadian Journal of Psychology* 1954, *8:* 70–76.

Borrie, R. A. *Sensory deprivation as a therapeutic facilitator in obesity treatment.* Ph.D. dissertation, The University of British Columbia, in preparation.

Borrie, R. A., & Suedfeld, P. *Arousal as an explanatory construct in sensory deprivation research.* Paper presented at the meeting of the Western Psychological Association, Los Angeles, April 1976.

Cappon, D., & Banks, R. Orientational perception: I. *Archives of General Psychiatry* 1961, *5:* 380–392.

Cohen, S. I., Silverman, A. J., Bressler, B., & Shmavonian, B. M. Problems in isolation studies. In P. Solomon, P. E. Kubzansky, P. H. Leiderman, J. H. Mendelson, R. Trumbull, & D. Wexler (eds.), *Sensory deprivation.* Cambridge: Harvard University Press, 1961.

Doane, B. K., Mahatoo, W., Heron, W., & Scott, T. H. Changes in perceptual functions after isolation. *Canadian Journal of Psychology* 1959, *13:* 210–219.

Fischer, R. Cartography of inner space. In R. K. Siegel & L. J. West (eds.), *Hallucinations: Behavior, experience, and theory.* New York: John Wiley & Sons, 1975.

Fiske, D. W. Effects of monotonous restricted stimulation. In D. W. Fiske & S. R. Maddi (eds.), *Functions of varied experience.* Homewood, Ill.: Dorsey, 1961.

Goldberger, L. Reactions to perceptual isolation and manifestations of the primary process. *Journal of Projective Techniques* 1961, *25:* 287–302.

Haggard, C., Ås, A., & Borgen, C. Social isolates and urbanites in perceptual isolation. *Journal of Abnormal Psychology* 1970, *76:* 1–9.

Harper, W., & Zubek, C. Short-term visual deprivation and critical flicker frequency. *Psychonomic Society* 1976, *7:* 525–526.

Hoffman, P. Personal communication, April 20, 1977.

Horowitz, M. J. *Image formation and cognition.* London: Meredith, 1970.

———. Hallucinations: An information-processing approach. In R. K. Siegel and L. J. West (eds.), *Hallucinations: Behavior, experience, and theory.* New York: John Wiley & Sons, 1975.

Jones, A. Stimulus-seeking behavior. In J. P. Zubek (ed.), *Sensory deprivation: Fifteen years of research.* New York: Appleton-Century-Crofts, 1969.

Kammerman, M. (ed.), *Sensory isolation and personality change.* Springfield, Ill.: Charles C. Thomas, 1977.

Kempe, P. *Bedingungen halluzinatorischer Phänomene bei Experimenten mit sensorischer Deprivation.* Ph.D. dissertation, Christian-Albrechts-Universität, Kiel, West Germany, 1973.

Kubie, L. S. *Practical and theoretical aspects of psychoanalysis.* New York: International Universities Press, 1950.

Leiderman, P. H. *Imagery and sensory deprivation, an experimental study.* (MRL–TDR62–28). Wright-Patterson Air Force Base, Ohio, May 1962.

————. Imagery and sensory deprivation. *Proceedings of the Third World Congress of Psychiatry,* 1964, Vol. III, pp. 227–231.

Lilly, J. Mental effects of reduction of ordinary levels of physical stimuli on intact, healthy persons. *Psychiatric Research Reports* 1956, *5:* 1–9.

————. *The center of the cyclone.* Des Plaines, Ill.: Bantam, 1973.

Lilly, J., & Shurley, J. T. Experiments in solitude in maximum achievable physical isolation with water suspension of intact healthy persons. In B. E. Flaherty (ed.), *Psychophysiological aspects of space flight.* New York: Columbia University Press, 1961.

London, H., Shubert, D. S. P., & Washburn, D. Increase of autonomic arousal by boredom. *Journal of Abnormal Psychology* 1972, *80:* 29–36.

Ludwig, A. M. Altered states of consciousness. *Archives of General Psychiatry* 1966, *15:* 225–234.

Murphy, D. B., Myers, T. I., & Smith, S. *Reported visual sensations as a function of sustained sensory deprivation and social isolation.* HumRRO Research Report. Monterey, Calif.: Human Resources Research Office, 1963.

Myers, T. I., Murphy, D. B., Smith, S., & Goffard, S. J. *Experimental studies of sensory deprivation in social isolation.* Unpublished technical report, HumRRO Technical Report. Washington, D.C.: George Washington University, 1966.

Neisser, U. *Cognitive psychology.* New York: Appleton-Century-Crofts, 1967.

Orne, M. T., & Scheibe, K. E. The contribution of non-deprivation factors in the production of sensory deprivation effects: The psychology of the panic button. *Journal of Abnormal and Social Psychology* 1964, *68:* 3–12.

Paivio, A. *Imagery and verbal processes.* New York: Holt, Rinehart, & Winston, 1971.

Savage, C. W. The continuity of perceptual and cognitive experiences. In R. K. Siegel & L. J. West (eds.), *Hallucinations: Behavior, experience, and theory.* New York: John Wiley & Sons, 1975.

Schultz, D. P. *Sensory restriction: Effects on behavior.* New York: Academic Press, 1965.

Smith, A. *Powers of mind.* New York: Random House, 1975.

Solomon, P., Kubzansky, P. E., Leiderman, P. H., Mendelson, J. H., Trumbull, R., & Wexler, D. (eds.), *Sensory deprivation.* Cambridge: Harvard University Press, 1961.

Suedfeld, P. Changes in intellectual performance and in susceptibility to influence. In J. P. Zubek (ed.), *Sensory deprivation: Fifteen years of research.* New York: Appleton-Century-Crofts, 1969. (a)

————. Theoretical formulations: II. In J. P. Zubek (eds.), *Sensory deprivation: Fifteen years of research*. New York: Appleton-Century-Crofts, 1969. (b)

————. Attitude manipulation in restricted environments: V. Theory and research. Paper read at the 20th International Congress of Psychology, Tokyo, 1972.

————. Social isolation: A case of interdisciplinary research. *Canadian Psychologist* 1974, *15:* 1–12.

————. The benefits of boredom: Sensory deprivation reconsidered. *American Scientist* 1975, *63:* 60–69.

Suedfeld, P., & Vernon, J. A. Visual hallucinations in sensory deprivation: A problem of criteria. *Science* 1964, *145:* 412–413.

Tart, C. T. Introduction. In C. T. Tart (ed.), *Altered states of consciousness*, New York: John Wiley & Sons, 1969.

Vernon, J. A. *Inside the dark room*. New York: Potter, 1963.

West, L. J. A general theory of hallucinations and dreams. In L. J. West (ed.), *Hallucinations*. New York: Grune & Stratton, 1962.

Wright, N. A., & Abby, D. S. Perceptual deprivation tolerance and adequacy of defenses. *Perceptual Motor Skills* 1965, *20:* 35–38.

Zubek, J. P. (ed.), *Sensory deprivation: Fifteen years of research*. New York: Appleton-Century-Crofts, 1969.

Zubek, J. P., Bross, M., & Harper, D. Changes in CFF during prolonged exposure of one eye to homogeneous illumination (Ganzfeld) and the other to darkness. *Studia Psychologica* 1976, *18:* 146–152.

Zuckerman, M. Hallucinations, reported sensations, and images. In J. P. Zubek (ed.), *Sensory deprivation: Fifteen years of research*. New York: Appleton-Century-Crofts, 1969. (a)

————. Theoretical formulations: I. In J. P. Zubek (ed.), *Sensory deprivation: Fifteen years of research*. New York: Appleton-Century-Crofts, 1969. (b)

▪10
Mysticism: Psychodynamics and Relationship to Psychopathology

MICHAEL R. ZALES

Evidence for the existence of mysticism and mystical trends is to be found in the history of both preliterate and civilized societies. This observation alone compels the conclusion that mysticism serves certain psychic needs, or that it constitutes an attempt to resolve certain ubiquitous problems.

There has been increased interest in mysticism in the United States and elsewhere during the past decade, and mysticism has been associated with social alienation and the rejection of a socially established morality. The similarities between mysticism and certain types of mental disorder, notably schizophrenia, as well as the likeness to temporal lobe seizures, are also receiving much attention. Mystical and hallucinogenic drug experiences show enough similarities in their formal characteristics that one might ask whether common mechanisms are involved. The creative aspects of mysticism are of interest, not only because they carry clues regarding underlying ideation and motivation, but also because they may shed light on the problem of creativity in general.

Perhaps the broadest descriptive statement that can be made about mystics is that they are individuals who view the world differently from others. In varying degrees, mystics derogate and detach themselves from the perceived, real world. They do so in either or both of two ways; first, by attributing a greater reality to their inner world or to belief in the transcendental or supernatural, and second, by attributing a higher reality to certain aspects of the perceived world, along with a complementary derogation of others. The first way suggests a similarity with schizophrenic detachment. It differs in that for mystics the detachment from consensual reality is sought, while for schizophrenics it appears to be obligatory. The second way resembles both the hallucinogenic drug experience and the temporal lobe seizure. In attempting to account for this, the psychiatrist may assume that that which is derogated or denied is that which disturbs, while that which is elevated and valued is that which is wished for. The mystic achieves this end by psychological means alone; the hallucinogenic drug user achieves it by pharmacological means; the temporal lobe seizure is attributable to organic factors.

Any attempt to understand mysticism must take into account the fact that the disposition of both individuals and groups to turn to it is influenced by environmental factors. Social, cultural, economic, political, and religious conditions play important roles in the origin and fate of mystical movements. These conditions vary from one sociocultural group to another and also from one time period to another. While the assessment of these factors may take the psychiatrist away from his area of special expertise, he cannot disregard them in evaluating the mystical phenomenon.

Mystical Union

The word *mystical* is used to describe experiences of union with supernatural power, in contrast to other experiences that are more appropriately called magical, esoteric, visionary, occult, or metaphysical. Differing from the usual practices of institutional religions, mysticism involves a relationship with the supernatural that is not mediated by another person. The goal of mystical union occurs during the course of this relationship. The union itself is considered ultimate reality, in comparison to which the events of everyday life are dim and uncertain.

The mystic asserts that the experience of union is not achieved by rational intellectual functions or through the ordinary senses, but from the depths of the soul. He is driven toward his goal by an outgoing love for the supernatural object. Although his description may employ sexual metaphors to describe this love, he asserts that it is not the sexually contaminated attraction between men and women. Neither is it the self-seeking love of a child.

There is probably a mystical element in all institutional religions —at least for some adherents. The tendency of the mystical approach to isolate individuals, however, is one of the reasons that churches tend to discourage it, inasmuch as they are dependent upon social organization. On the other hand, a mystical leader may dominate a religious group. In cases of secular mysticism, it may be denied that the practice is religious in nature, although here one becomes involved with questions of definition.

Although mystical experiences vary widely in content, they do share certain characteristics. The basic technique for achieving the mystical goal, used by mystics of all times and places, is commonly called contemplation. Successful contemplation requires arduous practice. Through it the mind gradually finds ways of eliminating thoughts of the self and the ordinary world, as well as abandoning all imaginative or reasoning thought processes. The ultimate direct encounter with the supernatural—the unitive state—occurs during a period of mental emptiness. It appears, as it were, on a blank screen. Although mystics have worked hard to find their way, they are passive recipients of the event.

The training process often begins with meditation—an exercise in which thought is consciously restricted to an isolated aspect of the potential mystic's belief system: a single sacred word, one aspect of God, or a short passage from the Bible, for example. All other ideas are rejected. This type of thinking is gradually succeeded by a state of emptiness in which rational thinking processes are eliminated. During this quiet period the mystic becomes aware of the supernatural while remaining distinct from it; an awareness of the self as an independent agency continues to exist. The state of true contemplation, or union, follows.

There are two aspects of the contemplative state—the transcendental and the immanent; they differ in relative strength from one mystic to another. From the transcendental aspect, the supernatural object is perceived as "the wholly other" or "the cloud of unknowing"; feelings of strangeness and awe in relation to it predominate, with corresponding feelings of humility concerning the self. On the other hand, a belief in the immanent nature of the supernatural, conceived as a part of the self, contributes to a more intimate and more joyful relationship with it.

The ultimate in the contemplative state is the occurrence of an ecstatic trance. The mystic is physically transfixed, unable to move or speak, and experiences a tremendous lucidity. A state of rapture is differentiated from the state of ecstasy by its sudden, violent onset and the occurrence of gross mental disorganization.

Great mystics, like great artists, take advantage of the ideas of their historical forebears, even though their search is private and creative. They usually have been adherents of traditional religious groups and make use of the religious forms to which they have been exposed. While doing this, however, their private and creative natures often put them on courses that defy traditional practices, and they find themselves at war with established authority.

Mystics agree that the mystical experience is ineffable, yet often they have felt the need to explain it. In reading the literature of the mystics, it is well to bear in mind that in attempting to describe the indescribable they have been forced to use symbolic terms. Images related to the pilgrim, the lover, and the alchemist are among those which have been commonly used. Mystical writers stress the limitation of such symbolic language and warn the reader of its dangers. They excuse it on the grounds that no other language is available to them.

The Mystic Way

The natural history of the contemplative process tends to follow a more or less typical course that has been called the Mystic Way. It is marked by alternating periods of joy and suffering. Indeed, suffering is considered essential to the attainment of the unitive state.

Typically, the Mystic Way is inaugurated by the sudden onset of an exalted experience, known as conversion. Mystical conversion, which should be distinguished from the usual conversion to a religious belief, is marked by the sudden expansion of the mystic frame of reference from a narrow, self-centered state to a broader view of oneself in the world and to a beginning awareness of the transcendent. This stage, as well as others in the Mystic Way, may be accompanied by visions or voices, a radiant light, and an increased lucidity involving one or all of the senses.

Clearly aware of their imperfections in relation to the supernatural, the mystics may now enter the state of purgation, a state that is filled with pain and suffering. In it they attempt to purify themselves by ascetic self-mortification; they simplify their existence, lead a life of poverty and chastity, and detach themselves from worldly pursuits and desires.

Once the mystics have succeeded in this initial divestment of their impurities and sensual claims, they emerge—both symbolically and literally—from the darkness into a bright light; this is the state of illumination. Suffering is again replaced with joy. There is a heightening of the sense perceptions and an apprehension of the supernatural. This is not as complete as in the later stage of union since the self is still perceived as a distinct entity. Auditory and visual hallucinations and phenomena such as automatic writing commonly appear during this phase.

Typically, illumination is followed by the most painful and horrifying experience of the Mystic Way. The bright light, the lucidity, and the perception of the supernatural object are replaced by a great darkness, a feeling of having been abandoned by the object, and finally, a conscious rejection of personal satisfactions. Similar to the earlier stage of purgation, it is deeper and more terrifying. The mystics, deprived and abandoned, feel so empty that contemplative activity is no longer possible, and the visions and voices of the earlier phase disappear. The emotions that accompany this period have caused it to be called the "mystic death" or "the dark night of the soul." It carries on the purification of the stage of purgation to its ultimate end—the total abandonment of any desire for self-satisfaction.

Thus prepared, the very few finally reach the mystical goal of union, a state of joy and absolute certainty. The actual experience is said to be timeless, yet often lasts for only a moment—"the space of an Ave Maria," according to St. Augustine. It remains forever implanted in the mystic's being. It is spontaneous, but at the same time the product of a long and difficult process. Although the mystics say that they seek no reward for their labors, they feel that their outgoing love has been returned in kind and that they have achieved an ineffable peace and a sense of moral perfection. The mystic who conceives of the supernatural object as an awesome, distant figure is apt to describe this union in terms of a godlike transformation called deification. When the supernatural is seen as a personal, intimate companion, the mystic may speak of a spiritual marriage between God and the soul. Once having attained this peak experience, brief as it may be, mystics are enabled to live their lives on "transcendental levels of reality." Endowed with great vitality and great certitude about the nature of their experience, the former recluses may now emerge as active leaders who regard the salvation of the world as their duty—not surprising in view of their identification with a godlike figure. It should be emphasized that all mystics do not reach this state of union. Jewish mystics, for example, describe only a clinging to God, rather than a merger.

The mysticism of the East insists on still another step on the mystical path: the total annihilation of the self and its absorption into the infinite, as expressed in the Sufis' Eighth Stage of Progress and the Buddhists' Nirvana. This suggests that the ultimate goals of Western and Eastern mysticism have opposing values: The Western mystic seeks the active life as a godlike figure or as one assisted by God, and the Eastern mystic seeks total passivity.

It is evident that the phenomena encompassed by, and related to, the term *mysticism* are numerous. They include states of mind of the individual, the nature of his relation to the world around him, and his behavior within the community in which he resides. It follows that a proper psychological account of mysticism that would do justice to all of these differing aspects must be correspondingly subtle and complex.

Trance State

I shall describe further the mystical trance state because, though it is less common, it is nevertheless the most dramatic and probably the most extreme phenomenon of those subsumed under the term *mysticism*.

Form

In the trance state, the external world is excluded from consciousness more or less completely, or its impact is muted; attention is turned away from it. To the extent that the external world is perceived, the impressions of it are distorted. Visual sensations seem brighter than their stimulus would warrant. Sounds seem louder. Sensations arising in bodily functions may be magnified. For example, there may be intense awareness of the beating of one's heart or the throbbing of one's blood vessels, or the sounds of one's breathing. Sensory experiences develop affective connotations. Inanimate objects seem threatening. Several of the modalities of sensation respond to a stimulus that ordinarily elicits only one; this phenomenon is known as synesthesia.

As the perception of the external world is suppressed, it may be replaced by hallucinatory experiences. These hallucinations are formed or unformed. Unformed, they appear mostly in the visual sphere. They are interpreted as water, mist, rocks, or jewels. The appearance of scintillation is described frequently, as is a sense of whispering or blowing. Formed hallucinations also are mostly visual, with only minor auditory components. The images are usually derived from the religious background of the individual. They may be described as unnatural or supernatural. There may be buildings, rooms, mountains, forests, oceans—all of immense magnitude and incomparable brilliance.

Some subjective sensations are encountered frequently. Subjects will usually say that their mystical experiences are more real than conventional reality. They experience a sense of elevation in any of the meanings of that term. They may describe feeling ecstatic, or they may say that they feel literally transported to a high place such as a mountaintop. They will commonly declare that their experiences are indescribable in conventional language. They usually experience some kind of contact or union with a divine being.

Anxiety may appear at the outset of the experience, but when the mystical adventure succeeds, anxiety is soon replaced by ecstasy. Sensations of familiarity are often encountered, as well as the experience of depersonalization or of expansion of the self. Commonly, the subject describes a sense of revelation, of new knowledge, of seeing the light, both figuratively and literally.

States of Mind Similar to the Mystical State

The mystical state, as described by those who experience it, reminds one of states of mind described under other circumstances. For example, the hallucinogenic drug experience resembles the mystical trance; in fact, hallucinogenic drugs have been and are used at times in rituals of organized religions and by individuals to induce the mystical state. Such a drug-induced mystical experience seems to satisfy the criteria of some theologians for religious validity.

The onset of schizophrenia is often marked by a similar aversion to, or detachment from, the world of reality, with a complementary turning to sensations arising intrapsychically. The incipient schizophrenic feels that something bad has been rejected, and a new and promising vision of life attained. Here, too, there are distortions or hallucinatory replacement of sensation. This acute schizophrenic state usually lasts from a few moments to a few days, and ultimately gives way to one of the more enduring and familiar syndromes.

In seizure states originating in the temporal lobe, caused by organic disease, states of mind are encountered that are accompanied by the perceptual distortions, the hallucinations, and the disturbances in the sense of reality, familiarity, or both, that are characteristic of the mystical state. The sense of ecstasy, expansion, or elation is usually not encountered.

The trance state may be considered to possess dynamic significance whether it is induced by mystical preparation, or hallucinogenic drugs, or occurs spontaneously in an acute schizophrenic attack. Consciousness is occupied by intrapsychic sensations. The external world has been removed from the individual's awareness, and therefore it seems to have been destroyed. The area of awareness that is usually occupied by the external world is now occupied by sensations that arise from within. These are illusorily interpreted as manifestations of the outside. The world of outer, consensual reality then is replaced by the world of inner sensation, which seems to be the world of reality. The sense of reality is usually transferred from the outside inward. The impression to which I have referred—that the outer world is destroyed—is complemented by an impression that it is being replaced by a new world, that the world is being reborn.

Content

I have been speaking of the *form* of the fantasy, which seems to be remarkably consistent no matter how the trance state is induced and from one individual to another. The *content* can often be understood as the resolution of the problem that motivated the divorce from reality in the first place, when the latter has come about as a result of psychic stress or as a result of deliberate, rather than fortuitous, intoxication. Usually the content represents a reunion of some kind with the individual from whom the mystic feels alienated. This reunion may take the form of an approach, an embrace, a sexual act, or a physical merging. The objects of the union often seem to be one or both parents, sometimes represented directly, occasionally by other humans, or frequently, in religious contexts, as God or other figures with supernatural or divine attributes.

Affect

The *affect* that accompanies the experience is determined by a number of factors. It includes some residue of the distressing affect that prevailed before the trance began and that may have played a role in inducing the trance. There is often anxiety generated by the dissociation from the world of reality. One also encounters the pleasure that follows the escape from the pressures of reality into a gratifying fantasy. Therefore, in some instances one encounters panic or dread; in others, ecstasy; and in others, fluctuations between unpleasant and pleasant states.

There are no reliable data that would permit me to study the psychological occasion for mystical withdrawal. Acute schizophrenic detachment, which resembles mystical withdrawal, is usually precipitated by some disappointment in relations with other individuals, whether that disappointment is initiated by the subject or by a loved one. Mystics are generally not mentally ill; it seems likely that difficulty arises not only in their relations with other individuals but also in their relations with their communities, since their behavior brings about a withdrawal from the societies in which they live. There are circumstances in which the demands the community imposes upon its members are so stringent that many cannot comply and use the mystical detachment as a way of escaping these demands. The term *community demand* applies to situations in which economic hardship or political oppression absorb major portions of the individual's energy, leaving him little opportunity for gratification. However, it may be just as difficult for an individual to find himself in a society that, because it has been disrupted by war or by revolution or by disaster, fails to protect the individual and provide him with the sense of belonging to a community which he requires. Here, too, there is a demand in the sense that the individual must do for himself what is ordinarily expected of his society.

Origins

Let us now consider the genesis of two aspects of the mystical trance, namely, the origin of the trance state itself and the origin of its contents.

The kind of psychic function one finds in the trance state can be compared to what one might imagine to be the psychic function of infants. In both instances, there is no awareness of hard external reality that is not immediately relevant to the individuals themselves. They give their full attention to sensations arising within their bodies and within their minds, hallucinating the fulfillment of their needs. (In psychoanalytic metapsychology, this state is called primary narcissism.) Ordinarily this state is left behind as an individual's perceptual capacities mature and as he acquires not only the images but the concepts of an outside reality with which he must contend. The readiness to revert to this primal state, while it may create vulnerability to mental illness, can be used defensively when external reality becomes too distressing. When this regression becomes obligatory, so that the individual cannot by an act of will prevent it or undo it, we consider him psychotic. When the regression proceeds to the point of transferring the sense of reality from outside inward and yet the regression can be voluntarily intensified or resisted or terminated, we see a trance-like state such as that which I have been describing. We have no difficulty in diagnosis when the situation is clear-cut. However, one sometimes encounters states of mind that do not fall clearly into one category or the other.

Some individuals, while participating in every visible way in the real world, nevertheless attribute personal "meaning," not consensually shared by the larger society, to the images of the ordinary individuals and objects they encounter. Here a residue of this primal state of mind flavors external reality and softens its impact.

What about the origin of the contents of the trance state? The creatures of the trance usually represent a deity. Sometimes there are two such figures, one male and one female, or a member of the divine court as it is given in the religious tradition of the subject.

The action of the fantasy focuses on the relation between the subject and the representation of the deity. It may be that the subject just sees this supernatural figure, but in such instances it is implied that merely seeing it is itself a wondrous experience. The individual may approach the deity. Something may be revealed or done to him by the deity, or he may unite with the deity. As he experiences this trance state the subject feels illuminated, expanded, inspired, or that he is acquiring wisdom and power.

In conclusion, when an individual is confronted with an unacceptable reality, intrapsychic, personal, or social, he rejects that reality and excludes it from consciousness, psychically destroying it. He replaces it with a new, inner reality that he has designed to gratify rather than frustrate him. This process represents a rebirth, a return to a state of mind characteristic of his infancy, when he was able to deal with frustration and disappointment by retreating to a world of fantasy, when he was supposedly blessed with a firm and intimate union with his parents. Achieving this union in fantasy, he now feels vigorous and powerful and no longer dependent upon the whims of other humans.

Individuals who experience the trance state usually speak of invigoration and a feeling of power that appear during the trance and persist for some time thereafter. The feeling of being energized contrasts with the feelings of dismal unhappiness and inertia that precede the trance, referred to previously as "the dark night of the soul." One may infer that the detachment from frustrating reality has liberated the individual from its depressing and enervating influences. Both this freedom and the illusion of uniting with the omnipotent parent create the feeling of alertness, vitality, and strength.

The Mystical Life

While the trance with its drama creates the strongest impression, it constitutes only a small part of the mystical life. Trances occur infrequently among those individuals who experience them, and are brief. The "mystical life" these individuals lead possesses its own qualities, even though these may be considered either preparatory to, or the consequence of, the trance. Many, in fact, who regard themselves as leading a mystical life never experience a mystical trance. In some mystical movements the trance plays no role. For example, in Jewish mysticism, both Cabalistic and Hasidic, the trance is absent. The emphasis in these cases is on the mystical way of life, not on the experience of dissociation.

The essence of the mystical life is described as seeing mundane things, people, and events of everyday reality as the worldly representations of a supernal world, invisible to the eye of the unilluminated. Awareness of this supernal world makes it possible for the individual to appreciate the otherworldly significance of this-worldly objects.

Behavior within the Community

Pursuing the psychological analysis, one might say that mystics continue psychically to reside in the world of consensual reality in the sense of behaving appropriately and performing their roles within the community. At the same time, to overcome the frustration and disappointment that seem to them to arise within the lower world, they look for satisfaction in the experience of reverting to a primal state, in feeling if not in behavior. They interpret what they see of the external world as a representation of the inner world, and thereby they make it possible for themselves to tolerate the external world. In a sense, the latter is made more palatable by being flavored by the inner world and its affects.

What mystics do that is different from what their fellow citizens do depends upon the basis of their mysticism and the nature of their relation to the community. Many of the important things that mystics do they relate to the mystical experience. They do some things to prepare for or to invite the experience; they say and they do other things because they are influenced by it. From a superficial point of view, one may accept their explanation. However, one may suspect that these activities, which they claim are determined by the mystical experience, are actually motivated by unconscious needs, probably the same needs that invoke the trance. It does no violence to the facts to infer that the adoption of the mystical attitude and way of life performs an adaptive function in the sense that it makes it possible for individuals to cope with social stresses that threaten to overwhelm them.

In order to prepare for mystical experience, individuals engage in activities that may be seen as methods of undoing sin. There may be confession, abstinence, penitence, or purification. One encounters such activities outside the religious context, in individuals who are trying to ward off depression by consciously or unconsciously inviting forgiveness, love, and protection of a parental figure. In a few bizarre instances, an indulgence in sinful behavior is seen as a way of purification, because by descending to what he sees as the depths of depravity the individual "destroys the power of evil." The desperate pursuit of sensual gratification can be used also in the attempt to prevent depression because it replaces the emptiness of impending depression with the excitement provided by sensual experience.

Mystics may say that the mystical experience encourages them to commit themselves to a purer, that is, abstinent, way of life. Such a commitment is sometimes seen as an attempt to prevent the return to depression after a period of relief and well-being.

Differences between Mystics and Schizophrenics

While mystics may seem to be following in the footsteps of schizophrenics in that they retreat from outer to inner reality, they differ from schizophrenics in three important ways. First, their retreat is facultative rather than obligatory. Second, it is partial rather than complete. Third, mystics find it possible, frequently desirable, to associate with others who share their view of the world; that is, they participate in mystical fraternities. Schizophrenics, on the other hand, are rarely able to form or maintain affectionate ties with others.

The "reality" from which the schizophrenic and the mystic retreat is the reality of the demands of affectionate ties. Schizophrenics find their difficulty either in emancipating themselves from their parents early in life or in coming to terms with their spouses as adults. Mystics, on the other hand, find the demands and constraints of the society in which they live too difficult. In a sense, then, both schizophrenics and mystics retreat from social reality in two ways. On a personal and psychological level, they withdraw interest from the world that presents itself to their senses. On a social level, they withdraw themselves from the society in which they live. They differ in that schizophrenics can and do maintain this withdrawal by sustaining their regression from normal psychic function to infantile narcissism. The mystics' withdrawal is overwhelming during the brief trance periods when they occur, and it is only partial at most other times. They must reinforce their withdrawal from the larger society by creating a smaller one held together by the common interests of its members.

The Mystical Society

Since it is the authority and the associated demands of the larger, older society that these individuals cannot accept, the new one must be democratic and fraternal and without an established hierarchy. In order to prevent a demand for intense, affectionate attachments, the new society usually requires abstinence and self-control.

The mystical society consciously rejects its matrix, but unconsciously may see itself as cast off and rejected. It considers itself elite and elect; that is, it defends itself against the unconscious view that it is undesirable by putting forward the opposite view. It disputes the religious basis for the authority of the larger society. The larger society claims that its authority derives from Divine recognition, while the new fraternity claims that its members experience God directly and, therefore, need not defer to established authority.

From a psychological point of view, one may conclude the following about mystics. They find living within society stressful. They retreat from society and the reality it sponsors by withdrawing their interest from both and reinvesting it in impressions that arise from within. They take advantage of their ability to retreat to the psychic position that existed during their infancy when the only reality that had access to their consciousness was the reality of inner sensation. They reinforce this retreat and overcome the loneliness it would create by joining with others to form an elite, democratic, and abstemious mystical fraternity. They claim authority for their departure from, or rebellion against, the religious establishment by asserting that they have been granted immediate experience of the Divine, which supersedes traditional authority.

However, it must not be forgotten that the mystical state resembles not just certain pathological conditions but also common psychological phenomena that are generally regarded as normal. In romantic love, for example, there is a changed sense of reality in which the overestimation of the loved one approaches the mystic's attitude toward the Divine; and in a course that never runs smoothly, ecstasy alternates with darkness and suffering. As another example, the esthetic reactions touched off by painting, poetry, and music are characterized by a change in the sense of reality in which the external world is significantly distorted or excluded and that is both sublime and ineffable. In still another example, those who are deeply affected by nature see natural objects in terms of human form and feelings, an experience they share with mystics; in fact, identification with nature is so complete for some persons as to be indistinguishable from mystical union.

Feelings of awe experienced toward another human being or nature—like love—can be compared to those phases of mysticism in which there is contact with the Divine. Some athletes experience a fusion between their bodies and the environment, and performance may be directly related to success in reaching this state of mind. Like the mystical union, ordinary flashes of insight, as well as these other states, are experienced passively and spontaneously; none can be elicited by logical thought, but they arise from unknown inner sources in which the boundaries between self and object fade or disappear. Such observations suggest that potential mystics abound —indeed, that everyone might tap these inner sources and become a mystic were it not for the inhibitions and rigidities imposed by early training and the want of proper motivation. Even so, recent surveys indicate that a high percentage of the population claims to have had one or more mystical experiences.

Creativity

Perhaps the mental phenomenon with the closest psychological ties to mysticism is creativity, the state in which the mind integrates a variety of information into a new configuration. This relationship is recognized not only by members of modern mystical groups who claim that their methods will enhance creativity, but by the man who is regarded by many as the foremost creative thinker of our time, Albert Einstein (1954). He wrote, "The most beautiful, the most profound emotion we can experience is the sensation of the mystical. It is the fundamental emotion that stands at the cradle of true art and science."

The idea of the relationship between mysticism and creativity was recognized in ancient times. Plato's dictum recognizes the fusion of God and the creative person (embodied in the poet) as well as the state of emptiness that is prerequisite to achieving the mystic goal:

> God takes away the minds of poets . . . in order that we who hear them may know them to be speaking not of themselves, who utter these priceless words in a state of unconsciousness, but that God himself is the speaker, and that through them he is conversing with us.

In the West, experimental empiricism—such as displayed by Galileo—found an ally in antiauthoritarian religious mysticism, with "rational" theology lined up against it. The addiction that some seventeenth-century biologists had for the Cabalah hinged on the belief that its mysticism might contribute to their studies.

In Islam, too, mystical theology was closely associated with early scientific developments. The same phenomena occurred in China at the time of the ancient philosophical schools. It was the mystical Taoists, rather than the rational, government-sponsored Confucians, who stimulated Chinese scientific discovery. Like mystics in general, the Taoists stressed spontaneity, "inaction," "emptying the mind," simplicity, tranquility, and "transcendental bliss." Emptying the mind was intended to rid it of distorting memories, prejudices, and preconceived ideas so that true practical knowledge would flourish.

The qualities of the mystical mind are not confined to the artist and the scientist. Some political figures also seem to possess them. It has been suggested that political leaders are effective not merely because of their position but due to gifts of grace (charisma) by virtue of which they are set apart from others and treated as endowed with supernatural, superhuman, or at least specifically exceptional powers or qualities. Like mystics, charismatic leaders tend to appear when large numbers of people are suffering some kind of distress and when rationalistic thinkers in positions of power are tied to worn-out, rigid systems.

Einstein (1954) pointed out two motives that lead people to art and science, motives that also lead people to mysticism. The first is negative: "to escape from everyday life with its painful crudity and hopeless dreariness, from the fetters of one's own shifting desires." The second is positive:

> Man tries to make for himself in the fashion that suits him best a simplified and intelligible picture of the world; he then tries to some extent to substitute this cosmos of his for the world of experience, and thus to overcome it. This is what the painter, the poet, the speculative philosopher, and the natural scientist do, each in his own fashion. Each makes this cosmos and its construction the pivot of his emotional life, in order to find in this way peace and security which he cannot find in the narrow whirlpool of personal experience.

When I suggest that mystics are motivated in their search by disappointment with society, by the need to escape from unacceptable external realities, or by the need to rid themselves of depression and the feeling of being rejected outsiders, I am saying much the same that Einstein said about creators. Similarly, when I suggest that in reaching this goal mystics at last achieve a sense of belonging, and that mystical union symbolizes union with a parental figure from whom they felt estranged, I am only adding details to Einstein's remarks about the positive goals of the creator. Indeed, under different cultural or personal influences the creative person might have become a mystic. While it is true that similar problems face all people, they seem to be especially significant to the mystic and the creator. This may account in some measure for the great amount of energy both put into their work in their need to solve these problems.

Thus, both the creator and the mystic appear to have antiestablishment tendencies; they defy authority and often find themselves in confrontation with church, government, and community. Both aim to create a new world image—whether in a spiritual or an ideological sense, in words, on canvas, in music, in mathematics, in the laboratory, or in political action. They often experience this new image as a phenomenon of rebirth or speak of the "pangs of birth." Their goal is to create new solutions to old problems, and in doing so, change their view of themselves and of the world as well. For the most part, they wish to create a revolution in people's minds, but when pushed to it, may become militant in the service of their cause. Those who are more passive or who feel more threatened by personal encounter may furnish the ideas for new movements, while more active physical types furnish the brawn. Whatever their contribution, both are often regarded with a mixture of suspicion and awe by the community.

Syncretism, a type of thinking that unites or reconciles diverse ideas, seems to be an important facet of the thinking of both mystics and creators, one that is essential to their aims. Perhaps related to it, the synesthesia noted in mystics is also seen in artists, for example, in their not uncommon references to a mutual relationship between colors and musical tones. Like mystics, creators frequently project their inner fantasies, self-image, and emotions on the external world, attributing personal meaning to objects and to other individuals.

Like the mystic, the creator seeks solitude. Indeed, the ability to tolerate solitude is required by the goals of both, for only in solitude can the mind work out the new mental configuration it seeks. While this ability may be autonomous, it may have developed out of fear of intimacy and the need to handle the loneliness that accompanies isolation. Some creative people find that the solitary quest for new ideas alleviates their loneliness, and this quest then becomes a powerful force that stimulates creative thinking.

Like mystics, creators often do not isolate themselves totally from human contact, but tend to form small, close-knit groups with common interests and goals. These groups may not only provide a source of new ideas but also help to contain loneliness while avoiding the feared or hated establishment. Furthermore, the democratic nature of the group discourages the development of new authorities and helps to maintain self-esteem.

The mystics' love of the Divine and their desire to be intimate with Him has its counterpart in the creators' devotion to nature and natural laws and their desire to understand them as no one has ever understood them before—whether this be in artistic, scientific, or philosophic terms. This relationship, like the mystics' with Divinity, is personal and direct. Both mystics and creators commonly find a haven in the use of symbols: artists, for example, in the color, form, or object to which they attach special significance; the scientist in mathematics (a subject also dear to the hearts of many mystics); others in an esoteric vocabulary known only to initiates.

The alternating moods of depression and joy characteristic of the Mystic Way find their counterpart in the powerful mood swings of many creators, forming a common enough pattern to warrant suggesting a creative-depressive personality comparable to that of the manic-depressive. The creative phase, like the manic phase, is marked by a tremendous output of energy, but differs from the latter in having clear-cut goals. The mystic's "illumination" is analogous to the "inspiration" of the creator. In both, the periods in which old information is brought together in new and exciting patterns seem to appear spontaneously and passively, as if on a blank screen. Inspiration is a time when previous ideas and observations fit together like the pieces of a puzzle; doubts and depression disappear, and the certainty of "ultimate truth" takes their place.

Conclusion

An inability to make a firm distinction between a mystical and a psychopathological state may be due, in part at least, to fundamental theoretical problems in psychiatry. The many ways in which human behavior and thought can be perceived make numerous points of view inevitable. For example, some draw fine lines between various psychiatric disorders and some regard all psychiatric diagnoses as irrelevant and perceive schizophrenia as a manifestation to be prized as a way toward better adaptation. Pathology may be uncovered in the nature and method of resolution of the conflicts in one who seems to be brimming over with mental health, while the thought and behavior of the most disturbed patient may be viewed as a contribution to his well-being. Therefore, one should not expect to be able to reach a definite conclusion that distinguishes mysticism from mental disorder (GAP report, 1976).

The ambiguity of the mystical personality, in history and on the current scene, is illustrated by the fact that no single generalization can be made to account for it. Historical studies or clinical observations of many mystics point primarily toward pathological variables and see mystical experiences as symptoms of mental disturbance. Studies of other mystics lead to an appreciation of their contributions and creativity, and point to their mystical experiences as marvelously adaptive. Observations of still other mystics show that these seemingly polar attributes can and do exist in the same personality. The mystic, however, learns to live with paradox, to accommodate himself to opposing views, and finally to unite them. The fullest understanding of mysticism undoubtedly requires a similar effort.

REFERENCES

Einstein, A. *Ideas and opinions.* New York: Crown, 1954, p. 75.
Group for the Advancement of Psychiatry (GAP). *Mysticism: Spiritual quest or psychic disorder?* New York: GAP, 1976.

■11
Drugs and Consciousness: An Attentional Model of Consciousness with Applications to Drug-Related Altered States

STEVEN M. FISHKIN and BEN MORGAN JONES

The question, "What's it all about?" (What am I? What are you? What's an atom? The world? The universe? What's my place in it?) has been asked countless times in countless settings and by individuals too numerous to tally. Ways of approaching this question have been developed by both scientists (physicists, astronomers, psychologists, etc.) and humanists (writers, philosophers, theologians, etc.) and in our society a new principle of very great importance is beginning to be generally recognized—spurred on, no doubt, by the contribu-

This work was supported in part by the Medical Research Service of the Veterans Administration and by U.S. Public Health Service Grant AA01444, "Effects of Alcohol on Women during the Menstrual Cycle," from the National Institute on Alcohol Abuse and Alcoholism, under the direction of Ben Morgan Jones.

We thank Sherrilyn Gillespie for typing the manuscript and for editorial comment.

273

tions of both. This principle is that the evidence, the experience, that is gathered in an effort to deal with the question "What's it all about?" —no matter what the approach or the level of technical or theoretical sophistication—is always handled by a system called consciousness. From this realization it follows that the answer to the question, in all its ramifications, depends in large measure on the properties of this system. If consciousness changes, the answer to the question may change, and to the extent that we desire a more or less complete answer, we will have to be concerned with the nature of consciousness in its various states.

In this society the use of consciousness-altering substances has increased in recent years. Understanding the effects of these is important for a variety of practical reasons relating to personal, legal, and social matters. However, in this chapter the study of their effects is important primarily because drugs provide a means of examining the nature of consciousness and its alterations.

We present here a very speculative model of consciousness. At present, many of the statements regarding the model and related issues are neither confirmed nor unconfirmed by scientific data. The value of such a model is that it may provide the reader as well as the authors with an occasion to stretch the imagination. More specifically, we hope that the reader may be provided with a context within which he can fit together some of the phenomena of consciousness and its alterations. We also hope that those readers who are interested in investigating these matters further may find some interesting ideas or starting points for their own work.

In addition to presenting the model, we attempt to demonstrate its applicability by focusing on altered states of consciousness (ASC) that can arise in connection with the consumption of certain common substances. The ones we have chosen to look at are marijuana and alcohol. These are pertinent examples not only because of their widespread use, but also because in some respects they appear to "produce" opposite sorts of alterations of consciousness.

Introduction to the Model

The model is illustrated in Figure 11-1. It should be understood that the purpose of the model is to depict relationships among the incorporated phenomena rather than to specify the physiological processes that may underlie the phenomena. Assuming a rational

PAC or Material Potentially
Available to Consciousness
(all the area within the
curved lines to the left of
the WINDOW)
CONSCIOUSNESS
WINDOW (variable in size and
movable; closed while moving)

Near the Working Edge
are subdivisions of the PAC
which can be readily accessible to CONSCIOUSNESS:
    External Perception
    Body Perception
    Brain Perception
    Verbal Thinking
    Nonverbal Thinking
    Unspecified
    Direct Access to Uncon-
        scious

Memory and Unconscious Material (represent parts of
the PAC which are ordinarily
less available to CONSCIOUS-
NESS)

Attentional Control
Energy
External World
Behavior

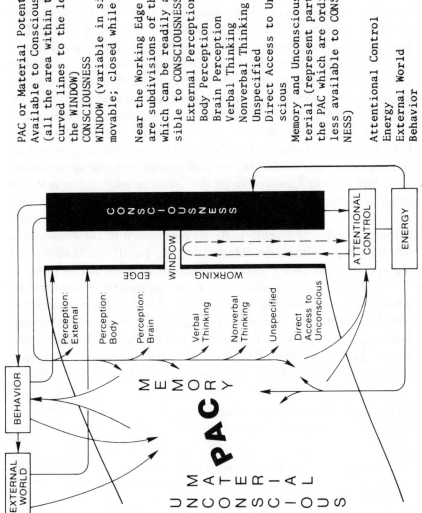

FIGURE 11-1. Model of consciousness.

275

universe, there would be a reasonable fit between an appropriate model of psychological phenomena and the underlying physiological mechanisms. In this chapter, however, no attempt will be made to elucidate the nature of the fit.

The model asserts that there are certain types of phenomena that are potentially available to consciousness (PAC). The major categories of phenomena contained in the PAC are listed in Table 11-1. Most of these phenomena, while potentially available to consciousness, are not in consciousness at any moment in time. The unselected phenomena remain in the PAC, and some of them (for example, incoming stimulation) are transformed and stored as memories. Memories are generally somewhat less available to consciousness than are ongoing events. This is represented in Figure 11-1 by the bulk of memory being further away from the "working edge," although some parts of memory are also readily available to consciousness. Still further removed from the working edge is the material called unconscious. This material is potentially available to consciousness, but reaches it only under certain conditions. A direct route through which unconscious material may pass into consciousness is also included in the model. This route is ordinarily not available but may be selected under special circumstances, such as dreaming.

The contents of consciousness at any moment is determined by what is being attended to. In the model, attention is represented as a moving window between the potentially conscious and what gets into consciousness. When the window is at a particular location along the working edge of the PAC, material from that vicinity will enter consciousness through the window. Thus, in terms of the model,

TABLE 11-1. Types of Phenomena That Are
Potentially Available to Consciousness (PAC)

1. Perception of external events.
2. Perception of body events (includes body position and movement as well as the state of muscle tension and glandular activity; "feelings" are included in this category).
3. Perception of brain-initiated events (imagery, hallucinations, dreams, etc.).
4. Verbal thinking (may or may not lead to speaking).
5. Nonverbal thinking (the "flash" or "it" that precedes words; that which words are an attempt to express).
6. Unspecified (psi phenomena?).
7. Direct access to unconscious material.

what is in consciousness is largely determined by the location of the window. Another feature of the window is that its size is variable. When attention is narrowly focused, the window is small. As the window grows larger, larger segments of the PAC material can move through it. This corresponds to a broadening of attention.

Shifts of attention are represented in the model as shifts in the location of the window to a new place along the working edge. The window is further assumed to have a shutter that is closed during movements and open otherwise. When attention has shifted and the shutter is opened, consciousness gets "loaded" with a segment of material from the PAC that stays there until the next loading period. Ordinarily, attentional shifts occur quite rapidly, that is, once a second or faster.

The PAC is assumed to have the characteristics of fluidity and structure. If the region of the PAC near the window is relatively fluid, more material from laterally adjacent and deeper lying areas can flow through into consciousness. Less-fluid regions will pass less material for a given duration and size of window. In this context the word *material* is used in a very general sense without implying, for example, that a physical substance moves from the PAC into consciousness. Structure refers to the connectedness or association of material in the PAC.

Another feature of the model is the energy source. This is assumed to be a reservoir of changing quantity with outputs to the attentional control mechanism, to consciousness, and to the PAC. The corresponding functions of each of these three uses of energy are: driving the attention shift mechanism, increasing the intensity of conscious experience, and maintaining low fluidity (high rigidity) of the PAC. At any given moment in time, a certain amount of energy is available for the three functions. Therefore, if more is used for one of the functions, less will be available for the others. For example, if a fixed amount of energy is used to maintain a given level of PAC rigidity, the intensity of conscious experience will vary inversely with rate of attentional shifting; other things being equal, the more rapidly attention shifts, the less intense the experiential world will be.

Overt behavior, while not the focus of the model, is included with its connections to other parts of the model. The direction of influence is indicated by arrows. Sometimes behavior is under the control of consciousness, and at other times it appears to be under the control of processes that are not conscious. Our behavior can affect the external world, and the external world affects behavior indirectly through its inputs into the PAC. Other arrows indicate the influence of consciousness on other aspects of the model. In its present state of development, the model does not attempt to explain how the various influences work, but merely acknowledges their presence. In addition to influencing behavior, consciousness can influence the attentional control mechanism. For example, one can consciously choose, within limits, to attend to various sections of the PAC. On the other hand, part of attentional control arises from sources within the PAC. It is also hypothesized that consciousness is a source of input to the PAC. This possibility is also depicted by the appropriate arrows.

Table 11-2 presents a summary of the parameters of the model and their psychological functions. It is on the basis of these parameters that a state of consciousness (SC) may be defined. Each SC is characterized by a particular set of values and/or attributes of the eight parameters. A characterization of the ordinary state of consciousness (OSC) is presented in Table 11-3. (The interested reader is urged to examine the tables closely since some information contained in them is not discussed in the text.)

Further Discussion of the Model

Many aspects of the model require further clarification. The following paragraphs attempt to deal with some of these issues.

The concept of nonverbal thought (part of the PAC) is used here in a special way. Some readers may have experienced "thinking" with pictorial images or with images in other senses. While this phenomenon is certainly real, it is not what is meant by nonverbal thinking, and is included in the model as category 3 in Table 11-1. What is meant by nonverbal thinking may be conveyed by the following exercise: Be aware of the next sentence you think of or say aloud. Now be aware of the possibility that while the whole sentence may have taken several seconds to say (outwardly or silently), there seemed to be a moment just preceding the formation of the sentence that in some way contained the whole thought. It is that preceding moment, that "it" which the words were expressing, that we mean

TABLE 11-2. Model Parameters and Corresponding
Psychological Functions

Model Parameter	Psychological Function
ATTENTIONAL CONTROL	
Location of window	Partially determines what gets into consciousness; is the locus of attention.
Rate of window movement	Determines rate of attention shifts; inversely related to intensity of consciousness.
Pattern of window movement	Determines temporal sequence of attentional shifts. Long-term standardized patterns are strongly related to such psychological phenomena as expectations, states, personality.
Size of window	Determines breadth of attention.
PAC	
Fluidity of PAC	Other things being equal, determines depth and amount of material that may enter consciousness.
Structure of PAC	Determines specifics of material that is likely to move into consciousness as an associated unit.
ENERGY	
Distribution of available energy	Determines trade-off among three factors: • rate of attention shift • intensity of consciousness • rigidity of PAC contents.
Amount of available energy	Determines total energy available for trade-offs in distribution of available energy.

by nonverbal thought. For many persons and for many sentences it will be difficult to become aware of the preceding "it." This is precisely because in the OSC our typical pattern of attentional shifts doesn't sample this domain of phenomena.

Each of the two ways of thinking represented in the model, verbal and nonverbal, has certain characteristics that may be suitable in different circumstances. For example, if an important concern is communication of one's thoughts, as is frequently the case, then the verbal mode is more suitable. However, the translation of "its" to words may be a clumsy one, and in any event takes considerable time. In situations where external communication is not needed and where speed and perhaps clarity is desirable, nonverbal thinking

TABLE 11-3. Parameter Characteristics of the
Ordinary State of Consciousness (OSC)

Parameter	Characteristic of OSC
Location of window	Tends to be located in one of the following areas: • Perception of external events (1)* • Perception of body events (2)* • Verbal thinking (4)*
Rate of window movement	Fast
Pattern of window movement	• Sufficient to maintain contact with external environment • Sufficient to maintain self-concept • 4 to 4, 1 to 4, and 2 to 4 shifts predominate (frequent talk to self or others)*
Size of window	Fluctuates about midpoint
Fluidity of PAC	Low to moderate
Structure of PAC	New associations form at moderate rate
Distribution of available energy	Low to moderate amount of energy available for intensity of consciousness. PAC rigidity moderately high.
Amount of available energy	Low to moderate

*Numbers refer to categories in Table 11-1.

may be more appropriate. For most of us, in the OSC the point may be moot since we do not know how to move the window to the place where nonverbal thinking will be in awareness. It may be, however, that in some ASCs this mode of thinking is more often selected.

One characteristic of the OSC is the preponderance of talking, particularly to oneself. Thus, a pattern of shifts in the Table 11-1 categories that include 1 to 4, 2 to 4, and within 4 is characteristic of the OSC. In particular, these shifts emphasize the degree to which we talk about (name and discuss) perceptual events and previous thoughts. For many persons, this characteristic of the OSC, certainly with reference to the internal verbalization, may not be apparent. Within the context of the model, this lack of awareness can be understood as resulting from the low level of intensity of these experiences as a consequence of rapid attentional shifts and from the maintenance of an attentional pattern that does not sample the memory of these internal verbalizations.

The subjective rate of the passing of time is a phenomenon that can undergo considerable change. In the model, the passing of time is determined by a joint function of rate of window movement and intensity of consciousness. It is possible that this function is a multiplicative one, so that if either factor is zero the apparent passage of time would be zero. This relationship could account for some of the phenomena of alterations of time perception in ASCs. For example, in various profound ASCs subjects report that time has stopped or doesn't exist. This can be understood as the expected outcome where rate of window movement has reached zero for the specified period. On the other hand, where attentional shifting has slowed but not stopped, subjective estimates of time might be greater than usual because the increased intensity of consciousness coincident with the slowed attentional shift rate more than compensates for the slow shifting.

Attention

Attentional mechanisms play a very important role in the model. Attention essentially is the location of the window since at any moment in time this location determines the area of the PAC to be sampled, and hence, what enters consciousness. Each window movement is a shift of attention; the rate of movement (or, inversely, duration) affects the intensity of consciousness as well as the availability of deeper-lying material. In addition, the breadth of material entering consciousness is partially controlled by the width of the attentional window. And finally, the pattern of window movement (attentional shifts) is intimately related to many of the more or less enduring psychological states and traits.

Given the importance of attentional mechanisms within the model, the question naturally arises as to what controls these mechanisms. Probably the most useful way to answer this question is to think of attention as under the control of "programs." The programs determine the location, rate, and pattern of attentional shifts, as well as the size of the window. They are the product of some combination of inheritance and experience, and are subject to modification by a variety of influences, including drugs.

Some of the programs that control attentional mechanisms are concerned with basic organismic survival. It may be necessary, for example, to sample rapidly those portions of the PAC concerned with external visual input and body position and movement when the person is engaged in operating a piece of heavy machinery. Other programs control attentional mechanisms when the person is involved in less physically dangerous tasks such as reading or eating. It is hypothesized that the various styles of attending in various situations may reflect and determine what we refer to as personality traits and states. This issue has been discussed by a number of investigators, including McGhie (1970) and Silverman (1964).

Drugs and Consciousness

It is very clear that many chemical substances can have profound effects on the experiential world. It is equally clear that any one-to-one description of these effects, wherein a given drug always leads

TABLE 11-4. Drug-Altered Experiences and Their
Explanation in Terms of the Model

Experience Potentially Altered by Drugs	Explanation in Terms of the Model
1. Shift from external to internal focus	1. Window location.
2. Alteration of mood or feelings	2. Location of window in 2* so that detection of alterations of muscles, glands, etc., are sampled. Strong feelings/moods associated with slow window movement at appropriate sites.
3. Breadth of attention	3. Controlled by size of window.
4. Intensity of experience	4. Controlled by energy available for consciousness. Inversely related to rate of window movement (attention shifts), and directly related to fluidity of PAC and total energy available.
5. Time distortions	5. Produced by alterations in either of the factors involved in determining time perception: • rate of window movement (the accumulation of "psychological moments") • the intensity of the experiences
6. Occurrence of strengthening of new associations	6. Events not usually entering consciousness at the same time do so because of high fluidity, slow attention shifts, or wide window. Their associative bond is strengthened so that on subsequent occasions they are more likely to enter consciousness together.
7. Persistent or enhanced internal imagery	7. Location of window; slow rate of window movement.

to specific alterations of consciousness, is inadequate. In talking about the effects of drugs we need to keep in mind that the precise dosage and form of the drug, the route of administration, the expectations of the consumer, and the setting in which the drug is taken all may influence the effect "produced." Indeed, it is sobering to speculate that each of the effects produced by drugs can in all likelihood be produced by procedures not involving the use of drugs. Notwithstanding the complexities involved, a number of alterations of experience are frequently associated with the use of certain drugs. Table 11-4 contains a list of some of these alterations and for each one an explanation in terms of the model.

TABLE 11-4. (Continued)

Experience Potentially Altered by Drugs	Explanation in Terms of the Model
8. Loss of memory	8. Fluidity of PAC decreased; memory not sampled by window.
9. Shift from verbal to nonverbal thinking	9. Location of window.
10. Availability of deep-lying memories or unconscious material	10. Directly related to fluidity of PAC and slowing of window movement; also accessible directly through special window location.
11. Alteration of complex psychological phenomena, e.g. values, attitudes, states, traits, personality	11. Complex events involving one or more of the following: • alteration of pattern of window movement • alteration of associative structure of PAC • alteration of rate of window movement Alteration of behavior associated with the above.
12. Loss of self-concept	12. Window does not sample appropriate areas of 2*; reduced sampling of other areas may be involved (e.g., 1 and 4*).
13. "Time doesn't exist"	13. Either factor involved in determining time distortions is zero.
14. Unity, oneness, connectedness	14. A combination of very slow rate of window movement, high PAC fluidity, and/or wide window.

*Numbers refer to categories in Table 11-1.

Marijuana

Much of our time is spent in doing things. We usually regard this activity as consisting of a set of physical acts such as talking, walking, pulling, pushing, manipulating, grasping, in order to get a task accomplished. Going along with this physical activity is the mental (verbal) activity of setting up expectations, reevaluating, devising alternative strategies, and so on. This active way of being in the world has been discussed by Deikman (1971), and he contrasted it with another way of being, referred to as receptive, in which the person is less concerned with doing or manipulating and more involved in sensing and observing. We wish to emphasize another aspect of these two ways of being: the rate of shifting attention. The active style of being is associated with rapid shifting of attention that is appropriate to the sequence of events necessary to plan, execute, evaluate, and revise a behavioral sequence. For the receptive mode, such directed shifting of attention is not required, and attentional shifting tends to slow down.

We hypothesize that the effects of marijuana can be understood in terms of facilitating movement from an active to a receptive style, and further, that the phenomena associated with this shift can be analyzed in terms of the model presented in Figure 11-1 (see Table 11-5). Each of the phenomena listed in Table 11-4 can occur under the influence of marijuana, although some of them are more likely to occur in association with the use of stronger drugs. One of the most commonly reported effects of marijuana is the enhancement of perceptual experiences; auditory, gustatory, tactual, olfactory, and possibly to a lesser extent, visual experiences are reported as occurring in a more intense fashion (Halikas, Goodwin, & Guze, 1971). In terms of the model, these phenomena are expected as a direct consequence of slower rate of attentional shifts, and they may be supported by an increase in total energy and in the fluidity of the PAC. It will be recalled that the energy not used to produce attentional shifts is available to consciousness, where it is manifested as an intensification of the contents of consciousness. The same sort of mechanism partially accounts for the sometimes reported "great insight" phenomena. When the window is moving slowly in the area of thinking, the thoughts, verbal or nonverbal, that enter consciousness will be imbued with enhanced intensity. Thus, even the simplest thoughts— which may occur in the same words in the OSC—are experienced

TABLE 11-5. Parameter Characteristics of the
Marijuana-Altered State of Consciousness (MASC)

Parameter	Characteristic of MASC
Location of window	• Less time spent in 4.* • Less time processing information required for task accomplishment.
Rate of window movement	Slower than ordinary.
Pattern of window movement	May spend considerable time without sampling the pattern required for maintaining "I" or "self." Other characteristic patterns may be altered.
Size of window	Increased range; small window size may predominate.
Fluidity of PAC	Possibly increased.
Structure of PAC	New associations may form at high rate (and may soon be forgotten).
Distribution of available energy	More available for intensity of consciousness.
Amount of available energy	More than usual may be present.

*Numbers refer to categories in Table 11-1.
Note: Descriptive terms, such as slower and increased refer to the OSC in Table 11-3.

with greater power or meaning. This process may be enhanced by the window sampling more often from the area of nonverbal thought, which is potentially a quicker, more direct, and clearer form of thinking. The model also suggests that some of the great insights that occur may also be seen as insightful or extraordinary when one regains the OSC. This results from the slow window movement allowing time for more adjacent and deeper-lying material of the PAC to flow into consciousness in new and different combinations that may be communicated to another person or retained after the ordinary state is regained.

Another phenomenon sometimes reported is enhanced, eyes-closed imagery. These experiences may range from the occurrence of geometric designs to the visualization of complete scenes. This phenomenon is understandable in terms of the attentional mechanism producing slow attentional shifts in the area of internally produced images.

Memory ability over periods of seconds and minutes of clock time have been found by several researchers to be diminished under the influence of marijuana (Melges, Tinklenberg, Hollister, & Gillespie, 1970; Tinklenberg, Melges, Hollister, & Gillespie, 1970). In the OSC it is necessary that memory be at peak efficiency in order to assist in the planning, executing, and revising of orderly sequences of task-oriented behavior. In the receptive mode much less demand is placed on memory, and in fact, the state seems to be characterized by less-frequent sampling of those facets of the PAC. The model also suggests, however, that should memory be sampled under the influence of marijuana, it could be done with greater intensity and with a greater flow of deeper-lying or unusual associations being brought into consciousness.

The mechanisms for altering time perception have been discussed above. The usual effect of marijuana on time perception is the "spaced out" feeling; for example, 10 minutes seem like 30 minutes. In terms of the model, this occurs as a result of the increased intensity of experiences more than compensating for the slow shift rate. Occasionally the "time doesn't exist" phenomenon is reported. This presumably is produced by complete lack of window movement for a specific period of time. During this "time" a "sequence" of events may flow into consciousness, but from the point of view of the experiencer, as long as the window remains stationary, the events are perceived as in some sense connected or unified and not consisting of a temporal sequence.

The various alterations reported occurring with marijuana may be ordered in terms of their departure from ordinary consciousness. This order roughly corresponds to the order of the listing in Table 11-4 with higher-numbered items being further from ordinary consciousness. The ordering also roughly corresponds to the probability of occurrence and/or the difficulty of achieving a given type of phenomenon. In general, the greater the departure from ordinary consciousness, the more difficult a phenomenon is to achieve and the less probable is its occurrence.

Several levels of marijuana-related alterations seem to be indicated. Each may be regarded as a separate SC—marijuana I, marijuana II, and so on—or they may be regarded as ordered variations of the marijuana-facilitated receptive mode of consciousness. The first level is characterized by a general feeling that "something is different," and is related to the switch from an active to a receptive mode. This is usually accompanied by feelings of well-being or relaxation, although in some individuals on some occasions anxiety may be present. This level includes the first three items of Table 11-4. The primary characteristic of the second level is enhanced sensory-perceptual and emotional functioning. In this state the world is experienced as fundamentally unchanged except that everything is more intense—or at least some things are. Also characteristic of this level are a general feeling of euphoria, time distortions, and memory alterations. This level includes the items of Table 11-4 roughly through number 10.

A third level involves what might be described as a qualitative reorganization of the experiential world. Ordinarily if one is at home watching TV, one is aware that he is sitting in a room and watching TV. However, under the influence of marijuana, one may profoundly not pay attention to (that is, not sample with his window) the outlines of the TV set, the room in which he is sitting, his own body feedback, or his talking to himself about these things; but only the scene on the screen. When that happens, that scene is all there is; that *is* "reality." In this example, if attention is focused completely on the screen, and no sampling occurs of those aspects of body feedback and verbal thought which are required to maintain the "fact" that "I" exist, then "I" do not exist. This level of consciousness can include the highest numbered items in Table 11-4.

Alcohol

The general effects of alcohol on consciousness are so well known that they are frequently ignored (Jones & Parsons, 1975). However, we still do not understand the details fully. The four alcohol-altered states of consciousness (AASC) that are related to the time course of the blood alcohol curve and the absorption and elimination rates of alcohol have been described (Jones & Jones, 1976a). Two sorts of data support these AASCs. First, the subjective reports of the individuals indicate that they are meaningful and distinguishable (Paredes, Jones, & Gregory, 1977). Second, objective data such as direction and change of blood alcohol levels, test performance, and physiological measures also exist that covary with the subjective experiences (Jones, 1973; Jones, Parsons, & Rundell, 1976; Jones and Vega, 1972).

The purpose of this section is to relate the subjective experiences of alcohol intoxication to our model of consciousness and then to speculate how changes in consciousness may be related to overt behavioral changes during alcohol intoxication (see Table 11-6).

Alcohol-Altered State of Consciousness-I (AASC-I)

AASC-I occurs during the absorption phase, when the blood alcohol level is increasing. This usually lasts from 20 minutes to one hour after a moderate dose of alcohol (for example, three ounces of 100-proof Scotch for a 150-pound person), depending on the individual's rate of absorption. The physiological and behavioral changes during this ascending limb of the blood alcohol curve resemble a state of activation and arousal in most social drinkers. Increases in heart rate, respiration rate, skin conductance level, and EEG frequency have been reported to occur during this time period (Jones, Parsons, & Rundell, 1976). Individuals become more talkative, often laugh, report that they feel euphoric, and report slight tingling and numbness in the arms, legs, and facial areas (Ekman, Frankenhaeuser, Goldberg, Hagdahl, & Myrsten, 1964). Performance on psychological tests reveals impairment in memory (Jones, 1973; Jones & Jones, 1976b, in press) and reaction-time tasks (Jones & Jones, 1977), although often the individual reports he feels he is doing very well. This is the positively reinforcing phase of the alcohol state. Most individuals report they drink to experience this "high" feeling and often request more alcohol during this time. Additional alcohol keeps them "going up," but more importantly keeps them from "coming down," a second AASC that will be discussed later.

Unlike many other drugs, there has been a considerable amount of research evaluating the effects of alcohol. While introspection and self-reported changes can be utilized in relating the alcohol effects to our model of consciousness, other data are also available from objective reports.

We have speculated that the location of the window partially determines what gets into consciousness. The individual often becomes talkative and disinhibited during AASC-I, suggesting that the window is moving more rapidly, allowing a greater variety of information to enter consciousness and be verbalized. In fact, it is not

TABLE 11-6. Parameter Characteristics of the Four Alcohol-Altered States of Consciousness (AASC)

Parameter	Characteristic of Alcohol-Altered States of Consciousness			
	AASC-I	AASC-II	AASC-III	AASC-IV
Location of window	More time in verbal thinking (4*)	Less time in verbal thinking (4*)	More time in verbal thinking (4*)	More time in perception of body events (2*)
Rate of window movement	Faster than ordinary	Slower than ordinary	Approximately ordinary	Ordinary
Pattern of window movement	More chaotic than usual	Restricted	Selective	Almost ordinary
Size of window	Generally small	Generally small	Slightly decreased	Ordinary
Fluidity of PAC	Increased	Decreased	Slightly decreased	Ordinary
Structure of PAC	New, fragmented; quickly-forgotten associations made	No new associations	Few new associations	Ordinary
Distribution of available energy	Most used for maintaining fast window movement	Little used for window movement, but not much available for consciousness	Approaching ordinary, but somewhat less energy than ordinarily available for consciousness	Ordinary
Amount of available energy	More than ordinary	Less than ordinary	Slightly less than ordinary	Ordinary

* Numbers refer to categories in Table 11-1.
Note: Descriptive terms such as increased and restricted refer to the OSC in Table 11-3.

uncommon to observe that individuals jump from topic to topic during AASC-I. It appears as though different ideas enter consciousness fleetingly, seem very important for a short interval, and then vanish.

The pattern of the window movement appears to be more random than in the normal state of consciousness. The topics that are brought to consciousness during AASC-I are varied and seemingly unrelated at times. Important thoughts may be rapidly replaced with trivial references to past events. The rather disorganized thought process is often associated with poor memory, particularly long-term memory, during this time. This may be due to the fragmented nature of the individual's consciousness and the subsequent feedback to the PAC of fragmented data. The rapid attentional shifting and, perhaps, the window locations selected might also operate against effective long-term memory.

The size of the window during this time appears to be relatively small since only fragments of many thoughts are likely to penetrate into consciousness. On the other hand, the fluidity of the material in the PAC appears to increase during AASC-I since many unusual associations occur. The individual seems to be aware of the often bizarre content of his or her associations, but doesn't appear to be disturbed by it. This may be a consequence of the low to moderate level of intensity of the experiential world in this state. The energy consumed to drive the rapidly changing attentional shift mechanism results in the individual experiencing a slight decrease in the intensity of conscious experience.

These particular changes in consciousness associated with AASC-I may be directly influenced by the peak blood alcohol level and the rate of the absorption of alcohol. For most social drinkers, few of the changes could be detected at a very low blood alcohol level of 0.01%–0.03%. Most of these changes would be apparent from a blood alcohol level of from 0.04% to about 0.15% during the time alcohol was actively being absorbed. Beyond a blood alcohol level of 0.15%, most social drinkers would begin becoming incoherent and so intoxicated they would soon either vomit or pass out or both. However, increased tolerance in many heavy drinkers and alcoholic individuals might result in fairly well integrated behavior up to blood alcohol levels of 0.30%, with the point of coma often not developing until 0.40%. This shift in the quality of consciousness experienced by individuals with an extremely high tolerance to alcohol may develop into their being in a chronic state of altered "unconsciousness" when sober (Parsons, 1975), possibly as a result of brain damage.

The second factor, alcohol absorption rate, may be intimately related to the model parameters assumed to change. For example, a rapid absorption rate and the accompanying rapid change in brain alcohol level may result in the rate and pattern of the window movement being considerably altered. On the other hand, a slow absorption rate would allow for a more complete ongoing biological adjustment to alcohol in the system and, hence, less profound effects would be produced.

Several other factors that might influence AASC-I experiences are time of day when the alcohol is consumed (Jones, 1974; Jones & Paredes, 1974) and the day of the menstrual cycle in women (Jones & Jones, 1976b). The interaction of alcohol with normally varying biological rhythms may be important in producing different types of consciousness during AASC-I. For example, SC experienced with alcohol in the early morning immediately after waking may be different from the SC experienced in the late evening after a long day. Recent evidence also suggests that alcohol may affect women differently than men. For example, women in general reach a higher peak blood alcohol level and have a faster absorption rate than men. This suggests that women may experience a more intense AASC-I than men if peak blood alcohol level and absorption rate are related to the intensity of the change in consciousness. The peak blood alcohol level in women has been reported to vary with the menstrual cycle, suggesting that AASC-I may be more intense during the premenstrual phase, the time of high peak blood alcohol levels (Jones & Jones, 1976c).

Alcohol-Altered State of Consciousness-II (AASC-II)

The rapid increase in blood alcohol level described for AASC-I dissipates after the individual finishes his last drink, and culminates in the peak or highest blood alcohol level being reached. After the peak is reached and no further drinking is allowed, the blood alcohol level may remain stable (plateau) in some individuals for a short period of time and then begin decreasing. For others, the blood alcohol level begins dropping rather rapidly almost immediately following peak. In contrast to AASC-I, this state is often signaled by a yawn and then a feeling of sudden tiredness and often sleepiness. The high is over. Another drink would probably reinstate AASC-I at this point. Without more alcohol, a relatively slow descent begins, with the depressive actions of alcohol taking hold. Everything begins to slow down, especially the thought processes. Ironically, objective performance on certain cognitive tasks is better on the descending limb than on the ascending limb. However, the reverse may be the case for tasks that involve sustained attention (Colquhoun, in press). This state lasts until the blood alcohol level has fallen about halfway to zero. During this time the individual is well aware that he is intoxicated and is having difficulty doing a number of tasks. He usually feels very "drugged," becomes quiet, and mainly wants to "sleep it off." He is no longer interested in having another drink.

The complete change in affect and behavior from the ascending to the descending limb of the blood alcohol curve suggests that a different SC is developing. The rapidly changing thought processes characteristic of the first state slow down, suggesting that the window is now shifting slowly. Both body events and external events are experienced with little intensity and appear unimportant. This lack of intensity in spite of slow window movement presumably occurs as a result of diminution of the total energy available to the system. The fact that few events appear to be reaching consciousness suggests that the fluidity of the PAC has been reduced and possibly that the window size is reduced.

The duration of AASC-II may be several hours, depending on peak blood alcohol level. If drinking takes place at night, the person might pass through most of what would have been AASC-II (and the next state) during the night while asleep. If an individual drinks enough alcohol to reach a peak blood alcohol level of 0.12% and then discontinues drinking, the AASC-II time may last for 3 to 4 hours. Males metabolize alcohol at an average rate of 0.015% per hour. The person would reach halfway, or 0.06%, in 4 hours. Most women, however, metabolize alcohol faster, about 0.02% per hour, and would take only 3 hours to reach 0.06%. Therefore, the rate of alcohol metabolism is related to the duration of AASC-II, and this may be related to individual variation, sex of the drinker, and time of day of ingestion (Jones & Jones, 1976a). Once the halfway blood alcohol level has been obtained, a third state of consciousness appears to develop.

Alcohol-Altered State of Consciousness-III (AASC-III)

The third AASC can best be described as a dissociation between thinking and doing. During both AASC-I and AASC-II, the person is aware that he is intoxicated and is having difficulty thinking and doing things. However, during AASC-III the feelings of intoxication seem gone, or at least greatly diminished compared to AASC-I and AASC-II. The drinker feels he is completely (or almost completely) sober even though his blood alcohol level may be approximately 0.06%, still too high to drive legally in most states. Many aspects of his intellectual functioning have almost completely returned, but his motor and judgmental abilities may remain impaired, and the drinker may fail to be aware of this problem. Feeling completely sober, he may judge that he is able to drive an automobile, but may find that his reaction time is still not back to normal. This is potentially a rather dangerous state.

In terms of the model, it appears that the window is usually located at the verbal thinking area and not moving to the part of working edge where perception of body events and spatial information are sampled. The various model parameters are apparently in the process of returning to normal levels, but, as suggested above, the pattern of sampling the PAC is selective. This state has been described as a return to left hemisphere rational thinking while right hemisphere performance ability is still impaired (Jones & Parsons, 1975). In relation to the model, differential hemispheric impairment may be understood as differential hemispheric parameter values.

Alcohol-Altered State of Consciousness-IV (AASC-IV)

The fourth AASC may develop as a consequence of drinking, but is still present for some time after alcohol is no longer detectable in the blood. This state may last for as long as 32 hours after drinking

(Collins, Schroeder, & Hill, 1973). Individuals report "not feeling back to normal" and having alcohol hangover, and there are physiological recordings of alcohol produced nystagmic eye movements during this time. The state may not be directly related to the alcohol per se, but may be a response to metabolites of alcohol still in the body or a rebound effect from the ingestion of alcohol. Lowered sex hormonal levels following prolonged alcohol ingestion also may be related to some of the subjective aftereffects (Gordon, Altman, Southren, Rubin, & Lieber, 1976; Rubin, Lieber, Altman, Gordon, & Southren, 1976). While this state has not received detailed study, it appears that intensified somatic complaints predominate even though verbal thinking and perception of external events are back to normal. In relation to the model, the chief feature of AASC-IV is the increase in the amount of time that the window is sampling in the area of body events. In many ways, this state is difficult to delineate from the OSC, and its existence as a separate entity is, therefore, debatable.

Conclusion and Extensions of the Model

The discussion of marijuana and alcohol suggests that these drugs produce rather different effects. We would like to emphasize again an important feature of the discussion by reminding the reader that individual differences and a host of other factors combine with drugs to determine effects that therefore vary considerably from person to person and from time to time. Also, the model parameter characteristics presented in Tables 11-5 and 11-6 must be regarded as tentative for similar reasons and because of the sketchy nature of the model in its present state of development. In general, though, our analysis indicates that the MASC tends to be associated with less verbal thinking, with slower attentional shifts, with a different pattern of attentional shifts, and with greater intensity of conscious experience.

The model may also be extended to an analysis of the effects of other drugs. Briefly, hallucinogenic drugs are likely to produce similar but stronger effects than marijuana. In terms of the model, rate of window movement would be slower and the fluidity of the PAC increased even more. The probability of encountering the effects listed near the end of Table 11-4 would thus be increased. Depressant drugs are likely to produce a profile similar to the second state associated with alcohol, including as major features a slow rate of window movement and low total energy. On the other hand, stimulants are likely to produce an opposite sort of profile with fast window movement and high energy. One might also speculate that high PAC fluidity and a structure resistant to change along with a chaotic pattern of window movement would also be characteristic of this state.

There are of course many ways of altering consciousness other than consuming drugs. A number of these have been discussed in other chapters of this book. We would like to suggest that the model developed here may have general applicability to alterations of consciousness regardless of the techniques used to achieve the alteration. The applicability of the model and, particularly, the importance placed on rate of attentional shifting is perhaps most easily seen in connection with meditation techniques. It seems clear that facilitating alterations in attentional mechanisms and perhaps bringing them under control is both the method and a goal of these techniques.

It will certainly not surprise the reader to hear that we believe that consciousness expansion can be understood in terms of the model and that attentional mechanisms play an important role in this process. We believe that consciousness expansion involves not only gaining control over what one pays attention to, but also involves gaining control over the rate of shifting attention. The latter point appears to be a key factor in controlling the intensity of consciousness as well as facilitating the melding in consciousness of a new mix of potential experience. It may be the case that the phrase "gaining control" is somewhat misleading since the actual process may involve the relinquishing of previously used methods of control, rather than a striving after some specific new one. In any case, we would like to close by suggesting that consciousness expansion is a more ubiquitous term than first meets the eye, since we believe that it applies with as much credibility to the favorable outcome of psychotherapy for the "contracted" individual as it does to the favorable outcome of meditation for the guru-in-training. The difference lies mainly in the starting point.

REFERENCES

Collins, W. E., Schroeder, D. J., & Hill, R. J. Some effects of alcohol on vestibular responses. *Advances in Otorhinolaryngology* 1973, *19:* 295–303.

Colquhoun, W. P. Estimation of critical blood-alcohol level in relation to tasks of sustained attention. In M. Horvath (ed.), *Adverse effects of environmental chemicals and psychotropic drugs,* Vol. 2. Amsterdam: Elsevier, in press.

Deikman, A. J. Bimodal consciousness. *Archives of General Psychiatry* 1971, *25:* 481–489.

Ekman, G., Frankenhaeuser, M., Goldberg, L., Hagdahl, R., & Myrsten, A. Subjective and objective effects of alcohol as functions of dosage and time. *Psychopharmacologia* 1964, *6:* 399–409.

Gordon, C. G., Altman, K., Southren, A. L., Rubin, E., & Lieber, C. S. Effect of alcohol (ethanol) administration on sex-hormone metabolism in normal men. *The New England Journal of Medicine* 1976, *295:* 793–797.

Halikas, J. A., Goodwin, D. W., & Guze, S. B. Marihuana effects: A survey of regular users. *Journal of American Medical Association* 1971, *217:* 692–694.

Jones, B. M. Memory impairment on the ascending and descending limbs of the blood alcohol curve. *Journal of Abnormal Psychology* 1973, *82:* 24–32.

―――. Circadian variation in the effects of alcohol on cognitive performance. *Quarterly Journal of Studies on Alcohol* 1974, *35:* 1212–1219.

Jones, B. M., & Jones, M. K. States of consciousness and alcohol: Relationship to the blood alcohol curve, time of day and the menstrual cycle. *Alcohol Health and Research World* 1976, *1:* 10–15. (a)

―――. Alcohol effects in women during the menstrual cycle. *Annals of the New York Academy of Sciences* 1976, *273:* 576–587. (b)

―――. Women and alcohol: Intoxication, metabolism and the menstrual cycle. In M. Greenblatt & M. A. Schuckit (eds.), *Alcoholism problems in women and children.* New York: Grune & Stratton, 1976. (c)

―――. Interaction of alcohol, oral contraceptives, and the menstrual cycle with stimulus-response compatibility. In F. A. Seixas (ed.), *Currents in alcoholism,* Vol. 2. New York: Grune & Stratton, 1977.

―――. Alcohol and memory impairment in male and female social drinkers. In I. Birnbaum & E. Parker (eds.), *Alcohol and human memory.* Hillsdale, N.J.: Lawrence Erlbaum, in press.

Jones, B. M., & Paredes, A. Circadian variation of ethanol metabolism in alcoholics. *British Journal of Addiction* 1974, *69:* 3–10.

Jones, B. M., & Parsons, O. A. Alcohol and consciousness: Getting high, coming down. *Psychology Today* 1975, *8:* 53–58.

Jones, B. M., Parsons, O. A., & Rundell, O. H. Psychophysiological correlates of alcoholism. In R. E. Tarter & A. A. Sugerman (eds.), *Alcoholism: Interdisciplinary approaches to an enduring problem.* Reading, Mass.: Addison-Wesley, 1976.

Jones, B. M., & Vega, A. Cognitive performance measured on the ascending and descending limb of the blood alcohol curve. *Psychophar-macologia* 1972, *23:* 99–114.

————. Fast and slow drinkers: Blood alcohol variables and cognitive performance. *Quarterly Journal of Studies on Alcohol* 1973, *34:* 797–806.

McGhie, A. *Pathology of attention.* Baltimore, Maryland: Penguin, 1970.

Melges, F. T., Tinklenberg, J. R., Hollister, L. E., & Gillespie, H. K. Marihuana and temporal disintegration. *Science* 1970, *168:* 1118–1120.

Paredes, A., Jones, B. M., & Gregory, D. Blood alcohol discrimination training with alcoholics. In F. A. Seixas (ed.), *Currents in alcoholism,* Vol. 2. New York: Grune & Stratton, 1977.

Parsons, O. A. Brain damage in alcoholics: Altered states of unconsciousness. In M. M. Gross (ed.), *Alcohol intoxication and withdrawal.* New York: Plenum, 1975.

Rubin, E., Lieber, C. S., Altman, K., Gordon, G. G., & Southren, A. L. Prolonged ethanol consumption increases testosterone metabolism in the liver. *Science* 1976, *191:* 563–564.

Silverman, J. The problem of attention in research and theory in schizophrenia. *Psychological Review* 1964, *71:* 352–379.

Tinklenberg, J. R., Melges, F. T., Hollister, L. E., & Gillespie, H. K. Marihuana and immediate memory. *Nature* 1970, *226:* 1171–1172.

Index